German Studies towards the Millennium

CUTG Proceedings

Series Editor: Allyson Fiddler

Volume 2

Peter Lang
Oxford · Bern · Berlin · Bruxelles · Frankfurt am Main · New York · Wien

Christopher Hall
David Rock
(eds)

German Studies towards the Millennium

Selected papers from the Conference of University Teachers of German, University of Keele, September 1999

Peter Lang
Oxford · Bern · Berlin · Bruxelles · Frankfurt am Main · New York · Wien

Die Deutsche Bibliothek – CIP-Einheitsaufnahme

German studies towards the millennium : selected papers from the Conference of University Teachers of German, University of Keele, September 1999 / Christopher Hall ; David Rock (ed.) – Oxford ; Bern ; Berlin ; Bruxelles ; Frankfurt am Main ; New York ; Wien : Lang, 2000
(CUTG proceedings ; Vol. 2)
ISBN 3-906765-65-2

British Library and Library of Congress Cataloguing-in-Publication Data: A catalogue record for this book is available from *The British Library*, Great Britain, and from *The Library of Congress*, USA

Cover design: Thomas Jaberg, Peter Lang AG

ISSN 1424-0408
ISBN 3-906765-65-2
US-ISBN 0-8204-5304-8

Jupiterstr. 15, Postfach, 3000 Bern 15, Switzerland; info@peterlang.com

Printed in Germany

Table of Contents

Preface

The present collection of papers forms the second volume of Proceedings from the annual Conference of University Teachers of German in Great Britain and Ireland (CUTG). The conference which generated this publication was held at Keele University in September 1999, and the sixteen contributions to this volume represent a selection of the papers given over the three days of the conference. Papers are submitted to one of three 'strands,' and the articles published here are grouped accordingly, beginning with papers on society, media, and institutions, followed by contributions on German literature, and completed by articles on language and linguistics.

It is hoped that the diversity of subjects explored in this volume will appeal to a large readership and that readers will not only enjoy the latest research in the 'strand' in which they themselves are active, but will seize the opportunity to inform themselves of new developments in some of the many different fields which make up German Studies today. The Series of CUTG Proceedings will continue to reflect the dynamic range of interests and expertise of its wide membership. The Editors and Officers of the CUTG warmly invite readers to attend its conferences and to participate in the scholarship generated by them. Further information about the CUTG and about its forthcoming conferences can be found on our website (www.cutg.ac.uk).

As outgoing Conference Secretary and Series Editor, I would like to extend my warmest thanks to the editors of the first two volumes of our proceedings; Steve Giles and Peter Graves (volume one), Dave Rock and Chris Hall (volume two).

Allyson Fiddler
Series Editor

Preface

[illegible]

MARIANNE HOWARTH

The Business of Politics; The Politics of Business. The GDR in Britain Before and After Diplomatic Recognition

For a little over half of her brief existence as a German state, the GDR was denied full international acknowledgement of her status and existence. In the 1950s, she established diplomatic relations with the Soviet Union and other members of the Warsaw Pact; in the 1960s she also made a little diplomatic headway in establishing relations with some of the newly decolonised states in Africa. In general however, until the conclusion of the *Ostpolitik* in 1972/73, the GDR occupied a position on the fringes of international diplomacy. The signing of the *Grundlagenvertrag* between the two German states in December 1972 enabled the GDR to normalise bilateral relations with the majority of states in the world and to gain membership of all international organisations, a process which culminated in the admission of both German states to membership of the United Nations in September 1973.

The reasons for this twilight existence, in diplomatic terms, lie in the uncompromising position adopted by the Western Allies and the Federal Republic in response to the founding of the GDR in October 1949. In his *Regierungserklärung* of 12th October 1949, Ministerpräsident Otto Grotewohl had called for states to establish normal diplomatic and economic relations with the GDR 'auf dem Boden der gegenseitigen Achtung und Gleichberechtigung'. This call had been anticipated by the Western Allied High Commission for Germany which, on 10th October 1949, had already issued a statement describing 'the so-called government of the GDR [as] an artificial creation [...] which is devoid of any legal basis [...] [and] has no title to represent Eastern Germany. It has an even smaller claim to speak in the name of Germany as a whole[1].'

Western solidarity on non-recognition

Less publicly, however, the Foreign Office considered the implications of the founding of the GDR in terms of the extent to which there should be any recognition of the new government. In a memorandum entitled Questions of Recognition, written in October 1949, the pros and cons of *de jure* recognition (i.e. full diplomatic recognition under the terms of international law) and the implications of non-recognition were thoroughly discussed. The principal conclusion was: 'it seems clear that the disadvantages of *de jure* recognition far outweigh those of non-recognition, despite the practical difficulties involved in the latter'[2].

Other Western governments were also considering their position on recognition and it was clear that Britain's stand was by no means shared by all her Western partners. Following a meeting between the political advisers of the three Western military governments and the military missions of the Benelux states in Berlin on 17th October 1949, the British representative sent a telegram to the Foreign Office describing the Benelux position as:

> [...] far from reliable in the matter of recognising the Eastern Zone Germans. They appear to be under the delusion that they may be able to save some Benelux property in the Eastern Zone by this means [...] I think this is a pure delusion and it would moreover be disastrous if this so-called Government were now to be recognised by a respectable power. I hope that the Benelux, Scandinavian etc. Governments will be encouraged to maintain a proper Western solidarity and to

1 *Manchester Guardian*, 11.10.49; see also Department of State Press Release, No. 790, 12.10.1949 [Press Conference addressed by Dean Acheson], PRO FO371/76617, 13.10.49.

2 Miss G. Brown, Questions of Recognition, 11.10.49, PRO, FO371/76617. *De jure* recognition implies acknowledgement of the legitimacy of the state, the likely permanence of its government and the support of the majority of its population. *De facto* recognition implies the recognition of the existence of a government for purposes of political or economic expedience.

> discuss this question with ourselves and the other occupying governments before they embark on any action[3].

Establishing this solidarity now became an urgent task. Following tripartite talks in Paris in November, the Permanent Commission of the Brussels treaty powers held a conference on 8th December 1949 where a joint policy of non-recognition of the GDR was agreed by Britain, France and the Benelux countries. (An official American observer was also in attendance and the United States adopted the same official attitude.) The five governments agreed to take a similarly hostile attitude to the GDR in the areas of commercial relations, protection of property and nationals and participation of the GDR government in international organisations, 'all of which, either directly or indirectly, are likely to involve the question of recognition'. They also called upon other governments to follow their example. In a telegram sent to all friendly governments on 23rd December 1949, the British government expressed its hope that the government concerned

> [...] will adopt a similar attitude towards these problems and that they will be prepared to exchange with His Majesty's Government and other interested governments information on the difficulties they meet in their relations with Eastern Germany and, if necessary, to consult them with a view to maintaining a common attitude[4].

In this they were enormously successful; by early 1950 Denmark, Norway, Sweden, Greece, Portugal and Italy had all adopted the same position, and in the same year the British government used its influence with Commonwealth countries, Latin America and Switzerland to persuade them also to take the same line on the non-recognition of the GDR. This solidarity was clearly a severe set-back to the GDR's diplomatic ambitions, and a major boost for the Federal

---

3 Telegram to Foreign Office, 19.10.49, PRO, FO 371/76617 .

4 Attitude of the Five Governments of the Treaty Commission and of the US Government to the Question of Recognition of the Pieck Administration in the Soviet Zone of Germany, Permanent Commission of Brussels Treaty Powers, Document No A/561, (Final Version), in Minute "Attitude towards the Soviet Zone in Germany", Miss G. Brown, 15.12.49, and telegram sent to all friendly governments, 23.12.49, in: PRO, FO371/76619.

Republic. As Ulrich Pfeil has commented: 'Die Aufwertung der DDR wurde durch diese Politik massiv erschwert und verschaffte der Bundesrepublik einen deutlichen Vorsprung auf internationalem Parkett' (Pfeil 1999:531). The Western Allied position with regard to the Federal Republic was subsequently to be enshrined in support for the *Alleinvertretungsanspruch.* As such, non-recognition of the GDR was a key component of the Western Allies' relationship with Bonn and of Western strategy for eventual German reunification.

Overcoming non-recognition barriers

In the light of the inflexible position adopted by Britain and others, much of the GDR effort – especially in the 1950s – was devoted to subverting the non-recognition policy and to attempts to secure recognition by the back door. A typical tactic was to circulate Western embassies in GDR-friendly capitals with official GDR responses to international events; courtesy demands that such communications are normally acknowledged, and the Foreign Office was obliged to draw up guidelines for Embassy personnel on the appropriate procedures for accepting delivery of such items, 'in order that the East Germans may not be emboldened by their success in distributing tracts, to try one day to put in a substantive communication'[5]. The West Germans were vigilant in their scrutiny of any public examples of the use of the title 'German Democratic Republic' in the UK and tireless in bringing such misdemeanours to the attention of the Foreign Office. In one well-documented incident in 1959, BOAC was forced to withdraw its in-flight maps of Europe which named the GDR, on the grounds that this would cause offence during Chancellor Adenauer's visit to London[6].

5 Instructions to Chancery, Bucharest, 15.1.1959, PRO, FO371/145745.

6 BOAC initially refused to withdraw the maps on the grounds of the expense of reprinting. Pressure was put on BOAC to reconsider after the matter had been raised at the Foreign Office by the West German Ambassador, 23.11.1959 and 10.12.1959, PRO, FO371/145793.

In the light of this extremely strict operation of the non-recognition policy, the East Germans' success in 1959 in obtaining permission to open a trade office (*KfA Ltd*) in London ranks as a major breakthrough, and on the face of it, as a major setback to the British position. The following year permission was also granted for the East Germans to open a travel information centre (Berolina Travel Ltd), though this was not actually opened until 1965. Both these offices took the form of private, limited companies and both employed GDR personnel. Following the establishment of diplomatic relations, *KfA Ltd* was formally wound up in 1975, its work having been absorbed into the commercial section of the new GDR Embassy. Berolina Travel Ltd retained its status as a private company and remained in operation throughout the period of official diplomatic relations between Britain and the GDR. It was formally dissolved in 1993, though it had ceased operations in 1990/91.

Trade and politics

The significance of trade in overcoming the barriers posed by Britain's non-recognition policy lies largely in the fact that Britain also had a potential interest in improved trading relations with the GDR, an interest the GDR worked to exploit to her advantage. By arguing for more formal arrangements, such as a bilateral trade agreement, within which trade and commercial relations could be established and developed, the GDR could be seen to be putting forward a common-sense and apparently ideology-free view which stood in stark contrast to Britain's seeming intransigence on this matter. The reasons for this intransigence lay as much in the scepticism on the part of the Foreign Office as to the potential for developing trade as in British government reluctance to permit any increase in status for the GDR.

But how could the GDR view be expressed? In the circumstances of non-recognition, the means available to the GDR to communicate with British authorities and government bodies depended on the use of intermediaries. Here the GDR was able to draw upon a range of political and trading contacts and links through personal and political/ideological association dating back to the 1930s.

The events leading to the setting-up of *KfA Ltd* derive in part from this background; they also reflect, however, the way in which arguments in favour of improved trading relationships had gained substantial ground in elite areas of public opinion in Britain during the course of the 1950s, as well as a recurring feature of trade relationships between Britain and the GDR during the non-recognition period, namely, the involvement of British MPs.

By the time *KfA Ltd* opened for business, the role of MPs in the development of trade relations between Britain and the GDR was an established feature. Some, like Ian Mikardo, [Lab., Tower Hamlets], had been regular visitors to the Leipzig Trade Fairs before the war. Others, like Arthur Lewis, [Lab., Newham, North West], had come to know Heinrich Rau, the first *Industrieminister* of the GDR, during the Spanish Civil War as members of the International Brigade. Both men were motivated by anti-fascist considerations in their desire to develop better trading links between Britain and the GDR, as well as by considerations of a more mundane commercial nature.

(George) Burnaby Drayson, [Conservative, Skipton], was one of the very few Conservative MPs to sustain an interest in trade relations with the GDR, and though he too derived a financial benefit, he was also motivated by ideas of East-West co-operation[7]. It was Burnaby Drayson who first contacted the Foreign Office to inform them of the GDR's readiness to conclude a bilateral trade agreement prior to his participation in the 1953 Autumn Fair at Leipzig. In line with the decision of the five governments on non-recognition, the Foreign Office rejected this opportunity, stressing that Britain regarded the Soviet Union as the competent authority in Eastern Germany and had no interest in concluding a trade agreement with the Soviet Zone[8]. However, Drayson's success in negotiating a contract for the import of potash which was extremely favourable both to the GDR and to British business interests cast some doubt on the Foreign Office

7 Interviews with Burnaby Drayson MP, House of Commons, 18.7.77, and Ian Mikardo MP, House of Commons, 19.7.77; see also Bell (1977:135 –147).

8 F. K. Roberts to Selwyn Lloyd, 12.6.53, PRO, FO371/103857.

position in the minds of the British company involved and increased his stock substantially with the East Germans[9].

Over the years of the non-recognition period, the GDR courted these and other MPs assiduously, mostly in the form of lavish hospitality and flatteringly high-level discussions during the Leipzig Fair, recognising both the propaganda and the irritation value they represented. Their visits were comprehensively reported in the GDR press, much to the annoyance of the West Germans in general and the SPD and British MPs friendly to it in particular. Within Britain, interest among British manufacturers in exhibiting at the Leipzig Fair grew steadily, partly as a result of the work of the Leipzig Fair Agency, established by Communist businessman, Denis Hayes, in 1954. Between them, the British exporters and the British MPs from the three main parties attending the Leipzig Fair acted as a regular source of pressure on the government to relax its policy in this area in order to benefit British industry. Harold Wilson was one of many Labour MPs to raise the matter in the House of Commons during this period. In March 1957 he stated:

> While we are aware that we have no diplomatic relations with Eastern Germany, is it not a fact that the Leipzig Fair is attended by sellers and buyers from all over the world? Are we not losing export trade by the rather slack attitude which the Government takes about East German relations[10]?

These and similar pressures eventually led to discussions with the West Germans about a possible relaxation of the British position. The discussions were initiated by the Board of Trade and reflect the competing priorities of two government Departments. The Foreign Office was anxious to protect the government's position on non-recognition, and reluctant to make concessions, especially as it was also sceptical about any likely increase in trade which might result were the non-recognition policy to be relaxed; the Board of Trade,

---

9 Over the years Drayson came to be held in much lower regard by the GDR who criticised him for 'seine politische Labilität und seine Konzeptionslosigkeit, [...] sein politisches Handeln [hängt] weitgehend von seinen geschäftlichen Interessen [ab].' Einschätzung, gez. Ludwig, Abt. WE/Sektion 11, 11.3.69, SAPMO-Bundesarchiv, [BArch] DY13/2102.

10 567 H.C. Deb. Cols. 534–535, 21.3.57.

however, was committed to increasing Britain's export activity. Agreement was reached with the West Germans that any negotiations with the East Germans must be conducted by a non-governmental body; thus, the Federation of British Industry (now the CBI) was invited to enter into discussions with the East Germans on the subject of a trade agreement and a trade office in London. These negotiations were concluded in early 1959 with a bilateral trade agreement to the value of £7m. on each side and permission for the East Germans to open a trade information office in London. For the East Germans, negotiations were conducted by the *Kammer für Außenhandel*, the department within the *Ministerium für Außenhandel* responsible for trade with non-socialist countries – hence the name *KfA Ltd*.

Establishing the GDR presence in Britain

The timing of these agreements was of particular significance to the GDR, coming as they did during the run-up to the 10th anniversary celebrations in October 1959. In GDR press coverage, *KfA Ltd*'s status as a private company was glossed over; there, as on its letter-head, it was always presented as 'die offizielle Vertretung der DDR in der britischen Hauptstadt', a description designed to convey a prestigious relationship with Britain based on mutual respect and equality. Further, the importance the GDR attached to its presence in London was underlined by the appointment of the Deputy Director of the *Kammer für Außenhandel* to be *KfA Ltd's* first Director.

The reality of *KfA Ltd's* situation was rather different. Its status as a private company enabled the Foreign Office to exercise great vigilance over its activities and these were very strictly controlled and monitored. Staff working for *KfA Ltd* had to renew their visas every six months, and whereas legitimate commercial activity was permitted, any form of political activity was strictly forbidden. The Foreign Office had always suspected that the GDR's motives in establishing the office were primarily political, and consequently its understanding of 'political activity' was likewise very strict, in particular where the public use of GDR flags or emblems in advertising or publicity material was concerned. Matters came to a head in November 1959 when *KfA Ltd* organised a repeat showing of an exhibition on life in the GDR, allegedly by popular demand, but in fact to coincide with Chancellor Adenauer's visit to London. Despite the FBI's warning of 'very grave consequences [...] if your efforts were in any way given a political slant'[11], advertisements for the exhibition bearing the GDR emblem appeared in the British national press. In fact, no action was taken against *KfA Ltd* as the Foreign Office could not be sure that the East Germans had been responsible for placing the advertisements concerned. But a warning shot had been fired, and within the Foreign Office there was no doubt as to the action that might be taken in the event of further breaches of the terms of *KfA Ltd*'s activity. A minute of November 1959 states: 'We should [...] watch *KfA Ltd* carefully and crack down on them by revoking a visa if they go beyond the bounds of legitimate commercial activity'[12].

Revoking a visa was the most serious sanction available to the Foreign Office at that time and clearly *KfA Ltd* did not wish to risk this happening. At the time, the office was staffed by only four employees, though this was to rise. At the end of the 1960s, the number of GDR staff, including the correspondents of ADN and *Neues Deutschland*, working in London, was estimated at 30 (Eymelt 1970: 15). But each increase in staff had to be approved both by the Board of Trade and by the Foreign Office, and *KfA Ltd* knew it had to tread carefully in implementing the next phase of its strategy which was to raise public awareness of the GDR and eventually to mobilise support for the recognition of the GDR. The founding of Berolina Travel Ltd was intended to contribute particularly to the first of these objectives, whereas *KfA Ltd*'s role was really to focus on the promotion and development of trade relations and to exploit the opportunities for influencing elite opinion in favour of recognition. To achieve this and to avoid falling foul of the Foreign Office, in 1960 the GDR engaged the services of a London PR company, Lex Hornsby and Partners, at an annual fee of £20,000, to promote the

11 The warning came from the FBI as the Foreign Office had no direct contact with *KfA Ltd.* However, the Foreign Office was fully aware of the action being taken by the FBI. Peter Tennant (FBI) to Kurt Wolf (*KfA Ltd*), 2.11.59, PRO, FO371/145935.

12 Minute, John Killick, 16.11.59, PRO, FO371/145784.

trade and commercial opportunities for British business in the GDR. Lex Hornsby and Partners held this contract throughout the period of non-recognition and clearly did an excellent job of issuing press releases, organising visits to the Leipzig Fair for groups of businessmen, MPs and journalists and of introducing the staff of *KfA Ltd* to useful contacts[13]. By the mid-1960s Lex Hornsby and Partners' role in publicising and developing these links had helped to provide *KfA Ltd* with access to a network of contacts in politics, business and media in Britain which could be – and were – mobilised effectively in support of arguments for the recognition of the GDR.

In terms of the campaign for recognition, it was the company's links with MPs which were to be the most useful for the aspirations of the GDR and also to be the most controversial. For a short time in the early 1960s, Lex Hornsby and Partners retained Burnaby Drayson and another Conservative MP as consultants to the GDR account, an action which attracted widespread critical comment when Drayson sought to intervene in the case of the London correspondent of ADN whose visa was revoked in December 1960 in compliance with a NATO ban on the issue of visas and residence permits to East Germans. The staff of *KfA Ltd* and their families were not affected (Howarth 1981:5). The West Germans had been very critical of the role of Lex Hornsby and Partners in furthering the cause of the GDR, especially as the numbers of MPs visiting the Leipzig Fair increased. In fact, in 1960 the SPD made a formal complaint to the National Executive of the Labour Party, specifically in relation to the propaganda use made by the East Germans of these visits, but despite some initiatives designed to increase contact between the Labour Party and the SPD, there was no discernible reduction in the number of MPs visiting the GDR. Even worse for the West Germans, the calls for recognition seemed to be coming thick and fast both in the House of Commons and in the political press[14]. In September 1961, following the building of the Berlin Wall in August, both the Liberal

13 Lex Hornsby and Partners, Monthly Reports to Interwerbung, February 1960 – June 1970, cited in Bell (1977: 163 –165); also SAPMO-BArch DY13/2100.

14 See, for example, Emanuel Shinwell and Viscount Hinchingbrooke, 617 H. C. Deb. Cols. 235 and 272 (11.2.60); Lord Boothby, *Sunday Times*, 16.7.61; Richard Crossman, 'Berlin Collision Course', *New Statesman*, 21.7.61.

and the Labour Party Conferences passed resolutions in favour of the *de facto* recognition of the GDR.

Berolina Travel Ltd

KfA Ltd had come into existence against the Foreign Office's will, and experience of *KfA Ltd* in operation had done nothing to lessen the Foreign Office's distaste for an East German presence in London. In the summer of 1960, the Board of Trade informed the Foreign Office of the GDR's application to open a travel information bureau in London to encourage tourism between the UK and the GDR. The West German Embassy indicated its hostility to the proposal to the Foreign Office on the grounds that the GDR would derive great propaganda benefit. The Foreign Office was in no doubt that 'we should do anything we can to sabotage the establishment of it', though it recognised that it might not be able to prevent it[15]. Permission was granted and Berolina Travel Ltd was registered on 30th September 1960 with a share capital of £5000, though only two £1 shares were issued to named members of the London firm of accountants representing the GDR in this matter[16]. The *Reisebüro der DDR* was the immediate East German body involved, but in due course the *Deutsch-Britische Freundschaftsgesellschaft* came to play the most influential steering role.

The establishment of Berolina Travel Ltd was designed to raise public awareness of the GDR and to encourage more 'ordinary' UK citizens to visit the GDR and thus to spread the word. Although the GDR did not describe it as such, Berolina's role was to target the masses while *KfA Ltd* concentrated on the elite. But whereas *KfA Ltd* is a success story for the East Germans, the history of Berolina Travel Ltd is one of setbacks of a political, ideological and business nature that were so great that it totally failed to realise its potential either in the campaign for recognition or as a business. In fact, in early 1969 its

---

15 John Killick to W. Wilberforce, 11.8.60, PRO FO371/154279.

16 Berolina Travel Ltd Annual Reports and Accounts, 1960-1993, Companies House, Cardiff.

own Managing Director suggested to the *Reisebüro der DDR* that it should be closed.

The political setbacks were present right from the start. The Foreign Office did not have to try very hard to find a means of sabotaging the venture as the Managing Director proposed by the East Germans had already made himself *persona non grata* in Britain and his request for a visa was refused[17]. Though normally this might only have been a delaying tactic, in 1960 and again in 1961, this time in protest against the building of the Berlin Wall, NATO operated a ban on the issue of visas and residence permits to East Germans. The ban remained in force until the mid-1960s. This and other reasons prevented the appointment of an East German to the staff of Berolina Travel Ltd until after recognition had taken place.

The immediate consequence of this was that for the time being the accountants were asked to take on the job of finding suitable premises. As the West Germans had foreseen, the East Germans were keen to exploit the propaganda potential of their new presence and for that reason they placed considerable value on a prestige location. Negotiations at a distance were very difficult and the lease on one possible office in Oxford Street was not secured because of delays in communication with the GDR. Part of the reason for the delay at the GDR end was that the question of staffing had not been resolved, and this added to the uncertainty. Approaches had been made to the Communist Party of Great Britain to recommend a candidate for the post of Managing Director, and at their suggestion an appointment was made. The man appointed, a member of the CPGB, took up his duties in February 1964. His brief was to find suitable premises which could be opened in time for the GDR's fifteenth *Jahrestag* the following October and to organise a lavish opening event in that connection. Soon, however, the East Germans came to have severe doubts as to their new MD's suitability for the post. In a minute for the Abteilung Außenpolitik of the Zentralkomitee written in

17 During a visit to London in February 1960, David Rummelsburg had engaged in political activity by showing a film on the Nazi background of Theodor Oberländer to a group of MPs in the House of Commons. Correspondence between Simon Midgeley of the Economist and David Rummelsburg, 15.11.60, SAPMO-BArch DY13/2099.

September 1964, a member of Reisebüro staff described him as having 'zu wenig Geschäfts- und Organisationstalent' and for being 'seinen Aufgaben nicht gewachsen'[18]. There were certainly grounds for dissatisfaction. With less than three months to go before the fifteenth anniversary celebrations, no plans for the celebrations themselves had been made and no premises had been taken. Lengthy and ultimately costly discussions were ongoing with an architect about alterations to possible premises in High Holborn but these came to nothing. The plans for the anniversary party had to be ditched and so did the MD.

In his place, the GDR appointed Denis Hayes, the Managing Director of the Leipzig Fair Agency and also a Communist Party member, to the post. In consultation with Jost Prescher of *KfA Ltd*, he took a lease on premises in Dover Street, a side street on the North side of Piccadilly at Green Park, and parallel to Albemarle Street where *KfA Ltd*'s own premises were situated. The premises were double-fronted and large enough to accommodate both the Leipzig Fair Agency and Berolina Travel Ltd. Though both Prescher and Hayes were well pleased with their choice, it did not go down so well in East Berlin. Following a visit to Britain in the summer of 1968, Erich Friedländer, the secretary of the Deutsch-Britische Freundschaftsgesellschaft, wrote in his report, 'Das Büro ist in einer [...] vornehmen Seitenstraße [...] gelegen, einem Ort, der wohl geeignet ist für aristokratische Schneider- und Putzmacherateliers, weniger aber für so eine profane Angelegenheit wie Touristenwerbung'[19].

The GDR was also less than satisfied with the staffing of Berolina Travel Ltd. The appointment of Denis Hayes was envisaged as a temporary measure, but when, in 1966, he was reminded of this, he put up very strong resistance to the idea of stepping down, so much so that only the merest tinkering with staffing arrangements actually took place. These proved even less satisfactory. Hayes' secretary at the Leipzig Fair Agency, believed also to be a member of the Communist

18 Aktennotiz vom Reisebüro der DDR, gez. Hennig, an das ZK, Abteilung Außenpolitik, Abteilung Verkehr und Verbindungen, MfAA Länderabteilung u. a., 16.9.64, SAPMO-BArch, DY13/2099.

19 Reisebericht Erich Friedländers für die Deutsch-Britische Gesellschaft, 3.7.1968, SAPMO-BArchiv DY13/2095.

Party, took over as the office manager, while Hayes himself retained the title of Managing Director but took a less prominent role in the day to day operation of Berolina. The secretary was clearly an extremely abrasive character, and letters of complaint about 'die sehr unfreundliche Behandlung der Besucher' were made to the Reisebüro der DDR. More importantly, her ideological commitment to the GDR was called into question. 'Für sie ist eine Reise in die DDR etwa dasselbe wie eine Reise nach Südafrika, mit dem Unterschied daß es im letzteren Land wärmer, schöner, bequemer und einfacher ist'[20]. There was, however, little the GDR could do until her contract ran out in the spring of 1969.

These were just a few of the difficulties attaching to Berolina's operation during the non-recognition period. Others included the negative publicity in the wake of the arrest, in January 1970, and subsequent trial on espionage charges of Will Owen MP [Lab., Morpeth], who had been appointed as a Director of the company in 1964. Will Owen had also been Chairman of the All-Party British-GDR Parliamentary Group, a sub-committee of the East-West Trade Group of the House of Commons formed in 1965 to lobby for improved trade arrangements with the GDR. Berolina's difficulties were also reflected in mounting trading losses. However, the GDR was not inclined to follow Denis Hayes' advice to close the operation down, because the prime interest for the GDR lay not in Berolina's commercial potential but in its role in the broad area of *Auslandsinformation.*

Auslandsinformation and the conduct of bilateral relations

The raising of the GDR's profile in Britain was primarily the area with which the *Deutsch-Britische Gesellschaft* [Debrig] was concerned. Founded in 1963, Debrig's role was to build a body of opinion favourable to the GDR in Britain. From the mid-1960s, its work was complemented by that of its counterpart in Britain, BRIDGE [Britain-Democratic Germany Information Exchange],

20 ibid.

which provided a vehicle for the expression of the GDR position on recognition, the principal policy goal at that time. Debrig soon realised that the efforts of BRIDGE alone would not be sufficient in this endeavour. The membership of BRIDGE was drawn largely from the ranks of the Communist Party, the British Peace Committee and similar political organisations. The bond holding the attachment to the GDR together had been forged by the strong personal links with German Jewish and Communist emigrés to Britain and their joint anti-fascist struggle of the 1930s and 1940s. Tireless though BRIDGE members were in promoting the cause of the GDR, the fact remained that they seldom succeeded in reaching beyond their own steadily declining circle of the already converted. For this reason, the role of Berolina Travel Ltd in reaching other areas of British public opinion was seen as crucial.

With the normalisation of relations between Britain and the GDR, the GDR anticipated an increase in interest in the GDR on the part of a number of different organisations and sectors of public opinion. As a travel and information centre, Berolina was expected to play a major role in promoting and supporting this interest. In part, these expectations proved correct. Awareness of the GDR's sporting prowess led to greater interest in selection and training methods (and suspicions of doping), but this interest did little to redeem the image of the GDR as a repressive regime which had to resort to building a cruel and ugly fortified frontier to prevent its citizens from travelling freely. In British academic circles, specialist interest in the literature, culture and society of the GDR grew, but its focus was on aesthetic considerations and theoretical analysis and could not be converted into a more general sympathy for the 'values' of the system, especially because of the prominence given to human rights as a result of the 1975 Helsinki agreement. Critical attention was drawn to the record of the GDR in this general area, particularly in the wake of the Biermann expulsion (1976) and the Bahro trial (1978)[21].

---

21 Recent revelations on the recruitment of alleged British informers for the Stasi during the 1980s have confirmed the importance the GDR placed on its *Auslandsinformation* activities. See *The Spying Game*, a four-part series shown weekly on BBC 2, 19.9 – 9.10.99.

During the course of the 1970s East German foreign policy towards the West was primarily concerned with consolidating the GDR's international position and with underlining its separate and distinctive existence as a German state at an elite level. Thus, the new East German Embassy in London focused on developing bilateral relations with Britain, specifically the negotiation of agreements to cover areas such as commercial co-operation, health and cultural exchange[22]. The activities of Berolina were secondary to this main undertaking.

Effectively therefore, the GDR came to pursue a two-tier policy in its diplomacy towards Britain. The upper tier was concerned with the normal and normalised trappings of diplomatic life, such as the negotiation of agreements and the round of meetings, briefings, receptions and socialising on which diplomatic life is based. In that way, the GDR sought to present itself as an uncontroversial actor on the London diplomatic scene. However, at the same time the lower tier was concerned to promote the GDR view on issues which were not so uncontroversial. In the Cold War climate of the late 1970s and 1980s, the interests of the GDR in presenting itself as a different (and in the GDR view, superior) German state needed to be communicated effectively and Berolina and the organisations associated with it provided the best means to achieve this objective.

Internally however, Berolina was once more beset by operational difficulties, this time in its relationship with the Britain-GDR Society (as BRIDGE had renamed itself following recognition) whose secretary had been detailed to run the 'GDR Travel Club', essentially a mailing list designed to promote further opportunities to visit the GDR. This arrangement did not operate to the satisfaction of Berolina or the GDR, partly because the then secretary of the Britain-GDR Society felt little allegiance to this area of activity and put almost no effort into its promotion as a consequence. In a small way, these and other difficulties reflect a broader area of disagreement evident as of the mid-1970s, namely the ideological splits developing between the

22 The Co-operation Agreement (1973) was designed to monitor bilateral trade on an annual basis. Other agreements were the Consular Agreement (1976), the Health Agreement (1977) and the Cultural Agreement (1979).

ruling communist parties of the Eastern bloc and the Euro-Communist tendencies of Western-based communist parties. The society's last secretary, though ideologically acceptable to the GDR, did not succeed in reconciling these tensions as they manifested themselves within the society, and splits developed. Under such circumstances, much of the propaganda initiative in Britain passed to Berolina.

In the 1980s Berolina was caught up in one of the few areas which were to bring these emerging tendencies back together, temporarily anyway, and in that sense it was to justify its existence – or some of it – at least in a small way. Its lifeline came in the form of the peace movement which mobilised sympathy and support for the position of both German states and increased public regard for the peace-loving aspirations of the GDR. In the entire history of the GDR no other single factor proved capable of engendering as much sympathy abroad for the GDR position, and the scope for Berolina to fulfil its potential as an information centre was greatly increased as a result.

Conclusions

The GDR maintained a presence in Britain for approximately thirty years and in various guises. During that time, the GDR never lost sight of her fundamental objective which was to score victories in small skirmishes on the edges of the battlefield of the Cold War, leaving more powerful allies to fire the big guns. By accumulating individual honours, the GDR hoped to claim her territory as a moral superior and to demonstrate her validity both to East and West. Though this accolade was ultimately to elude her, it was not to do so totally. The experience derived from the operation of *KfA Ltd* highlights the success of a clearly focused strategy in achieving defined but limited objectives. Though the scepticism of the FBI about the long-term trade potential of the GDR was ultimately borne out by events, it is questionable whether the development of trade relations with Britain was really the GDR's priority[23]. It seems more likely that the prime objective was to stimulate public opinion in favour of recognition. Much the same can be said of Berolina's sphere of activity. Though its chequered history underlines the vulnerability of a business operated for ideological rather than commercial reasons, the GDR's purpose was not primarily commercial. It was much more to do with winning hearts and minds in the context of the Cold War. The real lesson to be learned relates to the scope available to the GDR to use the mantle of diplomacy and an identity as a business in pursuit of these objectives.

Bibliography

Bell, Marianne (1977) *Britain and the GDR: The Politics of Non-Recognition*, unpubl. M Phil dissertation, University of Nottingham

Eymelt, Friedrich (1970) *Die Tätigkeit der DDR in den nicht-kommunistischen Ländern, V. Großbritannien*, Forschungsinstitut der Deutschen Gesellschaft für Auswärtige Politik, Bonn

Howarth, Marianne (1981) 'East Germany at Westminster', *GDR Monitor* 5, 1–12

Pfeil, Ulrich (1999) 'Die "anderen" deutsch-französischen Beziehungen, in Heiner Timmerman (ed.) *Die DDR, Erinnerung an einen untergegangenen Staat*, Berlin: Duncker & Humblot, 527–559

Public Record Office (PRO), Foreign Office General Correspondence (FO371)

Stiftung Archiv der Parteien und Massenorganisationen der DDR (SAPMO), Bundesarchiv Berlin Lichterfelde-West, Liga für Völkerfreundschaft (DY13)

23 In common with most other EU countries, Britain over-estimated the potential for increased trade with the GDR following recognition, and trade levels remained disappointing throughout the period of formal diplomatic relations.

MECHTHILD M. MATHEJA-THEAKER

The Collapse of the German Welfare State: Women and Poverty

Poverty in the Federal Republic

'Poverty? In Germany? Where?' Marek is Polish and has just returned from a lengthy trip through India. 'You can find poverty in Poland, there is poverty in India, that is really terrible, but not in wealthy Germany! Nobody is poor here!' – This is the introduction to Michael Schomers' documentary report *Alltag Armut* (1999:7). Marek is not alone in finding it difficult to reconcile his perception of Germany with the concept of increasing poverty. However, even a brief look through the most recent volumes of *Stern* and *Spiegel* soon reveals an increasing number of articles on rising poverty, growing numbers of people claiming social assistance [Sozialhilfe], in soup kitchens and in hostels for the homeless. The number of documentary reports during the late 1990s draw further attention to the fact that these assessments are not simply 'Dramatisierungen' (Leibfried et al. 1995:13f.) but facts, which are still subjected to a strategy of repression

This paper aims to investigate poverty in Germany at the end of the 90s and with particular reference to the situation of women. This will include an analysis of statistical data as well as sociological studies. In this context concepts such as the definition of poverty, the extent and time-spans involved, and the social groupings affected will also be addressed.

The changing face of poverty

As in any other industrial country there has always been a certain level of poverty in Germany, but the attitude of the government and the population has changed considerably since the end of the war. A brief profile of the changing faces of poverty in Germany is thus not only a suitable, but also a very useful starting point for an investigation of this kind. According to Eckardt (1997: 19) and Leibfried et al. (1995: 222) the changing perceptions fall into five time-spans, which can be quite clearly separated.

1945 onwards

Due to the devastation caused by the war and the country's economic collapse a general 'relief of the deprivation' ['Linderung der Armut', Konrad Adenauer] was imperative. The adverse weather conditions of the winter of 1946 brought the situation to a head. The alleviation of poverty was thus central to domestic policy.

1950s

In the 1950s a transition from *collective poverty*, i.e. the poverty of the people, to the poverty of the individual can be observed. By 1953 the debate on social reform was beginning to deal with problems caused by insufficient benefit provisions. The 1957 pension reform increased payments by around 60% and also clearly intended to alleviate poverty. During this period the concept of a social market economy was closely linked with the battle against poverty (see Leibfried et al. 1995:214f.).

1960s

In the 60s poverty lost its importance, as people believed themselves in Schelsky's 'nivellierter Mittelstandsgesellschaft'. Poverty was no longer seen as a problem affecting the whole of society. In 1961 social assistance [Sozialhilfe] was introduced. Despite numerous changes, at least some of its basic principles are still in force today. It not only embraces a legal entitlement to help and support but also obliges the state to ensure a life-style 'fit for a human being' [menschenwürdiges Leben] which it attempts to provide by standardising material benefits.

1970s

During this Social Democratic period, poverty was considered to be 'a thing of the past' and subsequently only discussed within the discourse on fringe groupings within society (Leibfried et al. 1995:218f.). It was not until the late 1970s that poverty was once more addressed and this time by Heiner Geißler in his debate on the *Neue Soziale Frage* (Eckardt 1997:19: Leibfried et al. 1995:222).

1980s onwards: Germany's 'new poverty'

Rising unemployment and the new poverty brought about discussions and theories on the 'two-thirds-society' [*Zweidrittelgesellschaft*], a concept used to describe a society in which it is acceptable that one third of the population lives in poverty, while two thirds do not. Not surprisingly, this notion always has been and still remains highly controversial (Klammer and Bäcker, 1998:363f.). But even though the new poverty started to affect the middle classes, its collective quality was not recognised in the same way as it was in the 50s. Consequently, it was not given the same unquestioning priority, and political measures for its alleviation were not implemented with the same urgency. Initially, the general public reacted by trying to repress what became increasingly obvious; to many, the existence of poverty was simply inconceivable. Instead, moral prejudices prevailed: Poverty is caused by an individual's own shortcomings, those afflicted are simply too lazy to work (Leibfried et al. 1995:11f.).

Demographic changes and shifts in the structure of the family caused the birthrate to dip, sent divorce rates soaring and subsequently the numbers of single parents and people living on their own increased. Socio-cultural changes such as the individualisation and pluralisation of life plans had a considerable impact, especially on women. All these changes are on-going and are likely to continue in the foreseeable future (Hübinger 1999:19f.; Miegel 1996:20).

Germany's unification brought a double helping of *new poverty* in east and west[1]. Nevertheless, at the beginning of the 90s poverty was still seen as relative and temporary – especially as regards the new *Länder*. It is often portrayed as a necessary evil that excessive consumerism needs to be restrained while Germany is trying to cope with the pressure of international competition (*Standort Deutschland*) (Leibfried et al. 1995:11f.).

The changing faces of poverty in the FRG have been summarised in the form of a table (Leibfried et al. 1995:231):

Table 1: The changing face of poverty

	1950s	1960s	1970s	1980s	1990s
Groupings afflicted by poverty	Poverty of the population	Poverty of the individual	Poverty of groupings	Poverty of groupings / lower third of society	Poverty of a region / part of society
Causes	Structural (consequences of war)	Individual (fate)	'Societal'; 'caused' by the welfare state	Structural (labour market)	Social upheaval
Duration of individual poverty	Temporary	Temporary	Long-term	Long-term	Long-term
Political Measures	Economic and housing policies, pension reform	Social assistance, social work	Social / welfare policies	Social / welfare policies; Policies supporting families	Regional development policies; socio-political transition regulations

1 In this context the consistantly rising figures of foreign workers and asylum seekers need to be borne in mind. In 1993, they were transferred to a different system, so that they are no longer included in the general statistics for social assistance.

Structure of society	'Social market economy'/ 'wealth for all'	'Nivellierte Mittel-standsge-sellschaft'	'Modern welfare state'	'Two-thirds-society'	Transition society
Approaches to poverty	Collective	Latency	Selective re-discovery	Re-discovery ('new poverty')	Broad

The face of poverty has changed considerably over the years: from collective poverty, via individual poverty and the poverty of fringe groups to today's form of poverty, which may be referred to as 'mobile poverty' or 'poverty on the move' [bewegliche Armut]. However, while there now is a much higher level of awareness, there is also a persistent lack of acceptance. The general public and the majority of politicians still do not wish to acknowledge (at least not publicly) that this problem is affecting a growing section of society.

Terminology of poverty

A new terminology has developed to cope with the various trends and observations. The term 'new poverty' relates to the poverty of the nineties, as opposed to the 'old' poverty, which was generally believed to be a thing of the past. 'New' poverty is also linked to 'concealed poverty', sometimes also referred to as 'bashful' [verschämt] and 'latent' (as opposed to 'open') poverty. The 'concealed poor' are those whose income lies below the threshold for social assistance and who – in spite of their legal entitlement – do not claim. The notion of having to expose one's financial situation to an official and the fear that relations might be called upon to contribute to one's maintenance is not only off-putting but also causes many – and especially older citizens – to forego their entitlement (Hunfeld 1998:64; Schomers 1999:145f.). The term 'concealed' is based on the fact that the people affected are not entered into any official statistic (Neumann 1999:27). Consequently, their existence is only known to experts, while the general public remains unaware.

'Absolute poverty' describes the problem of physical survival, the lack of food, clothing and housing. In today's Germany, poverty is no longer life threatening, it has become 'relative'. 'Relative poverty' is thus a concept whose meaning remains controversial and which is highly relevant to the study of women and poverty. Relative poverty generally implies that an individual's level of existence has fallen below the accepted socio-cultural minimum. Defining such a minimum standard requires the setting of norms, and opinions on how this should be achieved are divided. For many, even relative poverty in a welfare state is just as undignified [menschenunwürdig] as absolute poverty in developing countries (Leibfried et al. 1995:11).

What does being poor in Germany actually mean?

The former minister for the family, senior citizens, women and youth, Claudia Nolte, was by and large correct when she stated in an interview in *Der Spiegel* (Nolte and Schmidt 1998:69) that no one in Germany needed to starve and that everyone was clothed.But does this mean, as she claimed, that there is no poverty? Considering the rising unemployment and the growing numbers of people on social assistance, this notion is highly questionable. An increasing number of studies confirm that a growing number of citizens can no longer take part in normal everyday life, because 'there is more to poverty than simply having restricted funds. Poverty means life without the prospect of ever getting out of this situation, poverty means utter hopelessness' (Schomers 1999:12).

The European Commission defines the threshold of poverty at 50 per cent of the average national income per head, weighted according to the respective members of the household. The German Institute for Economic Research estimates that every citizen should have a minimum income of DM 941 a month to prevent him or her from sliding into poverty. According to this definition, around 10 million people in Germany are already poor (Hunfeld 1998:8). There is no official poverty threshold and thus the threshold to social assistance is frequently referred to as the 'quasi-official' line (Neumann 1999:27). Social assistance is available to those whose income is less than the minimum amount necessary for existence as defined by the Federal Social Welfare Act (BMfAS, 1999:9f.).

Social assistance

The standard level for social assistance for a single person or the head of a household stands at DM 539 per month[2]. While the Association for the Protection of Children [Kinderschutzbund] and other charitable organisations estimate the cost for one child to be DM 700 to 900 per month (Klein 1994:88f.), the actual payments available for children lie between DM 270 and DM 485 according to age. Dependants over eighteen years, e.g. the spouse, receive DM 431 (BMfAS 1999:84f.). The actual payments available thus barely come to half the sum recommended. Single parents are entitled to a supplementary payment of DM 216 per month for up to three children[3]. Social services will also cover housing costs 'within reason' (Federal Ministry of Labour and Social Affairs 1999: 82). The rules are strict: a single person is allowed a maximum of $45m^2$, a square metre must not cost more than DM 7,70 to rent or attract more than DM 3,50 in additional costs (heating etc.). There is an allowance of a further $15m^2$ for every additional member of the family (BMfAS 1999:16; Schomers 1999:21).

The basket of goods and the statistical model

According to the Federal Social Welfare Act, the social assistance office is obliged to enable every individual to lead a life in 'dignity' – but what is actually required to achieve this? Until July 1990 payments were based on the cost of a 'basket of goods' which was put together by representatives of the local authorities, the social ministries of the *Länder* and charitable organisations. The contents were very detailed, such as: ten eggs, 250g flour, 50g peas, 25ml

---

2 Applicable as of 1.7.1998.

3 Arithmetic average of the standard payments of all *Länder*.

shampoo, two rolls of toilet paper etc. In addition there were also one cinema ticket per month, twelve tickets for public transport, ten local telephone calls, four letters and thirty kilometres of rail travel.

Until July 1990 this basket of goods provided the basis for calculating the standard level of social assistance [Sozialhilferegelsatz] which then amounted to DM 420. The *Warenkorb* was always controversial, such a listing of items was considered shameful by many and it was also criticised for being unhealthy, the goods included had too few vitamins and too much fat (Hunfeld 1998:64). Nevertheless, there were further cuts: between 1978 and 1984 social assistance was no longer adjusted in line with price increases and the buying power of those on benefit fell by around 8 per cent. From then on the ministries of the *Länder* took over the responsibility of compiling the list of items deemed necessary. They did this by replacing the *average* prices the basket had been based on with *lowest* prices possible, as claimants had 'plenty of time to shop around' (Hunfeld 1998:65).

This measure did not achieve the desired effect. The 'cheap basket' [Billigkorb] was still 9 per cent more expensive than its predecessor. Subsequently, the concept of a basket of goods was abandoned and replaced by the statistical model, which bases its calculations on the earnings of the lowest income groups. All items considered superfluous were removed from such a budget, the rest provided the basis for the new standard level required for a 'life in dignity'. This regulation has been in force since July 1, 1990. Every time the income of the lower groups decreases, social assistance payments go down, even if this means that they fall below the minimum level for existence. Payments are no longer checked against basic requirements (see Hunfeld 1998:66).

What does a life on social assistance actually mean?

The listing below was published in 1997 in a journal for social welfare workers and is not offered to claimants. The leaflets they receive only refer to the sum of DM 539, but give no explanation as to how this amount is arrived at (Schomers 1999:23f.)

Table 2: Estimate of the standard level of social assistance

	Standard Allowance Per month		Daily Allowance
Food			
Food stuffs	DM 219.33		
Meals out	DM 17.68	Total food	
		DM 254.42	DM 8.21
Electricity	DM 51.39	Total electricity	
		DM 51.39	
Continuous provisions			
Purchase of clothes/ household items			
Socks, accessories	DM 8.40		
Crockery, household expenses	DM 9.39		
Washing and cleaning materials	DM 8.53		
Unspecified consumer goods	DM 2.58		
Services	DM 12.28	Total clothes/household	
		DM 41.18	DM 1.33
Repair of clothes and linens			
Repair			
Clothes and linens	DM 1.30		
Shoe repair	DM 2.06		
Shoe accessories	DM 0.22	Total repair	
		DM 3.58	DM 1.12
Personal hygiene			
Looking after one's health	DM 8.70		
Utility goods for health care	DM 2.29		
Personal hygiene	DM 7.04		
Shampoo, shaving cream etc	DM 2.31		
Toilet paper etc.	DM 3.24		
Utility goods for personal hygiene	DM 0.82		
Services for personal hygiene	DM 12.15	Total personal hygiene	
		DM 36.56	DM 1.18
Personal needs			
Books brochures	DM 10.54		
News papers	DM 14.23		
Education, entertainment, leisure	DM 2.54		
Theatre, Sport, Cinema	DM 2.61		
Education, entertainment, leisure	DM 3.74		
Public transport	DM 25.79		
Telephone, Postage	DM 41.79		

Flowers	DM 7.04		
Toys	DM 2.17		
Sport, Camping	DM 1.31		
Services banks etc.	DM 1.42		
Unspecified Repairs	DM 2.81		
Bicycle	DM 1.07		
Alcohol, Tobacco	DM 34.83	Total personal needs DM 151.88	DM 4.90
TOTAL		DM 539.00	

Schomers' documentary is based on Günter Wallraff's reports of 'hands-on experiences'. He describes his attempts of trying to survive on DM 539 a month and kept a detailed record of his experiences and thoughts which make compelling reading:

> I cannot manage. On day 15 I have already spent 60 per cent of my budget. But I don't really know how and where I could cut down further. [...] One really has to budget very carefully. [...]
>
> The experiment has failed. I have not been able to live on this amount; I have overspent by DM 43,63. In real life this would mean that next month I would have to restrict myself even more. But on the whole I already feel that I have restricted myself as much as I can. For a short time this should be quite manageable. But the idea of living like this for many years, perhaps my whole life, frightens me. And not so much on a material level. For me the feeling of being excluded from so many things, not being able to participate any more is much more important [...] (Wallraff in Schomers 1999:115f., 168).

Hunfeld (1998:66) explains in this context that even if social assistance were to be based on incomes between DM 800 and 1000, this would already entail a 10 per cent increase. To avoid this, standard rates are no longer based on the price increases of the goods required, but rather on the *general* price increase, which tends to be far lower. The fact that luxury goods such as cars, computers and similar consumer goods are hardly affordable for people on lower incomes seems to bear no relevance. The stability – and in some cases decrease – of the costs of these goods over the last few years thus appears to have been the deciding factor. The price increase for general goods between 1983 and 1988 came to a mere 4.6 per cent, while the prices for essential items such as bread, milk and clothes rose by about 12 per cent.

Initially, social assistance was introduced as a measure to combat poverty. But, as Ulrich Schneider, the Secretary of the *Deutscher Paritätischer Wohlfahrtsverband* (DPWV), points out, this is no longer working:

> On the one hand, politicians have kept the level of social assistance in check [...] for years, and on the other our society is beginning to split. Not so long ago it was quite sufficient to buy your child a pair of trainers when it wanted to play football, [...] today, being *in* or *out* is determined increasingly by expensive status symbols. This is costly. What poverty is and where poverty begins cannot be determined objectively. In the end this will always be a subjective decision. [...] Social assistance equals poverty, because social assistance is no longer sufficient to enable people, and especially children, to participate in society (quoted in Hunfeld 1998: 177f.).

What is life like below the poverty line?

An initial framework can be established by looking at who claims social assistance in the Federal Republic.

Table 3: Male and female recipients of social assistance (continuous support) 1980 – 1997 (in 1000). Source: Statistisches Bundesamt (1998b).

Year	Male	Female	Total
Old *Länder*			
1980	342	580	922
1985	613	858	1 471
1990	812	1 020	1 832
1991	829	1 046	1 875
1992	954	1 154	2 108
1993	986	1 222	2 208
1994	870	1 182	2 052
1995	993	1 321	2 314
1996	1 043	1 366	2 410
1997	1 102	1 426	2 528
New *Länder* and East-Berlin			
1991	113	141	254

1992	158	173	330
1993	150	171	321
1994	114	143	257
1995	128	158	286
1996	144	170	314
1997	178	211	389
Germany			
1991	942	1 187	2 129
1992	1 111	1 327	2 438
1993	1 136	1 393	2 529
1994	983	1 325	2 308
1995	1 121	1 478	2 599
1996	1 187	1 536	2 724
1997	1 280	1 637	2 917

Social assistance in its narrow sense, i.e. as continuous support, provides food, clothes and lodging. At the end of 1997, 2.92 million people in 1.51 million households received social assistance, i.e. 3.6 per cent of the population (1991: 2.7 per cent). Between the end of 1996 and 1997, the number of people claiming this benefit had risen by 7.1 per cent, 56.1 per cent were female, 43.9 per cent male, 2.53 million lived in the old *Länder* and 389,000 in the new. The number of recipients in the new *Länder* has risen considerably more from the previous year (+23.9 per cent) than in the old *Länder* (+ 4.9 per cent). The expenditure for social assistance for 1997 came to 17.1 billion DM (1991: 10.6 billion) (StBA 1998c, 1998b).

According to the latest (preliminary) figures, the situation is still deteriorating. A further increase of 2.6 per cent from the previous year is expected for 1999: in the old *Länder* a plus of 2.2 per cent, in the new a rise by 5.8 per cent. In 1998, the Federal Republic spent on average DM 484 per head (DM 523 in the old *Bundesländer* and 314 in the ex-GDR) (StBA 1999).

Is poverty still a female issue?

The share of women amongst social assistance claimants is continuously high and also still increasing. This fact alone provides a firm indication that poverty is still a problem which affects women more than men. But it is not only the sheer number of women who are affected: the reasons for their higher level of dependence on such benefits and the period of time spent in this dependence are also highly significant. The 1997 Welfare Report provides substantial data which further support the observations made above:

Table 4: Recipients of social assistance in Germany (rounded). Source: adapted from *Sozialreport* (1997: 88).

Children under 15		844 000	34.0 %
Over 65s		160 000	6.4 %
Persons between the ages of 15 and 65, Average age: around 36		1 510 000	60.1 %
Distribution:	In gainful employment (more than 50 % part-time)	109 000	7.0 %
	Registered unemployed	467 000 (approx. 300 000 without official support)	
	Men	1 100 000	43.2 %
	Women	1 430 000	56.8 %
Households affected	One-person-household		40.0 %
	Households of single parents		23.0 %
	Married couples with children		13.0
	Married couples without children		7.0 %

These figures show that there is a disproportionate number of women in most of the groupings affected. There are more women than men among the over 65s, more women than men live on their own, are unemployed and are single parents. The period of time spent on social assistance also varies considerably. On average, support is needed for about 27 months. But women living on their own require support longest: here the average is considerably higher (about 42 months).

Women's high risk factor is demonstrated further by their social assistance rate [Sozialhilfequote], i.e. the number of claimants per 1000 citizens of the same age and gender. While 34 women out of 1000 received social assistance, this applied to only 27 men. Indeed, for women, the risk of needing support has risen continuously over the last few years.

Since 1980 their number has doubled in the old *Länder*, from 17 per 1000 to 38. Clear changes as regards the age of the women affected can also be observed. While in the past women under the age of 65 were prime candidates for sliding below the poverty line, their number amongst the affected is now going down. Today, the risk of needing social assistance is higher, the younger the women are. Furthermore, female OAPs in the old *Länder* (38 per 1000 female citizens) have a higher risk than their counterparts in the new *Länder* (19 per 1000 female citizens) (StBA 1998a:137).

Women who have given up their jobs in order to look after their children are affected most. Due to their career break they only qualify for a rather modest level of welfare or pension payments. When unemployment strikes, or when they reach pension age, they are often made to pay the price. Single people and especially divorcees are also disproportionately affected. In 1992, every sixth person in east Germany (16.2 per cent) and every ninth person in west Germany (11.2 per cent) lived in a household below the poverty line even though they were in gainful employment. In 1996, there were 1.64 million single mothers in the Federal Republic who shared their households with 464,000 children who were also on benefit (Eckhardt 1997:45; StBA 1998a: 32f.).

The rising divorce figures indicate the fragility of any maintenance depending on marriage and family relations. Women are often, as Ulrich Beck put it, 'nur einen Mann weit von der Armut entfernt' (Beck in Eckardt 1997: 45). Almost 70 per cent of all single mothers have to survive together with their children on less than DM 1200 a month. Single mothers and female pensioners are those most frequently dependent on social assistance. The crisis of the family manifests itself in the fact that every third marriage fails and that cohabitation is becoming increasingly popular (estimates indicate numbers between 1 and 2.5 million) (Eckardt 1997:46). The risk of having to live on social assistance in old age is still twice as high for women as it is for men (Gerhard 1990:28).

Single parents

The number of mothers and fathers who bring up their children on their own has increased significantly over the last 15 years. The vast majority of single parents are women (1995: 85.7 per cent). The proportion of single parents amongst all families with children was considerably higher in the new *Länder* (1995: 25.8 per cent) than in the old (15.7 per cent).

Social assistance provides, especially for single parents, security for periods of child rearing (Leibfried et al. 1995:114, case study 25). The reason for this is often the lack of adequate childcare, but sometimes the mother is not allowed to work by the authorities, if one of her children is considered to be too young (Leibfried et al. 1995:117, case study 59). Some women try to work but then have to change their minds due to the negative affect they feel this has on their child (Leibried et al. 1995:114, case study 49). Others take their child-rearing responsibilities extremely seriously, so much so that they can become insurmountable obstacles. It is especially in these circumstances that the 'conscious decision for life on social assistance' can be observed (Leibfried et al. 1995:107f.).

Most of the women taking this step have every intention of getting back into their jobs and off benefit later on. They are 'subjektive Überbrücker mit Zeitperspektive' (taking the subjective decision of bridging the child rearing years by going on benefit) (Leibfried et al. 1995:110), they see their situation as a passing phase. However, there is the distinct risk of slipping into long-term dependence, and in view of the current economic climate it has been assumed that this danger is likely to increase.

Furthermore, mothers who concentrate fully on their child-rearing responsibilities often lose contact with the world of work and find re-integration difficult if not impossible. The Federal Government has established a number of special programmes and support schemes to help and inform women when they are looking for work (BMFSFJ 1998:124f.).

There is considerable evidence showing that women whose working life has been disrupted belong to a continuously growing grouping amongst the 'new poor'. Bieback and Milz (1995) talk of a 'deprivation index', which comprises of income poverty, abandoning the pleasures of life in a consumer society, debt, lack of time and limited social contact. Other research results are also alarming: Leibfried et al. (1995:117) found that more often than not an external impetus is required – e.g. a reconciliation with the husband or another job for their new partner – to enable women to stop claiming support. Only very rarely do they manage to achieve this under their own steam.

Work and Unemployment

Even when women have made it back into the workforce, they are still disadvantaged: their incomes, for example, are still considerably lower than those of their male counterparts.

Table 5: Distribution of income between men and women 1997

	Old *Länder*		New *Länder*	
	Women	Men	Women	Men
Workers	3.273 DM	4.552 DM	2.625 DM	3.316 DM
Employees in Industry	4.842 DM	6.931 DM	3.931 DM	5.257 DM
Employees in Trade, Banks, Insurance	4.055 DM	5.370 DM	3.327 DM	3.888 DM

Female workers in the west earn on average 72.1 per cent of the pay of their male colleagues, in the east they receive 77.1 per cent. Amongst the employees in the manufacturing industries, women earn 68.2 per cent in the west but 75.2 per cent in the east. The women in the new *Länder* fare better due to their higher qualifications (BMFSFJ 1998:67f.).

Today, these differences can be put down only very rarely to direct discrimination, and mostly to a persistent gender division of the labour market (BMFSFJ 1998:66f.). There are still far fewer women in the middle to high management positions and they are also often not in jobs which make full use of their qualifications. Women tend to work in sectors with lower wages and – due to their family commitments – they are less likely to work overtime. Because of their – sometimes lengthy – career breaks, it is impossible for women to clock up as many years of continuous employment as the average man can, many more of them are also working part-time. This uneven distribution of the participation in gainful employment not only has a detrimental effect on their careers and promotion prospects, but also on their pension entitlements.

But even when qualifications, length and continuity of work are the same, women are still frequently paid less. The notion that men as the 'providers' are entitled to higher pay has survived in some areas of industry in spite of legal regulations. Such attitudes can influence the promotion processes (BMFSFJ 1998:66) but are difficult to verify and prevent.

Unemployment also hits women harder than men. Since 1992 the number of unemployed women has risen continuously. The number of women affected is particularly high in the east (55.9 per cent, west: 42.4 per cent). Today, the transformation processes after unification can no longer be held solely responsible. Once again, the data show that it is generally more difficult for women to get back into the labour market. Indeed, women make up the vast majority of the long-term unemployed. In 1995, three out of every four of the long-term unemployed were female. Women's participation in job creation schemes [ABM] came to 63.5 per cent in 1997 (BMFSFJ 1998:76f.).

Conclusion

The observations made in this paper indicate one fact most forcefully: the number of people who fall below the line of poverty, and within the German context this means below the threshold for social assistance, is rising year on year. This is putting an ever-greater strain on the welfare state. Recent studies have shown that around 650,000 in the new federal states and 2,123,000 people in the old lead a life of concealed poverty. If one adds these figures to those of the people claiming social assistance, one arrives at a total of around 5.3 million people who are in need of continuous financial support (Neumann 1999:30). This problem, which could still be suppressed a few years ago, now needs to be recognised, acknowledged and addressed urgently:

> [The feeling of] helplessness is spreading. Many share the feeling that something has come to an end. [...] The era of promises has ended the [expectation] of 'better and better and more and more'. And many share that fear. They can see that capitalism is running out of work, that gainful employment will no longer be the determining factor of our children's lives. (Hunfeld 1998:9f.)

Current data show that the situation is still considerably worse for women than it is for men. At the end of the 1990s, poverty is still very much a female issue. Women earn less, their working lives are shorter, and the losses they incur through their childbearing role are still not fully counterbalanced by appropriate political and social measures.

Women are hit hardest by unemployment and they make up the majority of claimants for social assistance. Initially, many of them consider the latter a temporary throwback, but they are all too often denied the return into the labour market. Long-term unemployment and long years spent on social assistance are often pre-programmed. Once they have fallen into this poverty trap, it is very hard – if not impossible – to get out. The reasons are frequently periods of child-rearing and single parenthood. However, recent data also show that more and more married couples with children are falling below the poverty line.

Leibfried and Leisering's analysis of sample groups showed that poverty is 'more mobile' [beweglicher] than had generally been assumed: it is beginning to move into strata of society which had previously been deemed 'safe'. Their long-term study of male and female claimants (1995:103) also indicates that poverty and dependence on social assistance are often only temporary. They thus conclude that the long-term cases are only a minority, although they admit that this minority is by no means insignificant. Their findings, however, could not reveal whether people who stop claiming social assistance have actually escaped poverty. Hübinger (1999) has recently provided such data. Hübinger defines a new grouping of people who live in what he refers to as a state of 'precarious affluence' [prekärer Wohlstand]. Their incomes range between 50 to 70 per cent of the official average income, but – as Hübinger points out – they are by no means safe. Most of them are threatened continuously with slipping below the poverty line and only very few manage to improve their situation to the extent that they climb beyond the 80 per cent mark.

In view of Germany's high productivity, which is being maintained in spite of growing unemployment, it appears unlikely that the number of jobs available is going to rise within the foreseeable future. Since 1991 around 1.3 million jobs have been lost (StBA 1998b). A fairer distribution of the work actually available between men and women as put forward by Kurz-Scherf (1998:18f.) could provide a solution to the problem. However, this would require a drastic and far-reaching reorganisation throughout the economy and subsequently the whole of society and is thus unlikely. The Schröder government is currently experimenting with '620 DM-Jobs', but such measures can only provide a short-term solution, they can do little or nothing to bring about any discernible change. The alleviation of poverty will once more have to become a priority.

Bibliography

Bieback, Hans-Jürgen/Milz, Helga (eds.) (1995) *Neue Armut*, Frankfurt am Main: Campus

Bundesministerium für Arbeit und Sozialordnung (BMfAS) (1997) *Sozialbericht 1997*, Stand: April 1998, Bonn

Bundesministerium für Arbeit und Sozialordnung (BMfAS) (1999) *Sozialhilfe*, Stand: März 1999, Bonn

Bundesministerium für Familie, Senioren, Frauen und Jugend (BMFSFJ) (1998) *Frauen in der Bundesrepublik Deutschland*, Stand: März 1998, Bonn

Eckardt, Thomas (1997) *Arm in Deutschland. Eine sozialpolitische Bestandsaufnahme*, 2nd updated edition, Landsberg/Lech: Günter Olzog Verlag

Federal Ministry of Labour and Social Affairs (1999) *Social Security At a Glance*, Bonn

Geißler, Heiner (1976) *Die Neue Soziale Frage. Analysen und Dokumente*, Freiburg i.B.: Herder

Gerhard, Ute (1990) 'Geschlechtsspezifische Sozialpolitik und die soziale Unsicherheit weiblicher Lebenslagen', in Döring, Diether/Hanesch, Walter/ Huster, Ernst-Ulrich (eds.) *Armut im Wohlstand*, Frankfurt am Main: Suhrkamp

Hübinger, Werner (1999) 'Prekärer Wohlstand. Spaltet eine Wohlstandsschwelle die Gesellschaft?', *Aus Politik und Zeitgeschichte*, B18, 30.4.1999, 18–26

Hunfeld, Frauke (1998) *'Und plötzlich bist du arm'. Geschichten aus dem neuen Deutschland*, Reinbek bei Hamburg: Rowohlt Taschenbuch Verlag

Klammer, Ute/Bäcker, Gerhard (1998) 'Niedriglöhne und Bürgerarbeit als Strategieempfehlungen der Bayrisch-Sächsischen Zukunftskommission', *WSI Mitteilungen*, 51, 6, 359–370

Klein, Peter (1994) 'Regelsatzentwicklung und Wandel der Lebensformen', *Nachrichtendienst des Deutschen Vereins für öffentliche und private Fürsorge*, 74, 88–94

Kurz-Scherf, Ingrid (1998) 'Krise des Sozialstaats – Krise der patriarchalen Dominanzkultur', *Zeitschrift für Frauenforschung*, 16, Sonderheft 1, 3–48

Leibfried, Siegfried/Leisering, Lutz et al. (1995) *Zeit der Armut*, Frankfurt am Main: Suhrkamp

Miegel, Meinhard (1996) 'Der ausgefranste Arbeitsmarkt: Die Menschen in den Industrieländern müssen endlich die neuen Chancen nutzen', *Die Zeit*, 9.2.1996, 20

Neumann, Udo (1999) 'Verdeckte Armut in der Bundesrepublik Deutschland. Begriff und empirische Ergebnisse für die Jahre 1983 bis 1995', *Aus Politik und Zeitgeschichte*, B18, 30.4.1999, 27–32

Nolte, Claudia/Schmidt, Renate (1998) 'Nicken und brav sein. Gespräch über arme Kinder, Karrierefrauen und Hausmänner', *Der Spiegel*, 1998, 38, 69ff.

Schomers, Michael (1999) *Alltag Armut. Mein Leben mit 539.- DM Sozialhilfe – Ein Experiment*, 2nd edition, Köln: Kiepenheuer & Witsch

Statistisches Bundesamt (StBA) (1998a) *Im Blickpunkt: Frauen in Deutschland*, Stuttgart: Metzler-Poeschel

Statistisches Bundesamt (StBA) (1998b) *Mitteilung für die Presse, 19.08.1998, 2,9 Mill. Sozialhilfebezieher zum Jahresende 1997: Anstieg um 7,1%.* www.statistik-bund.de/presse/deutsch/pm/p8254081.htm, accessed on 15.7.99

Statistisches Bundesamt (StBA) (1998c) *Mitteilung für die Presse, 08.10.1998, Deutschland – ein statistischer Situationsbericht: Statistisches Jahrbuch 1998 erschienen.* www.statistik-bund.de/presse/deutsch/pm/p8328221.htm, accessed on 15.7.99

Statistisches Bundesamt (StBA) (1999) *Mitteilung für die Presse, 29.06.1999, Sozialhilfeausgaben 1998 leicht gestiegen.* www.statistik-und.de/presse/deutsch/pm/p9217081.htm, accessed on 15.7.99

JEAN-MARC TROUILLE

Germany and France – Promoting Mutual Understanding Through Cultural Bridges?

In the course of the last five decades, and in particular since the initial period of rapprochement between France and Germany, these two neighbouring countries have developed what is probably the closest relationship between any two nations, notwithstanding their profound differences and frequent divergences. This unique alliance, based on a spirit of reconciliation and mutual friendship, is even outlined by treaty: the Elysée Treaty, which has its historic roots in the early sixties. This treaty, signed on 22 January 1963 by de Gaulle and Adenauer, was an attempt made by the generation of the War to overcome the grief and resentment caused by not just three major conflicts between 1870 and 1945, but in total by twenty-three wars opposing the French and the Germans in the course of the last four hundred years since the times of the Reformation. Today, thirty-eight years after the signing of this friendship treaty, the degree of interdependence and interaction between the nations on both sides of the Rhine is second to none in the world: the thriving Franco-German relationship encompasses virtually all spheres of activity in society: not least politics and European affairs, but also the economy, finance, trade, industry, telecommunications, science, research and technology, aeronautics, space, defence and security, police, espionage, weapons, nuclear waste transportation and recycling, youth exchange, media, education, and last but not least, culture. Culture rarely comes as a priority in a list of societal concerns, and cultural cooperation is only one of numerous fields of activity where the Germans and the French work closely together. It is even often argued that culture is the poor relation in Franco-German affairs. And yet, the cultural dimension of bilateral French-German relations should not be underestimated. Despite frequent lack of attention in the

French and German media, this is sometimes a thriving area which has borne some very impressive results. The aim of this paper is to stress the role played by cultural cooperation and the importance of culture as a cement for better mutual understanding and for strengthening the ties between the French and the Germans. Firstly, this paper will look into the influence French and German cultures have exerted on each other's country in the past in order to assess their mutual impact. It will then examine the political steps made towards a deepening of Franco-German cultural interaction and highlight the strengths and limitations of this interesting case of binational cooperation in the fields of culture and education.

French cultural influence in Germany

Since the 17th century, French language and literature have occupied a privileged position in the German cultural consciousness. German authors were frequently inspired by French classical literature. German elites generally spoke French as their first foreign language, and sometimes even as their first language. Under Frederick the Great, the settlement in Brandenburg of 20,000 Hugenots, who were intermediaries between the French and German cultures, clearly reinforced French cultural presence in Prussia, and to some extent, at the expense of the German language. Frederick II of Prussia declared once: 'Je ne parle allemand qu'à mes chevaux et à mes soldats' (I only speak German with my horses and my soldiers). Voltaire, who spent all in all fifteen years of his life in Potsdam, prided himself on not having learned any German at all during these years. The considerable attraction of French culture was reinforced by the writers of the *Aufklärung* and by the French Revolution. French culture remained dominant in German states until the 19th century. During the Napoleonic wars, so-called 'nationalist' German writers such as Fichte, Jahn and Arndt elaborated the concept of *Erbfeindschaft* (hereditary enmity). Notwithstanding this, French culture continued to exert a strong influence on German intellectuals like Heinrich Heine, who spent many years of his life in Paris, where he is buried at the Montmartre cemetery, and Heinrich Mann. With Germany gradually ceasing to be a fragmented country, a more negative fascination for French culture appeared amongst those who were influenced by nationalist propaganda. This trend reached its height during the National Socialist period, with numerous publications on France between 1933 and 1944 whose purpose was to demonstrate the superiority of the German *Kultur* to the French *civilisation*. This obsessional quest indicated that there was still a considerable French intellectual influence on German culture, and that this influence was still too powerful for the taste of Nazi ideologists. After the War, however, there was a strong desire to make up for intellectual impoverishment imposed by the Nazis. French authors who were perceived as progressive and avant-garde, such as existentialist writers like Camus, Sartre, Beauvoir, and also others like Gide, Saint-Exupéry, Anouilh and Ionesco, became widely known. This was also the case in East Germany, where poets like Aragon and Paul Eluard were widely read. After the 1968 movement, however, and despite renewed popularity of the *nouveau roman* and of trends like structuralism and post-modernity, the interest in French culture and literature fell as quickly and abruptly as the Berlin Wall did in 1989. Never in the course of the last four centuries has French culture had so little impact in Germany than in the last decade: contemporary French philosophers and intellectuals are generally unknown on the other side of the Rhine, and translations of French literary works into German are becoming increasingly scarce. French films account for less than 2 per cent of market share in Germany (*Le Monde* 14.5.98:10). For some, this has to be interpreted as a sign of normalisation between the two nations. For others, in particular amongst the most dedicated or even unconditional defenders of the conception of a Franco-German osmosis, this evolution is perceived as a dangerous alienation which has to be put right rapidly. Knowledge of each other's language and culture has to be enhanced further, to fight what some already refer to as a new *Kulturmauer*.

German cultural influence in France

As far as German culture in France is concerned, there is also a long tradition of cultural influence. German cultural movements such as *Sturm und Drang*, German Classicism and Romanticism, featured in French cultural circles. During the 18th and most of the 19th century, when it did not represent any military or political threat, Germany was perceived in France in a very positive light. Madame de Staël described the Germans as 'virtuous and sincere people, meditative and cultivated, with a great passion for music'. French stereotypes in Napoleonic times reveal that the Germans were seen as romantic dreamers, musicians, writers and poets. Napoleon I, who was a guest at the first public demonstration of the use of telegraph wires, had not understood that Germans were already becoming technical experts: when the attempt failed, he is said to have declared: 'What else would you expect from a German invention!' Later in the 19th century, the writings of several French authors such as Lamartine, Hugo and Nerval attest to the fact that the German cultural influence in France did prevail and was clearly stronger at that time than French cultural influence in Germany. Then the first half of the 20th century witnessed the exacerbation of the Franco-German rivalry as well as an overall decline in the German cultural *Ausstrahlung* in France, despite several initiatives such as the opening of the first *Goethe-Institut* in France in the inter-war period. But even in the darkest times of hostility, the cultural dialogue between the two continental nations was never completely interrupted. Of course, the situation improved gradually after the War, when Germany was divided and perceived as less of a threat. The last forty years have witnessed a reversal in Franco-German cultural relations. In the 1950s, the German public was very keen on French lyric poetry, theatre and novels. But since the 1960s, Germany has had so much to offer that German culture has gathered momentum. German music, theatre and film are thriving on French stage and screen. Names like Fassbinder, Schlöndorff, Brecht, and Pina Bausch of the *Wuppertaler Tanztheater,* are well-known by the French public.

Institutionalisation of cultural cooperation – Cultural summits

A first binational cultural agreement was signed as early as October 1954 by Adenauer and the then French Prime-Minister Pierre Mendès-France. Both parties realised that no reconciliation or reliable cooperation could be envisaged without developing intellectual contacts. The agreement stipulated that the language and literature of the neighbour had to be promoted, and that opportunities for teachers, students and apprentices to visit the other country had to be developed. Artistic and literary contacts had to be encouraged, and recognition of qualifications was under consideration. But whilst binational relations were steadily improving, the Franco-German cultural dialogue remained limited. For this reason, educational matters and youth exchanges were high on the agenda of the Franco-German Friendship Treaty signed on 22 January 1963 by de Gaulle and Adenauer, and led to the setting up of the Franco-German Youth Office, a binational institution whose prime mission is to enhance contacts between French and German youth. Today, there is a large framework of institutions which is more or less directly involved in promoting the Franco-German cultural dialogue: the Franco-German Youth Office; the most concentrated twinning of towns in the world, involving 1400 French and German towns; close partnership between a number of universities and schools; various binational institutions in the field of education and culture; the German Academic Exchange Service (*DAAD*), which has helped to set up more than 200 new exchange agreements between French and German universities since 1987; the Franco-German cultural television channel *ARTE*[1]; seven *Goethe-Institute* located in France; and the *Instituts français* in Germany, whose number has gone up to 24 since unification to cater for the needs of the new Federal Länder. Franco-German *Gymnasien/lycées* were created in Saarbrücken, Freiburg and Buc, near to Versailles. In addition, 23 *Gymnasien* and 130 *lycées* have a bilingual Franco-German strand of studies leading to the Franco-German *Abitur*. The *lycée français de Berlin* and the *deutsche Schule*

1 Association Relative à la Télévision Européenne.

in Sceaux, near Paris, are prestigious grammar schools. In French universities, *Germanistik* is very strongly represented (though in Germany *Romanistik* includes other Romance languages). Experimental teaching of French and German from the age of six in primary schools, especially in border regions, has now become a matter of routine.

Within the framework of regular consultations as defined by the Elysée Treaty, the French and the Germans hold two bilateral summits each year, alternately in each country, of which the most recent one was the 73rd Franco-German Summit in Toulouse in March 1999. Out of the 73 bilateral summits which have taken place since 1963, only three were dedicated more specifically to cultural cooperation (Girod de l'Ain 1997): the first one in October 1986 in Frankfurt; the second one in September 1997 in Weimar; the third and most recent one in December 1998 in Potsdam, whose purpose was to follow up decisions taken in Weimar. At the Frankfurt Summit of October 1986, the French and German government delegations expressed their clear intention to boost their cultural relations in order to tighten further the links between the two countries. Cultural cooperation was to be intensified in the following areas: knowledge of the partner's language and country; cooperation in the field of teaching, professional training, arts, culture and media. As a result of this joint political resolution, three new institutions were created to reinforce the institutionalisation of Franco-German cultural relations:

- the *Haut Conseil Culturel Franco-Allemand, Deutsch-Französischer Kulturrat*[2] with representatives of the cultural life of both countries, which was only set up in December 1988, two years after the Cultural Summit in Frankfurt, and whose purpose is to encourage and support financially joint exhibitions, specific literary translations and co-productions in film and television.
- the *Collège Franco-Allemand pour l'Enseignement Supérieur, Deutsch-Französisches Hochschulkolleg*[3] based in Mainz and in Strasbourg, whose role was to facilitate student and staff mobility

2 The Franco-German Cultural Council.

3 The Franco-German Higher Education College.

and to expand the provision of integrated courses and binational degrees involving French and German institutions of higher education, leading to double qualifications acknowledged in both countries.

- the setting up in 1992 of a large-scale media co-operation project which was soon to be called ARTE, a Franco-German cultural television channel with a European mission.

The *Kulturrat* and the *Hochschulkolleg* were set up on the occasion of the 25th anniversary of the Treaty in January 1988 alongside other binational institutions: a joint Defence and Security Council, a joint Economic and Financial Council and a joint Council for the Environment (Trouille:1996).

Although the importance of improving the knowledge of the other language and culture was formally emphasized in Frankfurt, the expected results did not materialise. More than a decade later, at the Weimar Summit of September 1997, the same priorities as in 1986 were reiterated, with the accent on intensifying the Franco-German dialogue via education in secondary and higher education, and on replacing the Franco-German cultural dialogue within its broader European framework. The decision to hold this summit precisely in Weimar, the town of Goethe and Schiller and the cradle of German Classicism, was not a pure coincidence, since a governmental agreement was signed on the creation of the first Franco-German university, whose task will consist in supervising and coordinating existing networks and creating new ones involving a number of institutions in both countries in order to develop integrated Franco-German courses and joint research projects. The role of this new binational institution is to take over from the Franco-German *Hochschulkolleg*. It will have its administrative headquarters in Saarbrücken. However, the Franco-German university will remain a 'virtual' university, a university 'without walls', with neither faculties nor proper buildings: no teaching will take place on its virtual premises. It will be responsible for the amalgamation of study programmes jointly offered by Higher Education institutions of both partner countries. However, the Franco-German university will deliver its own Franco-German qualification which will, of course, be recognised in both countries. In a joint declaration on increased cultural cooperation, both governments also announced the project of setting up a Franco-German Academy, whose task will be to strengthen cultural and artistic exchange, and also, probably, to take over from the *Kulturrat* at some stage.

Rather than defining new fields of cooperation, French and German government officials in Weimar decided to deepen cooperation in cultural and educational areas where joint action had already been launched. Apart from the quite spectacular launch of the Franco-German university, which was in line with the decisions taken in Frankfurt in 1986, no major cultural initiative was taken. The 70th Franco-German Summit in Weimar was perceived as 'a routine meeting, leading to modest, but not insignificant results'[4].

Since 1988, the *Hochschulkolleg* has contributed to the setting up of about 60 integrated Franco-German study programmes, involving 400 students per year on both sides[5]. The areas of study concerned are wide-ranging: engineering, mathematics, computing, natural science, economy, law, humanities, architecture. It would be interesting, at this stage, to look more closely to one or two 'case-studies' of integrated Franco-German courses offered jointly by French and German universities. For instance, the *Diplom für grenz-überschreitende deutsch-französische Studien*[6] offered jointly since 1989 by the *Universität des Saarlandes* and the *université de Metz* and supported by the *Hochschulkolleg*, is a very interesting case. The chair in *Romanische Kulturwissenschaft und Interkulturelle Kommunikation*, based in Saarbrücken, and the specialisation in the field of Franco-German Relations of the *Centre d'Etudes des Périodiques de Langue allemande* in the German Department of the Faculty of Literature and Humanities in Metz offer coherent and complementary teaching. Students must already hold a *Zwischenprüfung*, or a French *DEUG*,[7]

---

4 Cf. 'In Weimar', in: *Frankfurter Allgemeine Zeitung*, 20.09.97.

5 Information from the *Deutsches Sekretariat*, Schillerstr.11, D-55116 Mainz Homepage: http://www.uni-mainz.de/~dfhk.

6 Transnational Franco-German Studies.

7 *CIRAC-FORUM, bulletin pour la coopération franco-allemande dans les sciences humaines et sociales*, No.45, April 1999, p.40.

which is obtained in French Higher Education after completion of the fourth semester. It combines thorough language training with a large choice of subjects, including history, geography, politics, law, economy and literature. This course of studies has a strong intercultural dimension, is well established in the so-called *SAR-LOR-LUX*[8] region and offers the opportunity not only to focus on Franco-German relations, but also to extend the field of studies to other domains such as the knowledge of an important European region. Students spend the first year at the *Universität des Saarlandes*, where they can obtain the *Licence d'Etudes franco-allemandes*. The second year is spent at the *université de Metz*, which delivers the *Maîtrise d'Etudes franco-allemandes*. In the course of the second year, a short placement in various institutions, administrations or companies is compulsory. The final year allows students to take simultaneously the French *DEA*[9] and the German *Diplom für grenz-überschreitende deutsch-französische Studien*[10]. Some of the teaching staff work outside higher education, and students can benefit from their more practice-oriented professional experience. The multidisciplinarity and flexibility of this training is a strong asset for French and German postgraduates: careers opportunities are good and range from media (*ARTE, Saarländischer Rundfunk, Südwestfunk*), trade and industry (*Bosch, BASF, Michelin, Siemens*), culture (theatres, cultural institutes) and tourism.

To take another example of a project in line with the framework of the Franco-German University defined in Weimar, the Integrated Franco-German Studies course offered jointly by the universities of Bordeaux and Stuttgart is the first Franco-German degree of its kind in political and social science. Four years of bicultural studies taking place alternately in Bordeaux and in Stuttgart lead to the *Diplôme de l'Institut d'Etudes Politiques de Bordeaux* and to the Master of Arts in Social Sciences (note that the title is in English, not in German) of the *Institut für Politikwissenschaft der Universität Stuttgart*.

---

8 Saarland-Lorraine-Luxemburg.

9 *Diplôme d'Etudes Approfondies*: higher degree normally leading to a French doctorate.

10 Diploma for Cross-Border Franco-German Studies.

Language learning: a key issue

Although a growing number of higher education institutions on both sides of the Rhine offer integrated Franco-German courses, the lack of knowledge of each other's language often remains a major obstacle preventing the culture of the partner country from being accessible and understood. Only 23.4 per cent of French secondary education students learn German, be it as a first, second or third language. The proportion of students learning French in German secondary education is a similar 23.6 per cent (Berchem 1999:47). Since the 1970s, the learning of the main partner's language in secondary education has lost considerable ground on both sides of the Rhine. In both countries, English comes first and Spanish is on the increase. In Germany, where Latin often determines the access to classes where students have higher abilities and better future prospects, French is rarely taken as a first foreign language, but remains relatively stable as a second language. Good students tend to take English as a first language. French is considered less useful except for holiday purposes or cultural interest. In France, the German language has declined as a first and as a second language. The proportion of secondary school students taking German as a first foreign language dropped from 33 per cent in 1945 to 12 per cent in 1995 (Rovan 1997:4). More recently, and in view of the hegemony of English and Spanish, this proportion has even dropped below the 10 per cent threshold (*Le Monde* 29.2.00:8). German is considered difficult: it opens the door to a country which is still too often looked upon by the young generation as boring, despite numerous youth exchange programmes, sports events and seminars on intercultural learning taking place under the aegis of the Franco-German Youth Office, which has organised or sponsored more than 155,000 events involving five million French and German young people in the course of the last 38 years. And also despite the fact that about 250,000 French and German students have been involved in university exchanges in the course of the last 30 years, of which more than 30,000 obtained a grant from the *DAAD* (Berchem 1999:48). According to the *Rektorenkonferenz* there are 1,000 existing partnerships and exchange agreements between French and German universities. However, behind such rather impressive figures, and although a number of dedicated francophiles and germanophiles are to be found among French or German elites and intelligentsia, France and Germany no longer appear to hold the kind of intellectual or cultural fascination for one another that they did during the 19th century and, to some extent, during the post-war period. Youth culture today is clearly oriented towards the Anglo-Saxon world or towards more exotic cultures. The proportion of the German student population studying in French universities amounts to 0.3 per cent, that is, 5245 German students in 1998. The French figures for French students studying in Germany is exactly the same: 0.3 per cent, that is, 5890 students in 1998 (Picht 1998:4). Half of these students stay in the other country within the framework of Socrates and Erasmus programmes. The situation is paradoxical, if not even absurd: France is Germany's first trade partner and vice-versa. There is considerable potential for development in Franco-German industrial cooperation (Trouille:1999). The significance of gaining international qualifications is undeniable. And yet, only very few students dare to make the step across the Rhine. It is also disheartening to note that the teaching of the partner's language is losing ground in both France and Germany, although jobs and needs generated by Franco-German cooperation increase all the time: in Germany nearly 400,000 jobs depend on Franco-German cooperation, and nearly 350,000 in France (Morizet 1999:45). Clearly, there is a growing discrepancy between the decline in linguistic competence and the increasing degree of integration and cooperation between the German and French societies. Filling this gap with the use of English would not prevent the threat of alienation in the long term.

Conclusions

The infrastructure of networks and cooperation projects between institutions is an expression of the sincere desire of the two nations on both sides of the Rhine to be good neighbours, and is at first glance very impressive. But the institutionalisation of the binational cultural dialogue also indicates that there is still a certain misapprehension, in the background, that this special friendship could be under threat. A chequered history punctuated by numerous conflicts has generated vivid memories amongst the French and German peoples. This, for instance, explains certain attitudes or irrational fears today. Amongst political elites, and in the ongoing French-German dialogue about their common European future, there are still deeply rooted fears that the old role of Germany could become the new one once again. The titles of some recent publications on the Franco-German relationship reveal its complexity: for instance, in France: *De la prochaine guerre avec l'Allemagne* (On the next war with Germany), by Philippe Delmas. Or, *Le retour de Bismarck* (The Return of Bismarck), by Georges Valance. In Germany: *Paris-Bonn: Eine dauerhafte Bindung schwieriger Partner* (An enduring relationship between difficult partners), by Klaus Manfrass. Or, *Ein glückliches (W)Ehepaar – Deutsche und Franzosen*, (An (Un)happy Couple – Germans and French) by Gérard Foussier. Or else, *Schwierige Nachbarschaft am Rhein* (Difficult neighbourhood on the Rhine), by Werner Rouget. Lothar Baier's highly controversial book *L'entreprise France*, in Germany: *Unternehmen Frankreich – Eine Fabrikbesichtigung*, contains some provocative chapters such as *Von der Republik zum Unternehmen, Der Nuklearphallus, Die Intellektuellen zwischen dem Schock des Gulags und Heideggers Kataklysmus*.

In spite of declared friendship, the relations between Paris and Bonn, now Berlin, have never been entirely harmonious. It seems that the closer both countries come together, the more striking and blatant are their differences. Their relations are special, but also very complex, difficult and often quite emotional. Misunderstandings and divergences of views are frequent. Not only are their respective languages, cultures and mentalities different, but also their ways of doing things and of tackling problems. For instance, in Germany the cultural domain is primarily the prerogative of the *Länder,* and the role of the new Minister of Cultural Affairs in the Schröder government is more limited than the role of his French counterpart. Even the definition of culture is different in France and in Germany: the French definition tends to associate culture with high culture or *beaux-arts,* whereas the German definition of *Kultur* has a more anthropological dimension. But whatever the differences, the necessity to reach a consensus has generally been stronger than the intrinsic weaknesses of Franco-German relations: there is undoubtedly a strong underlying commitment on both sides to sit down together, debate openly and attempt to resolve problems within the framework of regular bilateral consultations, whose purpose is precisely to facilitate communication between both countries' political elites. Other well-oiled mechanisms consisting of joint commissions of experts and civil servants, and specific bilateral institutions, reinforce the ongoing dialogue between the French and the Germans. The decision to foster better understanding of the main partner via improved knowledge of its culture and language is primarily a political one. It reflects genuine concern about the current situation, which bears the long-term risk of cultural alienation: after all, ultimately cultural relations tend to shape not only political and social behaviour, but also all types of relations, for instance economic practices. This concern exists not least amongst the lobby of the Franco-German cause, which consists of a large team of dedicated francophiles and germanophiles and advocates the furthering of the interpenetration of both societies, but it is also shared by the political elites in Paris and in Berlin. It is too early to evaluate the future impact of the steps taken in Weimar to consolidate the cultural dialogue between France and Germany. Will they just get lost within the endless list of symbolic initiatives which the French and the Germans launch every now and then, whenever there is a need to hide their differences and to raise the impression that the Franco-German axis is still the motor of European integration? Or will they contribute to building genuine cultural bridges and enhancing the Franco-German cultural dialogue not only to the advantage of a small elite, but also for the benefit of a wider audience? Quite clearly, the cultural domain, and also the competence in the language of the neighbour, are serious obstacles and a major challenge for the future evolution of French-German relations.

Bibliography

Baier, Lothar (1989) *Firma Frankreich – Eine Fabrikbesichtigung*, Frankfurt: Wagenbach Taschenbücher

Berchem, Theodor (1999) *Continuer avec la nouvelle génération* in: *Documents – Revue des questions allemandes,* special issue, Paris: 47–48

Delmas, Philippe (1999) *De la prochaine guerre avec l'Allemagne* Paris: Editions du Seuil

Foussier, Gérard (1991) *Ein glückliches (W)Ehepaar – Deutsche und Franzosen*, Stuttgart, Bonn: Reihe Burg

Girod, de l'Ain Bertrand (1997) *Le Sommet culturel franco-allemand* in: *Documents – Revue des questions allemandes,* Paris: 4/97, 97–103

Manfrass, Klaus (1984) *Paris-Bonn: Eine dauerhafte Bindung schwieriger Partner*, Sigmaringen: Thorbeke

Morizet, Jacques (1999) 'Renouveler la politique culturelle' in: *Documents – Revue des questions allemandes*, special issue, Paris, 33–36

Rouget, Werner (1998) *Schwierige Nachbarschaft am Rhein – Frankreich-Deutschland*, Bonn: Bouvier, 1998

Rovan, Joseph (1997) *Enseigner l'allemand aux Français* in: *Documents – Revue des questions allemandes*, Paris: 1/97, 3–4

Picht, Robert (1998) *Deutsch-französischer Hochschulaustausch: Stand und Perspektiven* in: *dfi Aktuelle Frankreich Analysen, Deutsch-französisches Institut Ludwigsburg* 11, 10/98

Trouille, Jean-Marc (1996) *The Franco-German Axis since Unification* in: Chafer, Tony/Jenkins, Brian (eds.) *France from the Cold War to the New World Order*, London: Macmillan

Trouille, Jean-Marc (1999) *Industries française et allemande: partenaires ou concurrentes?* in: *La Documentation Française – Problèmes économiques* No. 2.633, 29.9.99, 4–19

Valance, Georges (1991) *Le retour de Bismarck*, Paris: Flammarion

STEFAN WOLFF

Germany and Her Minorities Abroad

Invited by local and imperial rulers, Germans have migrated to various parts of Central and Eastern Europe as settlers and colonists since the twelfth century. For centuries before the emergence of nation-states, they preserved their cultural distinctiveness and lived peacefully with their neighbours. However, the advent of nationalism in the eighteenth century began to change this. Not only did other local national groups begin to strive for their own nation-state, but within Germany herself, the notion of German culture and a people linked to it by merit of descent rather than territory, became an increasingly important dimension of public debate. By the end of the second half of the nineteenth century, this initially cultural notion took on a more political shape – the wars of German unification in part succeeded in defining German territory through German culture in Holstein as well as in Alsace and Lorraine. Yet, even German settlements much farther away drew the attention of 'cultural activists' in the newly formed German *Reich* to themselves. Organised activities that would eventually lead to external minority politics becoming a fixed part of German foreign policy began in 1881 with the foundation of the German School Association (*Deutscher Schulverein*). Initially concerned with the preservation of German language and culture among Germans abroad, the *Schulverein* and other similar organisations had turned into instruments of German cultural and economic imperialism by the turn of the century.

External minority policy proper began with Germany's defeat in the First World War. The cession of territories and populations to France, Belgium, Poland, and to the newly established Czechoslovak Republic, led to Germany's external minorities becoming an important element in the foreign policy considerations of the Weimar Republic. With a different agenda and scope, this continued after 1945 when the Federal Republic of Germany also concerned itself with the fate of the German minorities in countries with which Germany had never had common borders, but which, as a result of migration, nevertheless hosted substantial populations of ethnic Germans who were subjected to discrimination by the Communist regimes in Central and Eastern Europe. Eventually, a qualitatively new stage of the relationship between Germany and her neighbours in Central and Eastern Europe began after the collapse of communism in the late 1980s, early 1990s. In all three periods, policy-makers operated on different premises, with distinct goals, and in diverse international environments. This essay will outline major events and processes in these three distinct periods, showing continuities as well as breaks in Germany's external minority policy.

First and second-class borders – external minorities and the policy of border revisions, 1919–1939

The Versailles Peace Treaty of 1919 altered the borders of Germany to a significant degree and left millions of ethnic Germans under the sovereignty of other states. In the east, Germany lost parts of East Prussia, Upper Silesia, and the territories assigned to the so-called Polish Corridor. In the west, France regained Alsace and Lorraine, Belgium acquired the areas of Prussian Moresnet, Eupen, and Malmedy, and the Saar territory was put under an international protectorate with considerable economic rights accorded to France. In the north, a referendum in 1920 determined the German-Danish border in Schleswig. Furthermore, the dissolution of the Austro-Hungarian Empire and the creation of the Czechoslovak Republic placed the ethnic German population of the *Sudetenland* in another state as well.

The substantial loss of territory and population and the enormous amount of reparations Germany had to pay to the allied and associated powers formed a considerable part of the background against which German foreign policy was formulated throughout the 1920s. The two major policy goals Germany pursued throughout the inter-war period were the revision of the borders in the east and relief from reparations payments. As both issues depended essentially on the goodwill of the western powers, they were closely interlinked with one another and related to the question of Germany's western borders, which, in turn, assigned an instrumental role in particular to the German-speaking populations of Alsace and Lorraine and South Tyrol.

Between 1919 and 1922, Germany had tried to turn the question of Alsace and Lorraine into a precedent for the right to self-determination to which not only defeated states, but also the victorious powers, had to bow. However, the German Foreign Office soon had to realise that the difficulties that existed in Alsace and Lorraine were an internal affair of the French Republic. Consequently, a 1922 analysis of the situation acknowledged that Alsace and Lorraine did not qualify as a minority problem in the strict sense of the concept, since the population did not insist on its different ethnicity (*Fremdständigkeit*), let alone on their German origin[1]. Although this assessment was accurate for the early 1920s, it had to be changed later, when Alsatians began to see themselves as a minority, in the way the League of Nations defined the term, and increasingly insisted on their distinctiveness, if not in terms of ethnicity, then certainly in terms of culture, language, and tradition. The rediscovery of their German roots and the recognition of the German element in Alsatian culture in turn led the Foreign Office to support cultural efforts in Alsace in addition to more political considerations and a policy of funding political parties there. German politicians had realised that regaining the former *Reichsland* was impossible. However, Germany could gain from a formal abandoning of all territorial claims vis-à-vis France, as this would assure the French government of the security of its eastern borders with Germany. This policy was implemented through the Treaty of Locarno in 1925[2]. At the same time, continuing problems in Alsace and Lorraine would weaken French resistance against desired

1 Internal policy document of the German Foreign Office, 1922. Cited in Rothenberger (1975: 74).

2 Article one of the treaty reads: 'The High contracting parties collectively and severally guarantee, in the manner provided in the following articles, the maintenance of the territorial *status quo* resulting from the frontiers between Germany and France and the inviolability of the said frontiers as fixed by or in pursuance of the Treaty of Peace signed at Versailles on the 28th June, 1919, and also the observance of the stipulations of articles 42 and 43 of the said treaty concerning the demilitarised zone.'

border changes in the 'German East', and the German Foreign Office could make sure that a certain level of tension continued to exist in Alsace and Lorraine through the funding of cultural activities and, especially between 1927 and 1929, also through the support of Alsatian particularist political propaganda[3]. Initially channelled through the private organisations of the Alsatian émigrés[4], political support was abandoned soon after Stresemann's death in 1929, not only because of a lack of success, but also because French suspicions about the true source of the funds grew, and alienating France was considered counter-productive. In 1930/31 cultural funding continued at a reduced level, and even after Hitler's take-over in 1933 it was not immediately abandoned. During the entire period, the objective of support was not to encourage Alsatian separatism, but rather to make France more willing to concede border revisions in the east.

The situation in South Tyrol, which had been annexed to Italy in 1919, was somewhat different, yet the area played a similarly important role in German foreign policy. While Austria had never accepted the loss of South Tyrol, international developments forced successive Austrian chancellors to recognise the importance of an alliance with Italy against German annexation plans. In 1928 chancellor Seipel declared that South Tyrol was an internal Italian affair, and in 1930 a friendship treaty was signed between Italy and Austria. Thus left with little support from Austria, many South Tyrolese vested their hopes in Hitler and his pan-German aspirations to remedy their situation.

After Hitler's seizure of power in 1933, the institutions of external minority policy were gradually turned into instruments of aggressive national socialist foreign policy[5]. The department in the ministry of

---

3 Rothenberger (1975: 138–151) gives the following figures of financial support: 141,247 *Reichsmark* in 1925/26; 548,331 *Reichsmark* in 1926/27; and 840,000 *Reichsmark* between 1927 and 1929.

4 The two organisations were the *Alt-Elsaß-Lothringische Vereinigung* and the *Hilfsbund.* While the organisations of the *Reichsland* émigrés were generally less willing to accept the fact that there would be no border revision, the two émigré organisations' and the Foreign Office's aims met in one crucial point – the attempt to minimise the impact of French assimilation policies in Alsace.

5 Increasingly, the 'foreign organisation' (*Auslandsorganisation*) of the NSDAP became active among ethnic Germans in eastern and Western Europe alike. Although its popularity and success in recruitment varied – it was more effective

foreign affairs responsible for co-ordinating ethnic German policy issues (*Volksdeutsche Mittelstelle*) and the Association for German Culture Abroad (*Verband für das Deutschtum im Ausland*) were taken over by committed followers of Hitler who replaced the foreign policy bureaucrats of the Weimar period. However, the basic premises of foreign policy were left unchanged, even though emphasis and rationales shifted. Hitler, too, saw the abandoning of territorial claims primarily from a tactical point of view, yet he also had ideological concerns. He considered the status of Alsatians to be 'racially questionable', but this did not make him lose sight of the strategic value of the territory of the former *Reichsland* in terms of the cohesion of the 'German heartland' (Kettenacker 1973). In the light of political developments in Italy in the early 1920s and the importance of the country as an ally for Germany, Hitler had made it very clear as early as 1922 that he was not willing to sacrifice his global interests, for whose realisation he needed an alliance with Italy, for the fate of 300,000 German-speaking South Tyrolese[6].

With respect to the former German territories in the east, the long-term policy objectives of the Weimar Republic, aiming at a 'recovery' of the lost territories in Poland, were complemented, from the early 1930s onwards, by a policy seeking the annexation of the German-populated areas in the Czechoslovak Republic, especially the *Sudetenland*. Even though the popularity of national socialist ideology increased in both areas and provided Nazi foreign policy with a very effective 'fifth column' in both Czechoslovakia and Poland, only the

---

in the South than in Alsace and Lorraine and had a stronger following in the *Sudetenland* than in Poland – local branches of the party were built up in all the external minority groups (e.g., Romania, Hungary, Yugoslavia) except in the Soviet Union.

6 Gruber (1974: 171) gives the following 1922 (!) quotation from Hitler: 'Germany has to join forces with Italy which experiences a time of national rebirth and has a great future ahead of it. In order to accomplish this, a clear and final renunciation of all claims to South Tyrol is necessary.' In an attempt to solve the South question, the German-speaking population in South Tyrol was asked in 1939 to choose between remaining in Italy and being subjected to further Italianisation, or to opt for relocation to the German Reich. Of the 267,265 German-speaking South Tyrolese eligible for participation, 43,626 abstained. Of the 223,639 participants in the plebiscite, 183,365 voted to leave and 38,274 to stay. (Figures according to Cole and Wolf 1974: 57. Slightly different figures in Alcock 1970: 45ff.)

Sudetenland was regained by Germany without going to war, when the Munich Agreement of 1938 obliged the Czechoslovak Republic to cede significant parts of its territory to the German *Reich.*

From 'Westintegration' to 'Ostpolitik' – the limits of external minority policy, 1949–1989

If the major problem facing German policy-makers after World War One was the territorial truncation of German territory and the reparations to be paid to the Allied powers, a new challenge presented itself after 1945. Ethnic Germans, in particular from Central and East European countries, were either expelled from their traditional settlement areas, such as in Poland and Czechoslovakia, or they were deported to forced labour camps in the Soviet Union, as happened in Romania and Yugoslavia, for example[7]. In any event, ethnic Germans were subjected to systematic popular and state discrimination as a result of the atrocious occupation policies of the Nazis during the war, in which many of them had participated. Even though this wave of repression and expulsion had ended by the early 1950s and ethnic Germans were gradually reinstated in their citizenship rights, their situation was still not considered satisfactory by the West German government, partly because they suffered all the 'usual' disadvantages of life under communism, and partly because the experience of the majority population during the years of German occupation made them vulnerable to continued discrimination.

However, in the early years of its existence, the Federal Republic was preoccupied with other issues both domestically and in its external relations. Domestically, the rebuilding of the political and economic foundations of society, including the integration of millions of refugees and expellees, took priority. On the international stage, the German Chancellor Adenauer had set a foreign policy agenda whose foremost aim was to ensure the integration of the country into the Western Alliance.

---

7 Ethnic Germans in the Soviet Union had been deported to the Central Asian Republics from their settlements in the European parts of the country after Hitler's attack in 1941.

This process of integration into the West, which provided a path to political security, economic recovery, and gradually also to social prosperity, was the preferred option of the overwhelming majority of the population. Yet, at the same time, the Western alliance as a symbol of post-war developments signalled, at least temporarily, an acceptance of the *status quo*, which, given the German borders in 1949, found significantly less support. While it was generally accepted that neither Alsace and Lorraine nor the *Sudetenland* could rightfully be claimed by Germany, the fixing of the German-Polish border along the Oder-Neiße line was renounced in public by West German politicians of nearly all political backgrounds, including the Chancellor and his cabinet ministers. Simultaneously, however, it was equally clear that the Federal Government was in no position to offer a credible political approach as to how to revise the German-Polish border. Not only was this contrary to the interests of all four allied powers of the second World War, West Germany itself no longer had a common border with Poland. Despite the claim of the Federal Republic to be the sole representative of the German people (*Alleinvertretungsanspruch*)[8]. It was a matter of political reality that the East German state had, in violation of the Potsdam Agreement of 1945, officially recognised the new border in a treaty with Poland in July 1950.

When integration into the western world had sufficiently progressed by the mid-1950s through membership of NATO and the precursor institutions of today's European Union, Germany could, more confidently, turn eastwards again. As a result of public pressure and political lobbying by the various expellee organisations, but also as a consequence of the *Alleinvertretungsanspruch*, the Federal Republic committed itself to a foreign policy vis-à-vis the communist countries in Central and Eastern Europe that included humanitarian efforts to improve the situation of ethnic Germans in these countries. The possibilities of direct involvement, however, were extremely limited throughout this period until 1989, so that the major instrument of German external minority policy was the negotiation of conditions

---

8 In a speech before the German *Bundestag* on 21 October 1949, Adenauer declared that 'pending German reunification, the Federal Republic of Germany is the only legitimate state organisation of the German people.'

with the host-states to allow ethnic Germans to migrate to Germany. A precondition for this was the establishing of diplomatic relations with the relevant states in the eastern bloc.

A first step in this direction was the Soviet-German treaty of 1955, followed by a verbal agreement in 1958 according to which all those persons of ethnic German origin who had been German citizens before 21 June 1941 were entitled to repatriation[9]. This policy was continued by all successive governments, and after 1970 it began to include a variety of other states in the Soviet zone of influence. Treaties with Poland (1970) and Czechoslovakia (1973) specifically addressed the sensitive issues of borders, confirming that the German government of the day respected the territorial *status quo*. Although both treaties thus included provisions to the effect that the signatory states assured one another of respect for each other's territorial integrity and of the fact that neither had territorial claims against the other, two rulings of the German Constitutional Court in 1973 and 1987 confirmed that Germany continued to exist within the borders of 1937, thus including territories east of the Oder-Neisse line.

The priority of promoting co-existence between East and West against the background of the political realities of the Cold War did not leave the West German government any other option apart from facilitating the emigration of ethnic Germans from Central and Eastern Europe to the Federal Republic, which included primarily ethnic Germans from the Soviet Union, Romania, and Poland[10]. German external minority policy was thus not very active between

9 This, however, solved only one part of the problem as it included only the Germans of former East Prussia, the so-called Memel Germans, and those ethnic Germans who, in the aftermath of the German-Soviet treaty of 1939, had been resettled to then German territories from the Baltic states, Galicia, Volhynia, Bessarabia, and the Northern Bukovina, but found themselves again on Soviet territory at the end of the war. Thus, it did not cover the by far largest group of ethnic Germans who had migrated to Russia during the eighteenth and nineteenth centuries.

10 The agreements between West Germany and some of the host-states on the repatriation of ethnic Germans included financial arrangements setting 'per capita fees' to be paid by the federal government. Average figures of annual emigration of ethnic Germans after 1950 are as follows: 1955–59: 64,000; 1960–64: 18,000; 1965–69: 26,000; 1970–74: 25,000; 1975–79: 46,000; 1980–84: 49,000, 1985–86: 41,000; 1987: 78,000 (*Infodienst* 1996: 2–5).

1945 and 1989, partly because it had always been suspected of a hidden revisionist agenda not only by the host-states, but also within Germany itself, and partly because to remain in their host-countries was not the preferred option of most ethnic Germans in Central and Eastern Europe[11], nor was it seen as an acceptable alternative by the federal government.

Promoting democracy, prosperity, and ethnic harmony – the new policy agenda after 1990

The general context of external minority policy after 1990

The transition to democracy in Central and Eastern Europe, which began in 1989/90, provided an entirely different framework of new and enlarged opportunities for Germany's external minority policy. On the one hand, democratisation meant the granting of such basic rights and liberties as the freedoms of speech, association, and political participation, allowing ethnic Germans in their host-countries to form their own parties, stand for election, and actively advocate the interests of their group. On the other hand, it also meant that there were no longer any restrictions on emigration, and given the experience of at least the past forty years, many ethnic Germans, particularly in Poland, Romania, and the Soviet Union and its successor states, seized this opportunity and emigrated to Germany. Both developments required a measured and carefully considered policy response from Germany – domestically to cope with the enormous influx of resettlers, externally to assure the neighbouring states in Central and Eastern Europe of the inviolability of the post-war borders, while simultaneously continuing the support for the German minorities at qualitatively and quantitatively new levels and ensuring their protection as national minorities. All this had to happen within the framework of general German foreign policy premises, such as the support for the transition process to democracy and a market economy, the creation of a new collective security order

11 Ethnic Germans in Hungary are something of an exception here.

embracing all states in Europe, and respect for international law and human rights

The domestic response – restriction of immigration

The most important legal act passed in response to the vast increase of ethnic Germans[12] leaving their host-states to migrate to Germany was the 1993 War Consequences Conciliation Act. Entitlement to German citizenship, formerly automatic, was revoked – ethnic Germans now had to prove ethnic discrimination in their host-states and a long-standing affinity to German culture, language and traditions in order to qualify. Furthermore, the annual intake of ethnic Germans was limited to the average of the years 1991 and 1992 within a ten per cent margin, i.e., a maximum of about 250,000 people. Since, prior to this in 1990, a bill had been passed that required ethnic Germans to apply for admission to Germany from their host-states, the annual intake could effectively be restricted to these quotas. In 1996, a language test was introduced that had to be passed by ethnic German applicants for citizenship as a way of testing their affinity to German language and culture. Together, these changed regulations have considerably reduced the influx of ethnic Germans to the Federal Republic – from around 220,000 each year between 1993 and 1995, the immigration figures dropped to 178,000 in 1996 and 134,000 in 1997. Since then immigration numbers have continued to fall to less than 100,000 ethnic Germans in 1999[13].

The international response – creating an alternative to 'repatriation'

Realising that the changed conditions after 1990 required a fundamentally different foreign policy approach, the German

---

12 In 1988, over 200,000 ethnic Germans 'returned' to Germany, in 1989, it was already 377,000, and in 1990, a figure of 397,000 was recorded.

13 This drop has two further reasons apart from legal restrictions: many ethnic Germans who have successfully applied for citizenship have not yet exercised their option to migrate to Germany, but keep it as a fallback position; in addition, the majority of people from Romania and Poland who had wanted to leave had already done so in the late 1980s and early 1990s so that the demand from these areas is now greatly reduced.

government embedded its external minority policy into the wider framework of its efforts to promote democracy, prosperity, and security in Central and Eastern Europe. Given the ethno-political demography of the region with its many national minorities, latent border disputes, and inter-ethnic tensions, it was obvious that the role of minorities would be a crucial one in two ways. The ultimate test of successful democratisation would have to include an assessment of whether or not members of national minorities, individually and collectively, were entitled to full equality and the right to preserve, express, and develop their distinct identities in their host-states. Furthermore, it would not be possible to operate a viable collective security system without settling existing ethnic and territorial conflicts and establishing frameworks within which future disputes could be resolved peacefully. Taking these assumptions as a starting point, the German government concluded that national minorities could play a crucial part in bringing about results in these two interrelated processes as they could bridge existing cultural gaps[14]. The Federal Government sought to create partnerships with the Central and East European host-states and the German minorities living there that, on the basis of international treaties and bilateral agreements, would promote the government's 'overall foreign policy concept of a European peace policy of reconciliation, understanding, and co-operation' (*Bundestagsdrucksache* 13/3195). Cultural, social, and economic measures to support German minorities, although primarily 'aimed at an improvement of the living conditions of ethnic Germans in their host-countries,' would naturally benefit whole regions and their populations independent of their ethnic origin and thus promote inter-ethnic harmony and economic prosperity while strengthening the emerging democratic political structures (*Bundestagsdrucksache* 13/3428 and *Bundestagsdrucksache* 13/1116). Thus, by creating favourable conditions for the integration of ethnic Germans in the societies of their host-states as citizens with equal rights, the German government hoped to provide an alternative to emigration (*Bundestagsdrucksache* 13/3428).

---

14 Cf., for example, 'Vertriebene, Aussiedler und deutsche Minderheiten sind eine Brücke zwischen den Deutschen und ihren östlichen Nachbarn', *Bundestags-drucksache* 13/10845, 27 May 1998.

However, not all of the projects have been successful. In the early stages of efforts to improve the situation of ethnic Germans in their host-countries, there was a general lack of co-ordination, and a comprehensive concept of external minority policy was still in the process of being formulated and adapted to the new conditions. Millions of Deutschmark were pumped into large-scale projects, such as the construction of houses for the settlement of ethnic Germans near St. Petersburg; yet, once the money had been allocated, there was little or no control of the progress of the project and its results in terms of increasing the willingness of ethnic Germans to remain in their host-countries. Closer to home, the *Verein für das Deutschtum im Ausland* has been involved in a financial scandal about the misuse of twenty-two million Deutschmark of support funds allocated to it by the Federal Ministry of the Interior.

Thus, it came as no surprise when the new red-green government began to reconceptualise German external minority policy soon after it came to power. In 1999, it was decided to abandon all large-scale investment plans as they did not have any measurable positive effect on the decision of ethnic Germans as to whether to emigrate to Germany or not. Instead, plans were drawn up, and have since been gradually implemented, to concentrate resources on projects to facilitate self-help, in particular through providing seed funding for small and medium-size businesses, to improve the services offered by the meeting centres (*Begegnungsstätten*), to increase training and qualification programmes, to provide more after-school German classes, to fund initiatives by communal partnerships, and to intensify social work with young ethnic Germans. Furthermore, a decision was made to focus these efforts primarily on Russia and Poland (*BMI-Pressemitteilung* 1 September 1999, *BMI-Pressemitteilung* 10 August 1999, *BMI-Pressemitteilung* 25 June 1999). Aid programmes for German minorities in other countries, such as Romania or the Baltic Republics, have not been phased out, but rather scaled down and concentrated on social work, as the new Federal Government, too, realizes that these programmes are an important instrument of a foreign policy aimed at 'the peaceful and tolerant coexistence of various national groups' in the states that also host German minorities (*BMI-Pressemitteilung* 2 July 1999 and *BMI-Pressemitteilung* 21 October 1999).

The restructuring and partial reconceptualizing of Germany's external minority policy is, on the one hand, driven by the desire for greater effectiveness, but, on the other, also by the need to decrease spending in all areas in order to consolidate the Federal budget. For the period from 2000 to 2003, annual cuts of twenty-six million Deutschmark have been proposed for 'Measures in Support of German Minorities in Their Host Countries'[15].

Conclusion

Germany's external minority policy has undergone significant changes since it became part of the country's foreign policy agenda after the First World War. Although there were 'geographic' differences between the approach to minorities in the east and the west, the inter-war period was primarily characterised by an instrumentalisation of the minorities question to change the borders established in the Treaty of Versailles in 1919. Border alterations in the east, facilitated by border guarantees in the west, were the foreign policy goal of the Weimar Republic as well as of Nazi Germany, distinguished only by the intensity and means with which this aim was pursued.

The east-west difference remained after 1945, but was, to some extent at least, externally determined. Collective victimisation of ethnic Germans in the form of expulsions (in Poland and Czechoslovakia) and deportations (in Romania and the Soviet Union) as a result of the Second World War affected members of the German minorities in Central and Eastern Europe much more than in their settlement areas in the west. Simultaneously, the foundation of the West German state and the importance of its integration into the

15 The total of the various budget titles had peaked in 1997 at almost 115 million Deutschmark, not including the payments made to various expellee organisations to support their activities in the host-countries (DM 5.1 million) and also not including institutional funding for the *Bund der Vertriebenen* (DM 24.8 million) before it was cut down to DM 85 million in 1998 and DM 75 million in 1999. From 1998 to 1999, there was however a significant increase in institutional funding for the BdV to DM 42 million. These cuts account for around 1% of the total savings in the Federal budget in 2000, decreasing to around 0.5% by 2003.

emerging western alliance set different priorities for foreign policy-makers in post-war Germany. Part of the acceptance of responsibility for the consequences of World War II was the tacit recognition of the geopolitical and territorial realities of Europe by successive German governments, while political engagement on behalf of German minorities in Central and Eastern Europe, even if was not set aside completely, was at least scaled down. In particular after 1969, when *Ostpolitik* was elevated to qualitatively new levels of reconciliation, the Federal Republic tried to facilitate the emigration of ethnic Germans from their host-countries and their smooth integration into German society, rather than to demand their recognition and protection as minorities.

From the end of the 1980s onwards, this began to change gradually. The democratisation of the formerly communist societies in Central and Eastern Europe opened new opportunities for Germany's external minority policy. Greater opportunities to support the German minorities in their host-states, the need to do so in order to halt, and eventually reverse, the mass exodus of ethnic Germans, and the genuine interest of the former communist countries in improving their relationship with Germany, which was seen as an important stepping-stone towards accession to the European Union and NATO, complemented each other in a unique way. Germany's desire to bridge the gap between cultures and across history could only be fulfilled through reconciliation and mutual understanding. Part of this was the eventual unconditional recognition of the borders with Poland and Czechoslovakia. Yet a common future of Germany and its eastern neighbours could not be secured without addressing the situation of the German minorities in these countries. On the basis of numerous treaties and within the framework set out by the 1990 Copenhagen Document of the Conference on Security and Cooperation in Europe, Germany and Poland, the Czech and Slovak Republics, Hungary, Romania, the Russian Federation, Ukraine, and Kazakhstan have developed relationships that allow both respective parties, with the participation of representatives of the German minorities, to tackle the issue of minority protection and external support for ethnic Germans. For historical as well as contemporary reasons, this has remained a very sensitive problem. Countries in Central and Eastern Europe have seen a resurgence of minority-related questions during the transition process to democracy. German external minority policy, therefore, has always only been one part of a more comprehensive foreign policy approach towards its eastern neighbours that aims at a stabilisation of democracy and the creation of a market economy in these countries as the wider social framework within which harmonious inter-ethnic relationships can develop that will inevitably benefit the German minorities as well.

Almost a century of external minority policy thus has seen different policy agendas being pursued by different German governments. These were partly determined by domestically formulated objectives, partly also by existing opportunities and the way in which they were perceived by policy-makers. Gradually since the early 1970s, however, the deliberate setting of a different foreign policy agenda in the form of the new *Ostpolitik* has also contributed to changing and eventually increasing opportunities for a successful external minority policy that does not treat minorities as objects of further-reaching policy goals, but makes them one of the beneficiaries of a co-operative rather than confrontational foreign policy.

Bibliography

Alcock, Antony E. (1970) *The History of the South Tyrol Question*, London, Michael Joseph

BMI-Pressemitteilung (25 June 1999) 'Unterstützung der deutschen Minderheit und ihrer Nachbarn in Rumänien', Bonn, Bundesministerium des Innern

BMI-Pressemitteilung (2 July 1999) 'Welt: Unterstützung der deutschen Minderheit und ihrer Nachbarn in Rumänien', Bonn, Bundesministerium des Innern

BMI-Pressemitteilung (10 August 1999) 'Aussiedlerbeauftragter zieht positive Bilanz seiner Rußlandreise', Bonn, Bundesministerium des Innern

BMI-Pressemitteilung (1 September 1999) 'Aussiedlerbeauftragter stellt Konzeption "Aussiedlerpolitik 2000" vor', Bonn, Bundesministerium des Innern

BMI-Pressemitteilung (21 October 1999) 'Neue Akzente bei den Hilfeleistungen: Der Schwerpunkt der künftigen Förderung liegt auf den gemeinschaftsfördernden Hilfen', Bonn: Bundesministerium des Innern

Bundestagsdrucksache 13/1116 (12 April 1995) Antwort der Bundesregierung auf die Kleine Anfrage der Abgeordneten Ulla Jelpke und der Gruppe der PDS – Drucksache 13/893 – 'Die Vertriebenenverbände und der angebliche "Aufruf zum Rassenkampf" gegen Deutsche von polnischer Seite', Bonn: Deutscher Bundestag

Bundestagsdrucksache 13/3195 (4 December 1995) Beschlußempfehlung und Bericht des Innenausschusses (4. Ausschuß) zu der Unterrichtung durch die

Bundesregierung – Drucksachen 12/7877, 13/725 Nr. 22 – Bericht der Bundesregierung über ihre Maßnahmen zur Förderung der Kulturarbeit gemäß § 96 BVFG in den Jahren 1991 und 1992 sowie die Fortschreibung des Aktionsprogramms des Bundesministeriums des Innern zur Förderung der deutschen Kultur des Ostens in den Jahren 1994 bis 1999', Bonn: Deutscher Bundestag

Bundestagsdrucksache 13/3428 (4 January 1996) 'Antwort der Bundesregierung auf die Kleine Anfrage der Abgeordneten Annelie Buntenbach und der Fraktion BÜNDNIS 90/DIE GRÜNEN – Drucksache 13/3344 – Die deutsche Minderheit in Polen in der Politik der Bundesregierung', Bonn: Deutscher Bundestag

Bundestagsdrucksache 13/6915 (7 February 1997) 'Gesetzentwurf des Bundesrates Entwurf eines Gesetzes zur Änderung des Bundesvertriebenengesetzes', Bonn: Deutscher Bundestag

Bundestagsdrucksache 13/10845 (27 May 1998) 'Antrag der Fraktionen der CDU/CSU und F.D.P. Vertriebene, Aussiedler und deutsche Minderheiten sind eine Brücke zwischen den Deutschen und ihren östlichen Nachbarn', Bonn: Deutscher Bundestag

Cole, John and Wolf, Eric R. (1974) *The Hidden Frontier*, New York and London: Academic Press

Gruber, A. (1974) *Südtirol unter dem Faschismus*, Bozen, Athesia

Info-Dienst Deutsche Aussiedler (1996) no. 82, Bonn: Bundesministerium des Innern

Kettenacker, Lothar (1973) *Nationalsozialistische Volkstumspolitik im Elsass*, Stuttgart: Deutsche Verlagsanstalt

Rothenberger, Karl-Heinz (1975) *Die elsaß-lothringische Heimat- und Autonomiebewegung zwischen den beiden Weltkriegen,* Frankfurt am Main: Peter Lang

RACHEL PALFREYMAN

Viewers and Villagers: Realism and Authenticity in Edgar Reitz's *Heimat*

A fascinating yet apparently contradictory aspect of the aesthetics of *Heimat* turns on the fact that it was made by an Oberhausen signatory – Reitz had put his name to the 1962 Oberhausen manifesto denouncing 'Papas Kino' and proclaiming that the future of the German cinema lay with those who had already begun to use a 'neue Sprache des Films' – and yet *Heimat* stands in the realist tradition. Indeed, some critics, such as Gertrud Koch (Kahlenberg et al. 1985:101,106) and Ruth Perlmutter (1987:21) have complained that it owes more to the aesthetics of the soap opera than the aesthetic innovation of the New German Cinema, while journalists Roland Hill (1985) and Gina Thomas (1986) reported that the British press often referred to the saga as a kind of soap opera, though in this context the term was not meant pejoratively. It seems obvious what was gained by embracing realism as the dominant mode of the film: an audience. 25 million watched one or more episodes in Germany in 1984, and around 2.5 million watched in Britain in 1986 ('Kein Stammpublikum' 1984; 'Heimat revisited?' 1986). However, Reitz's film was politically rather controversial, criticised for offering a nostalgic view of German history and promoting an unthinking German identity (Hoberman 1985; Saalmann 1988). Realism in the film was felt by Ruth Perlmutter to be aesthetically too close to the conservative Heimat films of the 1950s (1987:33–34). Gertrud Koch argued that Reitz had replicated rather uncritically the UFA realist mode, rendering the film too seductively pleasurable to encourage active spectatorship (Kahlenberg et al. 1985:103,106)[1]. Anti-Heimat

1 UFA, Universum-Film AG, was the leading German film company in the Weimar Republic. It continued under Nazi control until the end of the Second World War. UFA films, particularly in the 1930s, were noted for sophisticated lighting and

films in the 1960s and 1970s did function partly by breaking down the narrative 'pleasure' that viewers expected from Heimat films, and realism certainly is part of the pleasure of *Heimat*.

Leaving aside, however, the deeply held suspicion that pleasure and popular culture are in themselves escapist and reactionary and the argument (to which I shall return) about the political implications of *Heimat*, I am interested in the particular mode of realism used in *Heimat*. I have always felt uneasy about the implication that Reitz's filmic mode is the mimetic illusionism of the soap opera. The critique of *Heimat* as a slick and conservative product does not seem adequate, yet I would not disagree that 'realism' in various forms is dominant in the film. For while it is clear that *Heimat* remains for the most part in a realistic mode, it is difficult to ascribe to it one exclusive mode of realism. Reitz alludes in *Heimat* to various different modes of realism. Social realism is evident in the oral history project which underpinned Reitz's research for *Heimat*. One could also argue, however, that at times there is a gesture towards the poetic realism of the nineteenth century *Novelle*, though this gesture is shot through with historical realities that both heighten and disrupt this particular form of realism. And in addition to the poetic images, there is also a strong tendency towards naturalism in the use of local amateurs, authentic props and in the dialogue which sometimes allows rambling, sometimes incorporates long silences.

The poetic realist dimension in *Heimat* is seemingly underscored by Reitz's technique of imbuing certain objects or everyday situations with a particular aura, for example Maria carrying piles of washing, or Mathias working on a wheel hub in the forge, the red and white-hot metal shown in auratic colour to contrast with the black and white shots of Paul outside[2]. As Martin Swales puts it:

---

carefully designed interiors which contributed to a rather heightened but technically perfect realist style.

2 The changes from monochrome to colour in both *Heimat* and *Die Zweite Heimat* have been commented on perhaps more than any other aesthetic aspect of the film. As well as the effect of alienation, Reitz himself has commented that he used colour in *Heimat* emphatically where colour seemed particularly important to the scene, for example the red bicycle in 'Auf und davon und zurück', the shots fired at partisans on the Eastern Front in 'Die Liebe der Soldaten' and many of the landscape shots. Chronology was also an obvious factor in determining whether a scene should be shot in monochrome or colour and Reitz has linked this with his own

> Noch wichtiger ist es, festzustellen, daß sich Reitz mit der Tradition des provinziellen, will sagen, poetischen Realismus der deutschsprachigen Literatur auseinandergesetzt hat. [...] Was der deutsche Realismus literarisch erreicht, ist das, was Edgar Reitz filmisch erreicht'. (Swales 1992:129)

However, the appeal not just to various modes of realism, but in fact to 'authenticity' in the use of historically accurate and indeed 'original' sets and props, suggests that the dominant mode of *Heimat* might be naturalism rather than realism sliding into mimetic illusionism. The emphasis is less on the text *seeming real* than on it *being 'authentic'*. Of course the self-reflexive emphasis on the film's own textuality and the addition of surreal moments such as the gathering of the dead of Schabbach in Episode 11 'Das Fest der Lebenden und der Toten' and Paul's vision of the dead soldier in the first episode 'Fernweh' after his return from the First World War, mean that *Heimat* cannot be termed a naturalist film. But the long and in some ways unfocused scene of Paul's return and welcome in the Simon house owes much to naturalism and *Sekundenstil* in that Paul does not respond to people who address him for several seconds or minutes, and in that the dialogue wanders from Paul's return to local news to the political situation to Eduard's health. Paul's refusal, or inability, to speak about his experiences throughout a long sequence of about thirteen and a half minutes is more naturalist than realist. A soap opera with its attention to verisimilitude (*seeming* to be true/real) rather than authenticity might have focused on characters questioning Paul and on some sort of response from him.

Thus I would like to describe the mode of representation in *Heimat* as 'estranged naturalism', disrupted by poetic signs, surreal interludes and self-reflexivity. The use of amateur actors to play many major and minor roles is significant to this aesthetic mode[3]. For though many if not all of the lay performers are playing themselves or relatives a generation or two back, a more realist, perhaps in a paradoxical sense more *convincing* rendering of the roles could have been elicited from

---

memories, visual memories influenced by the cinema which slowly shifted from monochrome to colour. In *Die Zweite Heimat*, colour is often used for night scenes and black and white for day scenes (Birgel 1986:6–7; Reitz 1993:229–30).

3 There are 159 amateur actors in the film compared with the 32 professionals and in addition to 3863 extras.

professional actors. Though their performances have something 'authentic' about them, which would seem to indicate a naturalist approach, they also have certain alienating qualities in that such amateur performances are unexpected in a European art-house feature film. The performances, which vary greatly from being polished to slightly wooden and all things in between, go beyond the affecting charm many have praised in the film and are part of the alienated effect created by Reitz. In other words, the film's 'authenticity' is interfering with its realism, not adding to it. This paradoxical conclusion reveals the complexity of the grafting of 'authentic' villagers and their histories into the fictional film and suggests that the effects might not be a heightening of the realism of the film, but a pursuit of a naturalism that both does and does not seem 'real', a technique that is capable of alienating the viewer in a way that indicates a complete departure from the techniques and aims of the soap opera. The use of the 'authentic', whether 'authentic' local amateur actors, or 'authentic' oral history reminiscences, will be the focus of my investigation of the use of citation, or 'grafting', in the film.

I am particularly interested in the integration into the screenplay of reminiscences collected in informal oral history projects, and the biographical links between the amateur actors and the material woven into the fiction. All this raises theoretical issues about the fictionality of the film, which I shall examine with reference to Jacques Derrida's essay 'Signature Event Context' (1988a), a text I have found helpful in trying to deal with the film's anomalies and oddities which at first seem quite marginal. I shall also refer briefly to Roland Barthes's *Camera Lucida* (1984) where he considers the question of the authenticity of the photograph, as opposed to film.

The use of amateur actors in *Heimat* goes far beyond the practice of including local people as extras in crowd scenes. Firstly a number of main characters are played by amateurs, notably the characters of Katharina, Mathias, Marie-Goot and Pieritz, but secondly there is also a very large number of minor, or incidental, characters played by amateurs who might appear in small group scenes and speak a few lines. Many of these 'cameos' are based on incidents or routine activities remembered by local people and collected by Reitz for use in his film. Such oral histories were woven into the fictional text and some were performed in the fictional film text by people connected in some way with the original incident. A striking example is that in Episode 5 'Auf und davon und zurück', a baby is born just as war is declared. A small group of women talk about the birth on the street outside the family's window. One says 'Sieghild heißt es, wir wollen ja siegen.' The mother comes to the window with her baby and adds proudly 'Sieghild sollst du heißen'. The woman who plays the mother in that scene is herself the Sieghild of the reminiscence. She herself was born at the outbreak of the Second World War and was named Sieghild for patriotic reasons. In the film, she is in effect playing her own mother when the 'authentic' incident is grafted onto the fictional text[4]. One cannot be certain, of course, how many people might know about such techniques being used in the production process, but obviously some viewers would have had the information and others would have known about the kind of research and approach Reitz was using as this was documented in the popular and serious press (see '*AZ* Telefon-Aktion: Warum ist Ihre "Heimat" so grausam, Herr Reitz?' 1984, Hohmann 1982, Mayer 1981 and Gross 1984). One of the interesting questions thrown up by such a curious scene is what kind of status does the scene have, given the overlapping of fiction with oral history? Is it 'true' or not 'true'? Is it a fiction or a history? Why has this *mise en abyme* been introduced, with the daughter performing the role of the mother in her own oral history contribution to the text, and what is its effect? The effect of the citation goes beyond the personal '*mise en abyme*' where the daughter plays her mother naming her, and draws in other resonances. The personal, generational irony of the Sieghild baby performing in a fictional representation of her own naming is supplemented by the historical irony that there will be no victory and that the patriotic or nationalistic fervour of the mother is misplaced. But the most important general point is that this striking example of the layering of histories and fictions draws attention to techniques of mixing fictional and historical genres throughout the text.

Barthes considers the specific question of the relationship between the referent and the image in his late work on photography, *Camera*

---

4 From a discussion with Eva Maria Schneider, who played Marie-Goot, 9 September 1995.

Lucida. Barthes's pursuit of an essence of photography is bound up with his pursuit of his dead mother and her essence in a photographic image. Starting from the position that a photograph is tied to its referent in a way that is not true of any other medium, he nevertheless struggles to find 'her', her 'self' in any of the photographs he looks at.

> I never recognized her except in fragments, which is to say that I missed her *being*, and that therefore I missed her altogether. It was not she, and yet it was no one else. I would have recognized her among thousands of other women, yet I did not 'find' her. I recognized her differentially, not essentially. (Barthes 1984:65–66, his emphasis)

Finally, he is convinced by an image of her as a child, a generational reversal that has resonances for him in the generational role reversal that took place when he cared for his mother prior to her death (Barthes 1984:67–72). His comments about cinema, however, reveal the important differences from the related medium of photography. In cinema, there is a double turn of the referent which means the 'that-has-been' essence of the photograph is weakened in the filmic image (Barthes 1984:76–78).

> In the Photograph, something *has posed* in front of the tiny hole and has remained there forever (that is my feeling); but in cinema, something *has passed* in front of this same tiny hole: the pose is swept away and denied by the continuous series of images. (Barthes 1984:78, his emphases)

Fictional films have two 'referents': the actor and the role, with the result that the simple and strong adherence of the referent to the medium, which could be argued to be a fundament of photography, is already subverted by the fictional cinema. But in the case of *Heimat* the referential link is further subverted by the *mise en abyme* of the cited speech act. Barthes sees his mother as a child in a photograph and is convinced by some kind of essence of the maternal that he sees in the image. But Sieghild tells her story and then performs a role in front of the camera, but a different role, which in turn is removed from its context and functions as a part of a fiction[5]. In the pursuit of the

5 It is not only a different role, but also a different reversal: Barthes's mother becomes his daughter in old age, which he connects with the mother-as-child of the photograph, but Sieghild the daughter plays her own mother in *Heimat*.

'authentic' in the film, the referent is removed many more times than Barthes allows for in his comment on fictional cinema; there are more than two poses here, which results in a disengagement of the referent from the cinematic medium. The pursuit of the real unsettles the distinction between the real and the imagined.

The key theoretical issues raised by Reitz's citation of 'authentic' material can be usefully related to the questions considered by Derrida in 'Signature Event Context' (Derrida 1988a) and 'Limited Inc' (Derrida 1988b). In 'Signature Event Context', Derrida considers as in much of his other work the question of the binary opposition between speech and writing. He begins with a quotation from Austin's *How to Do Things with Words*: 'still confining ourselves for simplicity to *spoken* utterance' (cited in Derrida 1988a:1). Derrida identifies in Austin as in the whole of the mainstream philosophical tradition the view that while writing is essentially concerned with the absence of the writer and the iterability of the 'message', speech implies a presence and a connection with a 'pure' intention of the speaker. Derrida notes that writing, in order to be writing, has to be able to function in the radical absence of the writer.

> In order for my 'written communication' to retain its function as writing, i.e. its readability, it must remain readable despite the absolute disappearance of any receiver, determined in general. My communication must be repeatable – iterable – in the absolute absence of the receiver or of any empirically determinable collectivity of receivers. Such iterability [...] structures the mark of writing itself. (Derrida 1988a:7)

Such iterability means that writing can be disengaged from any context in which it was generated and grafted onto other contexts:

> By virtue of its essential iterability, a written syntagma can always be detached from the chain in which it is inserted or given without causing it to lose all possibility of functioning, if not all possibility of 'communicating,' precisely. One can perhaps come to recognize other possibilities in it by inscribing it or grafting it onto other chains. No context can entirely enclose it. (Derrida 1988a:9)

For Derrida, these features of writing have implications for spoken utterances. He argues that speech functions like writing, that it is 'writerly' or graphematic. His conclusion derives from a recognition that the iterability of the written sign as discussed above must also apply to the spoken utterance, that the same conditions of possibility exist for the phonic sign and that thus phonic signs as well as written signs could be called graphemes:

> [The] unity of the signifying form only constitutes itself by virtue of its iterability, by the possibility of its being repeated in the absence not only of its 'referent,' which is self-evident, but in the absence of a determinate signified or of the intention of actual signification, as well as of all intention of present communication. This structural possibility of being weaned from the referent or from the signified (hence from communication and from its context) seems to me to make every mark, including those which are oral, a grapheme in general. (Derrida 1988a:10)

From this point Derrida goes on to concern himself with the speech act theory of Austin, and particularly with the anomalies that Austin decides he should ignore for the sake of establishing a basic theory of speech acts. These comprise performative utterances that Austin calls 'parasitic' because they are fictional, spoken by actors, for example, as part of a performance. Such performances within performances (a marriage ceremony within a play, for example) troubled Austin and he found he could not formulate any kind of a theory until he had excluded them from his investigations. Derrida argues that it is these very anomalies that should concern us, not least because the structure and the very possibility of 'standard' ('pure', to use Austin's word) performatives are constituted by the parasitic performatives that Austin wanted to ignore. Derrida's point is that the iterability of a speech act, which allows it to be cited, is the same iterability which allows the 'pure' performatives to function:

> Could a performative utterance succeed if its formulation did not repeat a 'coded' or iterable utterance, or in other words, if the formula I pronounce in order to open a meeting, launch a ship or a marriage were not identifiable as *conforming* with an iterable model, if it were not identifiable in some way as a 'citation'? (Derrida 1988a:18, his emphasis)

Indeed, Derrida identifies one of Austin's greatest difficulties in the lecture where he considers the question of the intersection of writing and presence in the form of the signature. Austin finds that in verbal formulations there may be a reference (through a name or the pronoun

'I', for example) to the person who is making the utterance. Where this is not built into the formulation, the utterance-origin is established by the speaker '*being the person who does* the uttering' (cited in Derrida 1988a:19, Austin's emphasis). In writing, Austin sees the signature as performing this function. But a signature, as Derrida points out, far from being the exemplum of a written mark that is tied to an origin and that has a force by means of its singularity, 'the singularity of signature as event' (Derrida 1988a:20), is also constituted by iterability in order to create its general condition of possibility:

> In order for it to function, that is, to be readable, a signature must have a repeatable, iterable, imitable form; it must be able to be detached from the present and singular intention of its production. It is its sameness which, by corrupting its identity and its singularity, divides its seal [*sceau*]. (Derrida 1988a:20)

The relevance to *Heimat* of these theoretical insights is that local people performed within the fictional film their own oral history testimony, highly reminiscent of the 'parasitic performatives' that Austin identified and then excluded from his analysis. Such histories are iterable signs or chains of signs that can be taken out of their initial context and retold or re-performed in another. But in addition, they function as utterances by being iterable, by being able to be cited and by being able to function in the absence of 'original' context, receiver and author. The initial telling of the history, the iterable utterance, is removed from its context, from its syntagmatic chain and grafted onto another chain, given another context, the context of a fiction. Reitz's apparently illegitimate mix of signifying systems (history, oral history and fiction) is compounded by the fact that even his fiction draws on many different genre traditions (Heimat genre, 1950s rites of passage genre, romance, war stories), and thus lacks a unifying style. What is the effect of such grafting of iterable graphematic structures in the film, especially in view of the apparent attempt to introduce elements of 'authenticity', perhaps of a 'pure' origin into the fictional text? The status of the text is unsettled by the introduction of material which emphasises the iterability of graphematic structures and also the way in which their iterability constitutes the general condition of their possibility. In other words, is attention being drawn to the fact that these graphematic structures are always already cited? In the pursuit of the authentic, the naturalistic turn in Reitz's directorial style has at certain points disengaged the film from the pursuit of verisimilitude that characterizes the realism of, say, a soap opera, and has in fact thrown into emphasis theoretical issues concerning the nature of textuality and the intersections between history and fiction. *Heimat* could be seen as a questioning of the status of 'factual' and 'fictional' texts.

When Reitz grafts the oral history of Sieghild into the fictional text, the effect created is part of a naturalistic turn in the film drama. The woman playing the mother is easily recognizable as one of the amateur actors the viewer knows are performing in the film. Her slightly wooden performance marking her status as local amateur has an alienating effect in its gesture towards naturalism. In a soap opera, with its polished performances and attention to verisimilitude, the viewer can maintain a kind of double vision, where s/he simultaneously engages with the fiction as a 'reality' and with the characters as if they were real people, and engages critically with the programme as a piece of television drama subject to certain processes of production (Geraghty 1991:18–24). The viewer can be simultaneously internal and external to the text. In *Heimat*, the break away from the techniques of the soap opera at the point of the introduction of local amateurs means that the very boundary between the internal and the external to the text is being unsettled. The whole question of the grafting of fiction and history leaves the viewer unable to adopt a neat and clear position of double vision but might lead to a more active engagement with the text because the clarity of the realist drama is not always available to the viewer: the text can exist for the viewer as history, as oral history, as fiction, as documentary. But it seems that the more 'authentic' material is grafted onto the fictional story, the more the real/fiction distinction is unsettled, and the viewer is left without a comfortable position to adopt. When the Sieghild scene is viewed, it can be a part of the fictional narrative of Schabbach, or an ironic historical comment on the popular reaction to the outbreak of war. Or the viewer could be engaged by the generational irony of the mother being played by Sieghild herself, or by the strange effect of 'estranged naturalism' created by the integration of professional and amateur performers, the filmic techniques of verisimilitude, the powerful resonance of the auratic sign, and the *Sekundenstil* of naturalism.

But perhaps the key point about the use of cited graphematic structures is that they foreground the very iterability of the whole text, including sequences that are 'completely' fictional and those that are performed by professional actors. Thus, the textuality of the film, of oral history, of other histories, of fiction and ultimately of experience is raised as a conceptual concern of the film. The inclusion of the 'authentic', and more generally the pursuit of authenticity within the film, has led to an emphasis on iterability which in turn questions or unsettles the idea of viable boundaries between genres as well as between the real and the textual.

If this is indeed the case, then it touches on the central area of political disagreement between Reitz and his critics. For it might be argued that it is precisely his illegitimate mix and disruption of generic boundaries that has allowed Reitz to use German history irresponsibly as a source for a highly selective presentation which yet purports to have a more universal status. The way *Heimat* troubles the boundaries of the real and the fictional might be said to play into the hands of revisionist historians and commentators who would want to undermine the status of German history in terms of its defining function in contemporary German society. A presentation which, in blurring the boundaries of history and fiction, suggested that many different narratives of German history could be valid, could certainly be misappropriated or misinterpreted to support the claim that Germans should not feel so protective about the vital role of the Holocaust in defining contemporary positions and responsibilities. I do agree that there are differences between historiography and fiction, in that while historiography cannot or should not claim to bring us 'the whole truth', it does work with conventions of adequacy of evidence to a much greater extent than fiction. However, I feel that a more differentiated view of historiography, which would allow that it cannot be entirely separated from narrative modes, and would reflect on the effects of histories and fictions colliding and overlapping in a contested boundary, might ultimately be more honest and perhaps even more enabling in encouraging a more mature approach to the question of historical responsibility.

My interest in the contribution of amateurs, local oral histories and the performances of certain individuals' own histories in the fictional text is that these clear examples of citation and iterability foreground the way in which all graphematic structures are iterable and can be cited, reproduced and re-contextualized. Genre boundaries and distinctions that depend on contexts and certain kinds of readings are unstable. This is the kind of conceptual question that *Heimat* poses. It is, looked at closely, very far from the mimetic illusionism of a soap opera in its use of realism and authenticity. It is a history that is fictional. But it is also a fiction that might be 'true' in that oral history evidence is woven into the text. It crosses generic boundaries. It raises uncomfortable questions about the flickering interplay of the real and the fictional and it foregrounds the textuality of experience and history, in the sense that experience as it happens and history as it is written are necessarily processed through subjects located in belief or value systems. The word 'realism' ultimately turns out to be both aesthetically and politically inadequate for an assessment of Reitz's effort to represent German local history; the tendency in *Heimat* to slide from seeming 'real' to being 'real' to therefore seeming rather 'unreal' complicates the political and aesthetic questions raised far beyond the assertion that the film is realist and therefore conservative or revisionist.

Bibliography

'AZ Telefon-Aktion: Warum ist Ihre "Heimat" so grausam, Herr Reitz?' (1984) Abendzeitung, 9 October, 3–4

Barthes, Roland (1984) *Camera Lucida*, trans. Richard Howard, London: Flamingo

Birgel, Franz A. (1986) 'You Can Go Home Again: An Interview with Edgar Reitz', *Film Quarterly*, 39 (4), 2–10

Derrida, Jacques (1988a) 'Signature Event Context', trans. Samuel Weber and Jeffrey Mehlman, in Derrida Jacques *Limited Inc*, ed. Gerald Graff, Evanston: Northwestern University Press, 1–23

Derrida, Jacques (1988b) 'Limited Inc', trans. Samuel Weber, in Derrida Jacques *Limited Inc*, ed. Gerald Graff, Evanston: Northwestern University Press, 29–110

Geraghty, Christine (1991) *Women and Soap Opera: A Study of Prime Time Soaps*, Cambridge: Polity Press

Gross, Joachim P. (1984) 'Auf der Such nach den Bildern der "Heimat"', *Vorwärts*, 20 October, 3

'Heimat revisited?' (1986) *London Standard*, 2 May, 31

Hill, Roland (1985) 'Blick über den Hunsrück in deutsche Seelen', *Stuttgarter Zeitung*, 23 March, 37

Hoberman, Jim (1985) 'Once in a Reich Time', *Village Voice*, 16 April, 52, 56

Hohmann, Arnold (1982) 'Das Fenster öffnen und den elften Teil sehen', *Süddeutsche Zeitung*, 18 January, 19

Kahlenberg, Friedrich P. et al. (1985) '"Deswegen waren unsere Muttis so sympathische Hühner" (Edgar Reitz): Diskussion zu *Heimat* mit Friedrich P. Kahlenberg, Gertrud Koch, Klaus Kreimeier, Heide Schlüpmann', *Frauen und Film*, 38, 96–106

'Kein Stammpublikum' (1984) *Tagesspiegel*, 20 November, 25

Mayer, Alf (1981) 'Heimkehr in den Hunsrück', *Tagesspiegel*, 20 December, 52

Perlmutter, Ruth (1987) 'German Revisionism: Edgar Reitz's *Heimat*', *Wide Angle*, 9 (3), 21–37

Reitz, Edgar (1993) *Drehort Heimat*, ed. Michael Töteberg, Frankfurt am Main: Verlag der Autoren

Saalmann, Dieter (1988) 'Edgar Reitz's View of History: The New Religion of Regionalism and the Concept of "Heimat"', *Germanic Notes*, 19 (1–2), 8–14

Swales, Martin (1992) 'Symbolik der Wirklichkeit: Zum Film *Heimat*', in Rüdiger Görner (ed.) *Heimat im Wort: Die Problematik eines Begriffs im 19. Und 20. Jahrhundert*, Munich: Iudicium Verlag, 117–30

Thomas, Gina (1986) 'Ahnungsloser Applaus', *Frankfurter Allgemeine Zeitung*, 2 May, 26

STUART PARKES

'Auschwitz und kein Ende': The Recent Controversies Surrounding Martin Walser

In 1962 in his essay 'Vom erwarteten Theater', the then aspiring young dramatist Martin Walser spoke in the following unambiguous way about the relationship of contemporary German literature to the Nazi past: 'Ein deutscher Autor hat heute ausschließlich mit Figuren zu handeln, die die Zeit von 33 bis 45 entweder verschweigen oder zum Ausdruck bringen.' After a reference to the division of Germany he added: 'Jeder Satz eines deutschen Autors, der von dieser geschichtlichen Wirklichkeit schweigt, verschweigt etwas' (Walser 1965:64). Over three decades later in 1998 the spirit of these remarks, which is reflected especially in the two plays *Eiche und Angora* and *Der schwarze Schwan* of 1962 and 1964 respectively, seemed to have been entirely absent from his speech when he was awarded the 'Friedenspreis des Deutschen Buchhandels'. Here he spoke of his need to 'look away' when confronted with pictures of the worst Nazi atrocities. One thing, however, had not changed: the ability to provoke controversy[1]. Walser's early novels were generally not very well received, especially by conservative critics[2], whilst he was able to annoy his erstwhile allies in the world of literature when, despite being a former prizewinner, he suggested in 1964 that the Gruppe 47 should be 'socialised'[3]. In the 1970s it was his apparent closeness to

1 It is interesting to recall that one of the earliest general essays on Walser, by Marcel Reich-Ranicki, described him as a 'Provokateur' (Reich-Ranicki 1963).

2 The title of Friedrich Sieburg's review 'Toter Elefant auf einem Handkarren' speaks for itself. Sieburg found Walser's novel to reveal 'ungeheuerliche Taktlosigkeit' before going on to praise the value to society of 'Sitte und Anstand', through which 'Welten im Sturz aufgehalten werden [können]' (Sieburg 1970:36).

3 Walser's original article 'Sozialisieren wir die Gruppe 47!' (Walser 1997e) dates from 1964. The anger it provoked in the Group's convenor Hans Werner Richter can be seen from his correspondence (Richter 1997:507–13).

the Deutsche Kommunistische Partei that initially raised many eyebrows[4], but this was as nothing when compared to the reactions to his alleged espousal of German nationalism at the end of the decade[5].

The 1998 speech *Erfahrungen beim Verfassen einer Sonntagsrede* was interpreted by many as the ultimate proof of Walser's conversion to the right-wing, nationalist cause[6]. It provoked another of the major debates that have been a feature of cultural life in the Federal Republic since unification. The 'Vorsitzender des Zentralrats der Juden in Deutschland', the late Ignatz Bubis, accused Walser of 'geistige Brandstiftung' (Schirrmacher 1999:34), which then brought a response from the former prominent SPD politician and son of a murdered resistance fighter against Hitler, Klaus von Dohnanyi. Dohnanyi's hypothetical and, given historical reality, preposterous suggestion that Jews might not have resisted the Nazis any more forcefully than the mass of the German people if other groups had been targets provoked a separate exchange between the two men that began to alarm such a prominent figure as former President von Weizsäcker (Schirrmacher 1999:146–50, 158, 164, 174–5, 186, 187–8). Elsewhere there was a variety of reactions to Walser's speech, with, for example, Monika Maron seeking to defend him and others, for example Eva Demski and the prominent critic Wolfram Schütte of the *Frankfurter Rundschau*, worrying that there seemed little difference between Walser's stance and that of the extreme Right (Schirrmacher 1999:54, 181–2, 220–3). Joachim Wehnelt in *Die Woche* devoted an article to the way in which Walser's comments had found favour with right-wing journals such as *Junge Freiheit*

---

4 Walser's essay written prior to the 1972 Federal Election 'Wahlgedanken' (Walser 1973), which, if not an outright endorsement of the DKP, criticizes the way it is treated in the public sphere, was rejected for publication by *Der Spiegel* before it appeared in *Die Zeit* (10. November 1972), but only accompanied by a counter essay by Marion Gräfin Dönhoff.

5 One of Walser's first clear espousals of German unity came in a 1977 speech. It includes the sentence: 'Wir müssen die Wunde namens Deutschland offenhalten' (Walser 1979a:101).

6 Possibly the most extreme, and highly dubious because of the tone of insinuation, condemnation of Walser can be found in a contrast between him and Günter Grass made in 1999 by Marcel Reich-Ranicki. Ranicki speaks of Grass having learned the necessary lessons from Auschwitz, 'Walser nicht unbedingt' (Reich-Ranicki 1999:306).

(Wehnelt 1998:15). In this context it is possible to quote in Walser's defence Hans Magnus Enzensberger, whose criticisms of *Der Spiegel* in 1957 had gained him plaudits from ideological opponents. His response to those who pointed to 'Beifall von der falschen Seite', was that freedom of thought was a greater good than such tactical considerations which amounted to a kind of totalitarianism (Enzensberger 1964:103–5). Indeed, as a general rule, it would surely be undesirable if writers were to succumb to self-censorship out of fear of reactions to their work that remain beyond their control.

Given such problems it becomes evident that the only way to assess Walser's 1998 speech and the controversies surrounding it is by reference to the text itself. This essay will seek to concentrate on those comments that provoked the greatest amount of comment, compare them with earlier writings by Walser, in particular the two essays 'Unser Auschwitz' of 1965, which is a reflection on the Frankfurt trial of Auschwitz guards, and 'Auschwitz und kein Ende' of 1979, originally a speech given at the opening of an exhibition of art work done by Auschwitz prisoners, assess reactions to them and, I think rightly, given the nature of the subject, which challenges not only all Germanists but arguably the whole of humanity, include some personal response. It is not the aim to castigate apparent 'inconsistencies' for their own sake, as no writer is likely to repeat the same views over three and half decades. Moreover, attitudes towards and knowledge of the National Socialist era within German society – the context of Walser's comments – have changed over the period in question.

The first such point is the topos of 'looking away', as referred to at the beginning of this paper. This idea, it would appear, is to be taken literally. Walser speaks of 'looking away', 'wenn mir der Bildschirm die Welt als eine unerträgliche vorführt' (Walser 1998a:10). When it comes to National Socialist crimes he confesses: 'Von den schlimmsten Filmsequenzen aus Konzentrationslagern habe ich bestimmt schon zwanzigmal weggeschaut' (Walser 1998a:17f). This stance represents a major change from Walser's previous attitudes. In the 1965 essay, he adopts the position of the majority of critical intellectuals of the time who castigated their fellow citizens for not wishing to recognise the continuing significance of the Nazi past. He sees the importance of the trial in the way that it offers an opportunity for 'Enthüllung, moralische und politische Aufklärung einer Bevölkerung, die offenbar auf keinem anderen Wege zur Anerkennung des Geschehenen zu bringen war' (Walser 1997a:187). Fourteen years later the temptation to 'look away', an action that is now to be taken literally, is acknowledged, but rejected on moral and political grounds:

> Ich möchte immer lieber wegschauen von diesen Bildern. Ich muß mich zwingen hinzuschauen. Und ich weiß, wie ich mich zwingen muß. Wenn ich mich eine Zeitlang nicht gezwungen habe hinzuschauen, merke ich, wie ich verwildere. Und wenn ich mich zwinge hinzuschauen, merke ich, daß ich es um meiner Zurechnungsfähigkeit willen tue. (Walser 1997b:235)

Clearly, Walser's stance has changed over the years. Ignatz Bubis's charge of 'geistige Brandstiftung' suggests that Walser has forgotten his own warning about losing his civilising humanity. Whereas the emotionality of his particular phrase is open to question, Bubis was on stronger ground when he pointed out that 'looking away' was not a productive response. Moreover, he was surely right to castigate Walser's admission that he preferred not to believe reports of right-wing excesses in the former GDR. Walser's, on his own admission, trivial reaction, 'Hoffentlich stimmt's nicht' (Walser 1998a:16), is, one fears, another manifestation of Palmström's celebrated dictum: 'Nicht sein kann, was nicht sein darf' (Morgenstern 1972:166).

The other side of Walser's expressed desire to 'look away' is his attack on those who wish to make such a response impossible by repeatedly drawing attention to the horrors of National Socialism, namely left-wing intellectuals. This aspect of his speech encompasses two other comments that attracted particular attention, namely the charge of 'instrumentalisation' of Auschwitz by intellectuals (Walser 1998a:18) and the inappropriateness of using Auschwitz as a 'Moralkeule' (Walser 1998a:20). The difficulty with the first term is that any reference to any event can be classified as 'instrumentalisation'. By his own standards, Walser is certainly guilty of this in his 1965 essay. He links the failure of West Germans to understand Auschwitz with the prevalent mood of anti-communism and other populist ideas. Moreover, in what amounts to a demand for 'instrumentalisation', he specifically demands that people look beyond the more historical facts of Auschwitz, concentration on which he describes as 'sinnlos', (Walser 1997a:202) if further catastrophes are to be avoided. At the same time, much of this essay is a warning against a different kind of instrumentalisation. The title 'Unser Auschwitz' is significant here; Walser argues that on the basis of newspaper reports of the guards' bestiality, most Germans have created their own image of Auschwitz which allows them to claim that they had and have nothing to do with such excesses. In the case of the 1998 speech, Walser's defenders could point to examples of grotesque use of the Auschwitz metaphor: for example, the claim by scientologists that official reaction to them in the Federal Republic was akin to Nazi treatment of those who did not conform (Schirrmacher 1999:175). Nevertheless, the Israeli historian Moshe Zuckermann was correct to point out that Walser is himself guilty of instrumentalising Auschwitz for an attack on his intellectual opponents (Schirrmacher 1999:264). Moreover, by his approach, he provided ammunition to those who claim that many people manipulate Auschwitz to extort money from the German government. Manfred Fuhrmann, in the *Frankfurter Allgemeine Zeitung,* spoke of those who seek 'handfeste materielle Vorteile' from instrumentalising Auschwitz (Schirrmacher 1999:43).

The coinage 'Moralkeule' encapsulates Walser's critique of left-wing intellectuals who allegedly set themselves up as the 'conscience of the nation', when conscience is essentially something individual. Although he does not mention names, the passages he quotes show that he is thinking of, for example, Günter Grass and Jürgen Habermas[7]. The other derogatory term used about such people is 'Meinungssoldaten' (Walser 1998a:25). It has to be stated straight away that such terminology does little to advance the argument. At the same time, Walser's writing throughout his career shows an undoubted concern about gratuitous intellectual comment that lacks any real substance[8]. More recently, this can be seen in the essay 'Vormittag eines Schriftstellers' (Walser 1994). This contrasts the outpourings of the opiniated intellectual with true literature; the title of the essay is reminiscent of Peter Handke's *Nachmittag eines*

7 Walser's failure to mention names earned him strong criticism from Klaus Harpprecht (Schirrmacher 1999:51–3).

8 See, for example, Taberner (1999).

Schriftstellers, whilst the essay itself is full of praise for Botho Strauß, who, along with Handke, is generally seen as a writer who is at odds with conventional ideas of literary commitment.

The same dichotomy between facile opinions and true writing is to be found in the 1998 speech. Walser claims, for example, that the true Thomas Mann can be found in his fictional work rather than in his essays (Walser 1998a:24f). He also points out that Goethe and Schiller were able to develop their friendship despite their different 'consciences' (Walser 1998a:24). In as far as Walser is pleading for tolerance, this argument is perfectly acceptable; on the other hand, there is in all his work a tendency to idealise the 'true writer', for example in the essay 'Wer ist ein Schriftsteller' (Walser 1979b:36–46). In this connection Walser also uses his speech to defend himself against the critics of his novel *Ein springender Brunnen*, in particular Marcel Reich-Ranicki, who deplored the lack of any reference to Auschwitz. Against such demands Walser sets the concept of 'Perspektivität' as the 'Urgesetz des Erzählens' (Walser 1998a:19). Whilst the point is valid in general terms, it can still be argued that certain extreme perspectives cannot be reconciled with true literature.

Walser's attack on leftist intellectuals also extends to the media, the vehicle by which such intellectuals are seen as disseminating their opinions. The essay begins with a reference to the media: 'Als die Medien gemeldet hatten, wer in diesem Jahr den Friedenspreis des Deutschen Buchhandels bekommen werde' (Walser 1998a:9), which may seem harmless enough but which implies their omnipresent nature, before turning to the type of speech that is expected on such occasions: namely something that is so polemical 'daß die Medien noch zwei, wenn nicht gar zweieinhalb Tage eifrig den Nachhall pflegen' (Walser 1998a:9). The reference to the fleeting nature of media news, underlined by the added reference to two and a half days, underlines Walser's scepticism towards something that, unlike great literature, deals in the shortest of time spans. In fact, the whole essay is constructed on the basis that there is a group of intellectuals ready to give their easily expressed opinions at the drop of a hat to insatiable media. This criticism is at the core of a 1994 essay 'Über freie und unfreie Rede' (Walser 1997c) in which Walser launched into an attack on 'political correctness'. Given his own unrivalled access to the media, however, the claims about the dominating position of the politically correct have a somewhat hollow ring.

A similar claim is already apparent in the title 'Erfahrungen beim Verfassen einer Sonntagsrede'. The pejorative term 'Sonntagsrede' achieved notoriety in the 1950s and 1960s when it was used of ministerial speeches, delivered outside the normal political context, which made unrealistic demands, such as a revision of the Oder-Neisse frontier with Poland. In other words, it referred to a discourse in which rhetoric was more important than reality. Walser is claiming that such an offering will be expected from him on this occasion. This kind of reflection can be seen on one level as self-deprecating irony. At the same time, by introducing what might be called a 'meta dimension' to his speech, Walser is arguably allowing himself greater freedom to express his own opinions in a polemical way. Having conceded that such speeches have a ritual dimension, he can indulge himself to the full, as he surely does with some of the terms referred to above, not to mention other related ones such as 'Meinungsdienst' and 'Moralpistole' (Walser 1998a:25).

The clash of opinions between Walser and his opponents is ultimately about the course and relevance of German history. In his Friedenspreis speech, Walser makes a brief reference to German-Jewish relations, claiming, 'wer alles als einen Weg sieht, der nur in Auschwitz enden konnte, der macht aus dem deutsch-jüdischen Verhältnis eine Schicksalskatastrophe unter gar allen Umständen' (Walser 1998a:19). Here Walser is taking up arguments that are found at greater length in his – again controversial – essay that coincided with the publication of Victor Klemperer's diaries, *Das Prinzip Genauigkeit. Laudatio auf Victor Klemperer*, published in 1996. Here Walser stresses the 'Germanness' of Klemperer, his apparent willingness, if forced to choose, to abandon his Jewish identity in favour of 'Deutschtum' (Walser 1996:21). Whilst Walser is radically at odds with those extremists who throughout history have claimed that no Jew can ever be truly German, his stress on Klemperer's Germanness leads him to some dubious conclusions. Having quoted Klemperer's view that the Nazis were not true Germans (Walser 1996:31), he concludes the essay with the following eulogy: 'Nirgends sonst habe ich den Verbrecherstatus der damaligen Machthaber und Funktionäre so erleben und erkennen können wie in diesen

Tagebüchern. Daß es die Bevölkerung gab und eine Bande von Verbrechern als Machthaber' (Walser 1996:52). This effort to distinguish between the Nazis and the people, to cast the Nazis into the role of intruders into German history, which is also found in relation to language in the novel *Ein springender Brunnen* (Walser 1998b:263), flies in the face of the fact that the Nazis were a mass party with wide support. One does not have to be adherent of A.J.P. Taylor's view of German history to see that Walser, whilst being correct to reject historical determinism, is indulging in revisionist obfuscation by denying the links between Nazism and a large part of the German people[9].

In the essay on Klemperer, Walser attacks the plan for a Holocaust Memorial, contrasting the precision of Klemperer's prose with the monstrous nature of the planned memorial (Walser 1996:50f.). This theme is taken up in the 1998 speech. He speaks of '(d)ie Betonierung des Zentrums der Hauptstadt mit einem fußballfeldgroßen Alptraum', before concluding: 'Wahrscheinlich gibt es auch eine Banalität des Guten' (Walser 1998:20). This linkage of the proponents of the memorial with mass murderers – it will be recalled that Hannah Arendt spoke of the 'Banalität des Bösen' in connection with Adolf Eichmann – is clearly unacceptable. One can of course have different views about the aesthetics of the planned memorial or even the need for it; nevertheless it is interesting to note that Walser underlines his case with nationalistic pathos by his reference to the centre of the capital city. Whilst rejecting the memorial, Walser seems keen to suggest that the Federal Republic is now a 'normal country', although the intellectual consciences of the nation are unwilling to accept this. He asks the rhetorical question: 'In welchen Verdacht gerät man, wenn man sagt, die Deutschen seien jetzt ein normales Volk, eine gewöhnliche Gesellschaft?' (Walser (1998:20).

In fact the responses to this part of the speech show that Walser was to a large extent being disingenuous. Two Jewish intellectuals György Konrád (Konrád 1998) and Saul Friedländer were both willing to accept the point of normality. However, Friedländer goes on

---

9 Taylor sees an apparent inevitability in German history leading to the defeat of 1945, hence his closing sentence: 'German history had run its course' (Taylor 1945:225).

to point out that part of normality is facing up to history, asking 'ist eine normale Gesellschaft eine Gesellschaft ohne Erinnerung, eine, die sich der Trauer entzieht, eine, die sich von der eigenen Vergangenheit abwendet, um nur noch in Gegenwart und Zukunft zu leben?' (Schirrmacher 1999:233–40). Accordingly, 'normality' and the construction of the memorial are in no way contradictory. The SPD politician Freimut Duve, whilst generally defending Walser, also supported the idea of the memorial as a warning against the excesses of nationalism, referring in his article to the situation in former Yugoslavia (Schirrmacher 1999:175–7).

Despite his rejection of the Holocaust Memorial and the problematical nature of the idea of 'looking away', even if restricted to presentations of the worst excesses of Nazism, it is obvious from the above that Walser is unable to ignore the Nazi past. Moreover, he is far removed from those who claim that Auschwitz never existed, stating categorically in his Friedenspreis speech: '(k)ein ernstzunehmender Mensch leugnet Auschwitz' (Walser 1998a:18). This speech can be seen, as Monika Maron does, as an exhortation 'zu einem Umgang mit der Geschichte, der das Verdrängen nicht herausfordert und das Erinnern nicht zu ritualisierten Lippenbekenntnissen degradiert' (Schirrmacher 1999:181). Nevertheless, his attempts to come to terms with the past remain controversial and at times somewhat contradictory, as the reference to Auschwitz as 'unsere(r) Schande' (Walser 1998a:18) shows. The use of the term 'unser' underlines how much Walser thinks in national terms, a difference between herself and Walser that Maron points out. This is also ultimately true of the much earlier 'Unser Auschwitz', not just because of the use of the possessive but because of the way that essay comes close to espousing the idea of collective guilt, as the term was used in the immediate aftermath of war. How problematic this kind of thinking in collective terms can be surfaced in Walser's conversation with Rudolf Augstein that was published in *Der Spiegel* in late 1998. Walser showed himself totally unwilling to accept that Augstein came from an anti-Nazi family and that therefore Germans had a choice (Augstein 1998:48–72). Not only does this appear to contradict the distinction between Nazis and Germans Walser makes elsewhere; it also comes close to a kind of historical determinism. Nevertheless, it is important to stress that Walser never denies the existence of

German guilt, in the manner of the extreme Right. His essay 'Die Geburt der Tragödie aus dem Geist des Gehorsams' from as late as 1996 speaks of German guilt as of undeniable 'Unbestreitbarkeit und Schwere' (Walser 1997d:594).

In the debate that followed the 1998 speech, it was the word 'Schande', which is used seven times over two pages (Walser 1998:17f.) with and without the possessive, that attracted particular attention. In *Die Zeit,* Thomas Assheuer castigated Walser for preferring this term to 'Scham'. According to him, 'Scham' implies a moral dimension, whereas 'Schande' might be applied to something that happens as a result of evil fate 'das nur schuldlos Schuldige zurückläßt' (Assheuer 1998:56). The significance of the same terms was raised by two academics from the University of Duisburg, Klaus-M. Dogal and Michael Brocke, in a letter to Walser to which Walser replied in a speech at the same institution. Their claim was that 'Schande' as a word was part of nationalist discourse, as in such phrases as 'die Schande von Versailles', which prevented discussion of the 'philosophisch-ethische Kategorie der Schuld' (Schirrmacher 1999:253). Walser's reply, mixed with some probably justified mockery of professorial pretention, was that he was not concerned with the issues of guilt of the kind raised by Karl Jaspers in the immediate post-war era and referred to by the Duisburg academics, but with a critique of the media 'die bei den meisten Menschen am meisten bestimmen, wie unsere Vergangenheit in unserem Bewußtsein rangiert' (Schirrmacher 1999:256). As for Assheuer's distinctions, he claims that they are beyond his comprehension because of the use of such vacuous phrases as 'ein moralisch souveränes Bewußtsein' (Schirrmacher 1999:257).

It is difficult to mediate between all these interpretations. It is true, as shown, that Walser is concerned with the media, but not exclusively. It is also worthy of note that he too uses the term 'Scham' in the 1979 essay (Walser 1997b:230) and 'Schamgefühl' in 1965 (Walser 1997a:198) in a way that suggests that this is the feeling experienced or that ought to be experienced by most Germans. In the light of comments made over the past three decades and referred to here, it cannot be claimed that he ignores the question of German guilt. The change between the two earlier essays and the Friedenspreis speech is the different stress on the individual. In the first two essays, individualistic reactions to Auschwitz are seen as preventing an adequate response, whereas in the 1998 speech, despite the emphasis on the national dimension, the individual response is at the centre of the rejection of moralistic strictures. In the earlier essays, individualism, the refusal to face up to the collective past, was seen as the danger. 'Unser Auschwitz' closes with the warning that this can lead to new dangerous ideas which might be 'der Anfang des Schrecklichen' (Walser 1997a:202). It is to be hoped that this fear, which Walser linked to the end of the century, remains unfulfilled.

It is now necessary to set Walser's comments and the surrounding controversies into a number of wider contexts. In the case of Walser himself, this essay has clearly shown the significance German themes have in his oeuvre, as underlined by the publication in 1997 of the volume *Deutsche Sorgen* (Walser 1997a-d), which collects in its 600 closely printed pages his writings, fictional and non-fictional, on German themes between the years 1960 and 1996. What matters in such a collection and in the subsequent treatment of the theme is of course the nature of his comments. The main question that inevitably arises is the extent to which he has adopted a nationalistic stance that aligns him with unsavoury right-wing forces. Given his acceptance of German guilt, any such claim is clearly ludicrous. The problem is rather a way of thinking that sees everything in national terms along with a desire, born, one must assume, out of the awareness of the horrors of Nazism, to seek exoneration in other parts of German history, for example the 'success' of unification, and in the positioning of alternatives to historical reality, as in the Klemperer essay. This leads to historical distortion, for example the view that the 1914 war was some kind of natural catastrophe (Walser 1996:34), and to injudicious blanket attacks on those who take opposing views.

It goes without saying that Walser's concern with Auschwitz and Nazism generally is not unique within German intellectual circles. Enzensberger, for example, sought to justify the Gulf War by comparing Saddam Hussein to Hitler, a perfect example of 'instrumentalization' in the Walserian sense (Enzensberger 1997). In his 1992 essay *Hauptsache Deutsch* (Morshäuser 1992), Bodo Morshäuser speaks of how both left and right use Auschwitz to bolster their political arguments. Nor is this interest with the past confined to intellectuals. Gerhard Schröder is reported to have approved of the substance of Walser's 1998 speech, whilst saying that he, as a politician, was constrained on such topics in a way that writers are not (Schirrmacher 1999:221). On the basis of his age, Schröder is the first Federal Chancellor who belongs entirely to a post-war generation and therefore cannot at all be directly linked with Nazism. What this generational change should mean is that a new understanding of history which is not obscured by the burden of direct responsibility becomes possible. In a book that appeared in 1999 entitled *Niemand ist frei von Geschichte* and which reviews the various Bundestag debates about the Nazi past, the sociologist Helmut Dubiel stresses this point. He adds that it is only in the context of generational debate that the vexed question of guilt can be resolved (Dubiel 1999:289).

The continuing significance of the Nazi past for the Federal Republic is also visible in the context of practical politics. Whereas British involvement in Kosovo can be linked to the 'Munich metaphor' – the need to confront rather than appease 'dictators' – in the Federal Republic it was the 'Auschwitz metaphor' that was used to justify the sending of German troops in an operation the size of which can be said to mark another stage in the development of German foreign policy since it was deemed constitutionally acceptable for German troops to be deployed outside the NATO area. Hans Christoph Buch, in the *Frankfurter Allgemeine Zeitung* of 16 April 1999, spoke of 'Nie wieder Völkermord!' as being the lesson to be learned from the Second World War that had to be applied in this case[10]. By contrast, other writers, most notably Peter Handke but also, for example, Dieter Forte and Martin Walser, opposed the war, the kind of dichotomy that led Jan Ross to comment in *Die Zeit* that anyone can pick up the 'Moralkeule' of Auschwitz 'je nach Bedarf, und für seine Zwecke' (Ross 1998:3).

Whatever the truth of such a comment, it would be wrong to become sceptical about continuing concern with National Socialism and, specifically, Auschwitz. What is more, this concern goes beyond Germany and, in parallel to the development outlined by Dubiel, is taking on new forms. The attention, both positive and negative,

10 Buch's comments appeared originally in the *Frankfurter Allgemeine Zeitung* of 16. April 1999. For an overview of writers' attitudes towards the Kosovo war see: *Fachdienst Germanistik* 17/5, May 1999, 1–6.

attracted by Roberto Benigni's 1998 film *Life is Beautiful*, which again was linked with Auschwitz in the German press, although the camp in the film bears little direct relationship to it, is just one example of this[11]. In the United States, Art Spiegelman's *Maus*, a cartoon depiction of the fate of Europe's Jews under the Nazis and of how the shadow of Auschwitz never left one survivor to the detriment of those around him, gained the Pulitzer Prize (Spiegelman 1986/91). An explanation for this international concern was provided by Saul Friedländer in the speech already referred to: 'Der Nationalsozialismus mit allem, was er geprägt und angerichtet hat – die Austrottung der Juden vor allem –, ist im Lauf der Jahrzehnte in der Vorstellungswelt des Westens (und vielleicht sogar darüber hinaus) zum Inbegriff des Bösen geworden, "Auschwitz" zur zentralen Metapher für das Böse in unserer Zeit' (Schirrmacher 1999:235f.). This, Friedländer argues, cannot be explained in terms of manipulation any more than out of a desire to speak of German 'abnormality', but is rather 'ein tiefgreifender, ungesteuerter Prozeß' (Schirrmacher 1999:237). Or perhaps it is directed by the universal challenge Auschwitz poses to our common humanity and particularly our consciences, which need to be kept fully awake if the world is not entirely, to use Walser's own term, to 'verwildern'.

Bibliography

Assheuer, Thomas (1998) 'Ein normaler Staat', *Die* Zeit, 47/12 November, 55–6

Augstein, Rudolf (1998) 'Erinnerung kann man nicht befehlen'. Martin Walser und Rudolf Augstein über ihre deutsche Vergangenheit', *Der Spiegel* 45/2 November 1998, 48–72

Dubiel, Helmut (1999) *Niemand ist frei von Geschichte*, Munich, Vienna: Hanser

Enzensberger, Hans Magnus (1964) *Einzelheiten I*, Frankfurt am Main: Suhrkamp

Enzensberger, Hans Magnus (1997) 'Hitlers Wiedergänger' in H.M. *Zickzack*, Frankfurt am Main: Suhrkamp, 79–88

Konrád, György (1998) Die Freiheit des Erinnerns', *Die Zeit*, 53/22 December, 38–9

Morgenstern, Christian (1972) *Alle Galgenlieder*, Frankfurt am Main: Insel

11 See, for example, Seesslen (1998). The sub-title of the article is: 'Roberto Benignis Auschwitz-Komödie: Darf man über das Grauen Märchen erzählen?'

Morshäuser, Bodo (1992) *Hauptsache Deutsch*, Frankfurt am Main: Suhrkamp
Reich-Ranicki, Marcel (1963) 'Der wackere Provokateur' in M.R-R *Deutsche Literatur in West und Ost*, Munich: Piper, 200–215
Reich-Ranicki, Marcel (1999) '"Ich bedauere nichts", Spiegel-Gespräch mit Marcel Reich-Ranicki', *Der Spiegel*, 40/4 October, 306–12
Richter, Hans Werner (1997) *Briefe*, ed. Sabine Cofalla, Munich and Vienna: Hanser
Ross, Jan (1998) 'Aus Auschwitz lernen', *Die Zeit*, 49/26 November, 3
Schirrmacher, Frank (ed.) (1999) *Die Walser-Bubis Debatte*, Frankfurt am Main: Suhrkamp
Seesslen, Georg (1998) 'Kalter Blick und kleine Hoffnung', *Die Zeit*, 47/12 November, 56
Sieburg, Friedrich (1970) 'Toter Elefant auf einem Handkarren' in Beckermann, Thomas (ed.) *Über Martin Walser*, Frankfurt am Main: Suhrkamp, 33–6
Spiegelman, Art (1986/91), *Maus. A Survivor's Tale*, New York: Pantheon Books, 2 vols.
Taberner, Stuart (1999) 'Fictional Reflections on the Gruppe 47 in Martin Walser's Kristlein Trilogy' in Parkes, Stuart/White John J. (eds.), *The Gruppe 47 Fifty Years On A Re-Appraisal of its Literary and Political Significance*, Amsterdam and Atlanta: Rodopi (German Monitor 45), 139–58
Taylor, A.J.P. (1945) *The Course of German History*, London: Hamish Hamilton
Walser, Martin (1965) 'Vom erwarteten Theater' in M.W. *Erfahrungen und Leseerfahrungen*, Frankfurt am Main: Suhrkamp, 59–65
Walser, Martin (1973) 'Wahlgedanken' in: M.W. *Wie und wovon handelt Literatur*, Frankfurt am Main Suhrkamp, 100–18
Walser, Martin (1979a) 'Über den Leser — soviel man in einem Festzelt darüber sagen soll' in M.W. *Wer ist ein Schriftsteller?*, Frankfurt am Main: Suhrkamp, 94–101
Walser, Martin (1979b) 'Wer ist ein Schriftsteller?' in M.W. *Wer ist ein Schriftsteller?*, Frankfurt am Main: Suhrkamp, 36–46
Walser, Martin (1994) 'Vormittag eines Schriftstellers' in M.W. *Vormittag eines Schriftstellers*, Frankfurt am Main: Suhrkamp, 9–26
Walser, Martin (1996) *Das Prinzip Genauigkeit. Laudatio auf Victor Klemperer*, Frankfurt am Main: Suhrkamp
Walser, Martin (1997a) 'Unser Auschwitz' in M.W. *Deutsche Sorgen*, Frankfurt am Main: Suhrkamp, 187–203
Walser, Martin (1997b) 'Auschwitz und kein Ende' in M.W. *Deutsche Sorgen*, Frankfurt am Main: Suhrkamp, 228–35
Walser, Martin (1997c) 'Über freie und unfreie Rede' in M.W. *Deutsche Sorgen*, Frankfurt am Main: Suhrkamp, 468–86
Walser, Martin (1997d) 'Die Geburt der Tragödie aus dem Geist des Gehorsams' in M.W. *Deutsche Sorgen*, Frankfurt am Main: Suhrkamp, 593–601
Walser, Martin (1997e) 'Sozialisieren wir die Gruppe 47!' in M.W. *Werke in zwölf Bänden,* Frankfurt am Main: Suhrkamp, vol. 11, 144–47
Walser, Martin (1998a) *Erfahrungen beim Verfassen einer Sonntagsrede*, Frankfurt am Main: Suhrkamp

Walser, Martin (1998b) *Ein springender Brunnen*, Frankfurt am Main: Suhrkamp
Wehnelt, Joachim (1998) 'Unser Walser', *Die Woche*, 18 December 1998, 15

INGO CORNILS

Romantic Relapse? The Literary Representation of the German Student Movement

Introduction

Wolfgang Kraushaar, an authority on the German Student Movement, recently wrote about the difficulty of unearthing the experiences of the movement from under the 'Misthaufen der Medien' (Enzensberger 1985:9), and suggested:

> Vielleicht besitzt nur ein Schriftsteller oder Künstler die nötige Freiheit, Erinnerungen, in denen die Imagination lebendig geblieben ist, vor dem aufdringlichen Zugriff der Historisierung zu schützen. (Kraushaar 1999:188)

In the 1970s, a number of German writers attempted just that; to represent, in literary form, the 'heady' experience of the German Student Movement. These texts not only allow the rebels to re-live their youth, but also – and this is my thesis – modern readers to step 'inside' the movement and gain an understanding of its essence.

Given that most of these texts are still readily available, it is surprising to note that on the occasion of the 30th anniversary of the 'magic year', there were few new studies looking at the literary reflections of the movement itself. Whilst there is still significant interest amongst UK Germanists (Riordan 1995, Basker 1999, Plowman 1998), in Germany, in spite of great activity amongst the historians (Gilcher-Holtey 1998, Becker 2000), there is little academic interest in the literary representation of the movement. The reason for this may be a feeling that everything has been said about this literature, or even that most of these texts were so bad anyway that it would be a waste of time going back to them.

I would suggest that there are two other reasons: one is the strong conservative counter-current against a positive interpretation of the student revolt and associated social developments. The other reason is the confusion inherent in the German expression 'Literatur der Studentenbewegung', in that it implies a literature emanating from the movement, which we therefore expect to be somehow 'revolutionary' in form and message, as opposed to 'Literatur über die Studentenbewegung' for which such expectations are not applicable.

It is the 'Literatur über die Studentenbewegung' which I propose to revisit, to see whether the three decades' distance from the German Student Movement has not also had an effect on the way we read these texts.

History and Memory

All great literary 'Gedächtnisprojekte' of recent decades wrestle with the tumultous changes that have taken place in Germany this century. They write against forgetting – insights and experiences which have been hard won must not be lost again. And yet time seems to be winning. If we compare the following two statements by Hans-Magnus Enzensberger, we see how quickly we can lose what we once felt was a permanent achievement. In 1978, he writes, almost sentimentally, about the student revolt: 'Ich erinnere mich, kaum zu glauben, keine zehn Jahre ist das jetzt her, an die sonderbar leichten Tage der Euphorie' (Enzensberger 1978:14–15).

Years later, he has begun to mistrust his memories:

> Ein Gewimmel von Reminiszenzen, Allegorien, Selbsttäuschungen, Verallgemeinerungen und Projektionen hat sich an die Stelle dessen gesetzt, was in diesem atemlosen Jahr passiert ist. [...] Jeder Versuch, den Tumult intelligibel zu machen, endete notwendig im ideologischen Kauderwelsch. Die Erinnerung an das Jahr 1968 kann deshalb nur eine Form annehmen: die der Collage. (Enzensberger 1985:6)

If an individual or collective memory becomes undermined by the 'noise' of 'Historisierung', we lose the confidence of our convictions built on our experiences. One way to assure ourselves of the validity of our memory is the autobiographical novel. Andrew Plowman has shown in his study *Radical Subject* how German writers like Inga

Buhmann and Berward Vesper used this form to describe their personal development and how they were changed and affected by the Student Movement.

Plowman claims that his chosen texts work as historical documents and as contributions to the genre of autobiography, but I would argue that reading about the movement as history denies us emotional involvement, whilst a personal biography eclipses its wider significance. For readers trying to understand what drove the movement and made it unique, both approaches are unsatisfactory without a literary mediation which, in its best moments, makes the events and experiences come alive again. In such texts, the protagonist does not have to be the author's alter ego, nor to prove that he/she is particularly interesting or unique. The rebellion of the students, today widely regarded as a watershed in West German history, can itself become the protagonist and the focus of literary reflection.

Literature and the Student Movement

What exactly do we mean, more than 30 years after the revolt, when we talk about the 'Literature of the German Student Movement'? Is it literature written in a way that only became possible after 1968? Is it literature that uses the Student Movement as a background, setting, or catalyst for the narrated events or the development of the protagonists? Is it literature that requires the reader to have been part of the events, or is it literature that actually seeks out the aesthetic quality of the movement?

We could tick all four options, but be none the wiser. There has been a steady stream of novels 'dealing with' or 'coming out of' the German Student Movement, but, if we accept Wolfgang Kraushaar's view that 1968 was 'das Jahr, das alles verändert hat' (Kraushaar 1998), we are dealing with pretty much all literary production post 1968. In a way, this is what progressive Germanists have attempted to do, arguing that German literature was not and could never be the same after the revolt of the late 60s when literary concerns entered the revolt, and the revolt entered literature (Briegleb 1992:21ff).

The reactions to the literary representations of the movement, however, have been by and large negative. In the 1970s, the critical response was drowned in ideological squabbles, discussions about literary techniques, the 'death of literature' and the 'Tendenzwende'. The new terms for any attempt at literary representation of the movement were 'literarische Verarbeitung', 'Besinnungsliteratur' or 'Erinnerungsliteratur'. They implied a dealing with, a coming to terms with the past in literary form. In the eyes of the critics, these texts were marred by self-pity, their ambivalent political message and their traditional narrative structures.

It was W. Martin Lüdke who tried to point to the positive aspects of the ever growing number of texts, not because of their inherent literary value, but because, in his view, they were transporting 'ein zunehmend verdrängtes und unterdrücktes Widerstandspotential' (Lüdke 1977:11). Against the background of the 'Deutscher Herbst', Lüdke felt it necessary to retreat even further and diagnosed that an 'Überwintern der Idee einer freien Gesellschaft' (Lüdke 1979:8) was only taking place in literature.

The (unpopular) view that the literature from, of and about the Student Movement might actually be doing something valuable eventually found its way into the canon of 'progressive' literary histories (Beutin 1979, Schnell 1993). Indeed, Ralf Schnell has single-handedly categorised and labelled the 'literarisierte Revolte' for future generations of Germanists. But even here we find a 'yes, but…' approach. While on the one hand Schnell accepts that these texts are more than autobiographical, he still finds that they are lacking something, i.e. that they are conventional from an aesthetic point of view: 'Die Romane freilich, die von der politischen Revolte handeln, repräsentieren [...] keineswegs eine literarische Revolte' (Beutin 1979:495).

To bridge the gap, Schnell set about developing a new set of aesthetic criteria for this new literature. He absolved the literary representations of the revolt both from having a role in the political struggle, and from scrutiny according to conventional aesthetic criteria. Instead, he constructed a hermetic cage for the texts.

He argued that they had been written 'ohne literarische Ambitionen' (Schnell 1982), simply to describe the possibility of an alternative way of living, to pass on the experiences of the movement, and to illustrate new forms of perception. In order to compare the texts with each other, he suggested one look at how 'authentic' they seemed, how well the reader could share the 'Betroffenheit' of the author, and how well one could 'tune into' the 'Trauerarbeit' as a productive coming to terms with the experiences of a generation.

1986 saw the publication of Ingrid Eichelberg's study of the literature of the French Student Movement and the events of May 68 (Eichelberg 1986). This study focuses on the impact of the May 'revolution' on the attitudes of French intellectuals. Eichelberg argues that the 'Folgeliteratur' contributes to an unspecified memory project which she in turn sees as helpful in conveying 'Bewußtseinskunde' for a psychology of French social life.

Like Schnell, Eichelberg steers clear of any critical judgement on the literary merit of her chosen texts – she looks for statements about contemporary history, not how these statements are formulated in literary form. Given that she is prepared to concede that most of the novels she analyses can be regarded as 'ästhetisch nicht gelungen', it is not surprising that her tentative conclusion is fairly damning:

> Die Romane zeigen, daß der Impetus des Mai verschiedene Regungen auslösen kann: übersteigerte Ichbetonung, zuweilen rücksichtslos egoistische Suche nach Selbstentfaltung, andererseits die Tendenz zur Selbstnegation und nostalgischen Rückblicken auf die euphorisch erlebte Symbiose des einzelnen Individuums mit der Masse im Mai 68. (Eichelberg 1986:17)

It is at this juncture that one would have expected a response in the form of a similar study on the literary reflection of the German Student Movement. After all, the gap in research was obvious. But there was one problem: there was no equivalent 'euphorisch erlebte Symbiose des Individuums mit der Masse' in the German Student Movement. The veterans of the movement had spent long years after 68 coming to terms with this bitter fact, and only reluctantly managed to regroup in the form of a much wider alternative political project, namely the Green movement.

Meanwhile, in the English-speaking world, Keith Bullivant and others pointed out that the term 'new subjectivity', with its negative connotations of abandonment of the revolutionary cause, had been adopted too hastily, and that the literature about the student movement had retained its anti-capitalist critique, as well as exploring 'new perceptions'. According to Bullivant, a work like Uwe Timm's *Heißer Sommer* was politically realistic in spite of an 'unconvincing utopian ending', because it sought to 'influence opinion and to help to play a part in bringing about political action and, thereby, political change' (Bullivant 1989:50). He later classed such literary representations as 'political prose works', which were 'attempting to learn important lessons' (Bullivant 1994:40).

In Germany, however, academics like Klaus Briegleb are highly critical of the 'Erinnerungsmarkt', which in his view represents a counter-revolutionary trend whilst ignoring the more experimental, democratic and political literature that had developed from the mid-60s. Briegleb believes that the wave of 'neue Subjektivität' undermined the 'Aufbruch' of a new aesthetics. It is no surprise, therefore, that texts which do not adhere to his precepts of revolutionary aesthetics receive only short shrift from him :

> Einige Studenten wurden zu Schriftstellern, nachdem sie sich besiegt glaubten als Revolutionäre und sich bleibende Anerkennung versprachen als Bürger im belletristischen Kontinuum. Es begann 1973 mit Peter Schneiders ungedecktem Wechsel seines gekränkten Revolte-Ichs auf Büchners Lenz-Figur und verlief sich in einer Menge meist peinlich selbstgerechter Sohn-Vater-Schriften um 1980. (Briegleb 1993:11–12)

In 1998, the Deutsches Literaturarchiv in Marbach organised an exhibition entitled *Protest! Literatur um 1968*. Announcing the exhibition on the internet, the organisers asked 'Ist die Literatur vor den Ereignissen und Zielen der Studentenbewegung eher verstummt?', but the body of texts which could have provided the answers, namely the literary reflections of the movement, was by and large ignored. Instead, and in explicit reference to Briegleb's approach, a broad collection of German literature of the time was scrutinised for stylistic changes and 'revolutionary innovations' which one could attribute to the cultural revolution of the 1960s.

Only in Helmuth Kiesel's concluding essay in the exhibition catalogue do we learn anything about the crucial connection between the experience of the protest and its aesthetic reflection. Kiesel argues that literature had brought a new form of thinking *to* the movement, but that central experiences *of* the movement, such as the experience of collective political awakening and the sense of participating in a movement of global liberation, had in turn become legitimate material for literary representation:

> Die Literatur [...] folgte nicht mehr dem politischen Denken, sondern durchkreuzte und bereicherte es. Alle Versuche, das Dominantwerden des genuin poetischen Denkens in der Literatur unter je einzelnen Etiketten wie 'Entpolitisierung', 'quietistischer Rückzug', 'existentialistische Wende', 'Neue Subjektivität', 'Romantischer Rückfall' usw. zu begreifen, können der Kontinuität und Vielschichtigkeit dieses Vorgangs nicht gerecht werden. Es ging nicht einfach 'gegen Politik' oder um den 'Rückzug aus der Politik', sondern um 'mehr als Politik': um Dichtung. (Bentz 1998:624)

According to Kiesel, texts like Peter Schneider's *Lenz*, Uwe Timm's *Heißer Sommer*, and Jochen Schimmang's *Der schöne Vogel Phönix* began the 'epische Aufhebung der Protestbewegung', in that they 'ziehen Bilanz, eröffnen weiterführende Perspektiven, retten, verabschieden (Bentz 1998:625)'. This is nimble footwork, but cannot disguise the fact that, now elevated to the lofty heights of 'Dichtung', the literary representation of the Student Movement has been stripped of its subversive potential.

If future readers were to follow this interpretation, they might be tempted to view these texts simply as a convenient distillation of a time of upheaval, without any connection to their own lives. The historical 'fact' of the student movement neatly aligns with the political need of the new political elite to have 'respectable' revolutionary credentials, but after relegation to the realm of fiction, its utopian vision of an alternative to the present system no longer represents a threat.

However, I believe that the literary representation of the movement is still capable of having an unexpected effect on the reader, that it continues to have the potential to influence political culture. The reason for this subversive potential lies in its essentially romantic quality.

Romantic Relapse?

The German Student Movement has long been suspected of romantic tendencies. Marion Gräfin Dönhoff perceived the revolt as a 'Rebellion der Romantiker', and a 'neue Variante charismatischer Erlösungsvorstellungen' (Dönhoff 1968:1). Jürgen Habermas criticised the 'vorsätzlichen Irrationalismus' (Habermas 1969:9) of the students, and Richard Löwenthal saw it as a 'romantischer Rückfall' (Löwenthal 1970). By this he meant that the student unrest was in fact a complete refusal to accept the reality of the modern industrialised world. By attempting to destroy its institutions instead of humanising them, and negating all values instead of reformulating them, the intellectual leaders of the movement had given in to a 'romantic nihilism' that prefered romantic utopia over any reform. Although the revolt was politically inconsequential in the short term, Löwenthal feared that the romantic 'Glaubenssucht' would make the followers of the movement easy prey for totalitarian ideologies.

In *The Germans*, Gordon A. Craig pointedly linked his chapters on German Universities and on German Romanticism. The Romantic Movement, he argued, was essentially a youth and protest movement, searching for a world of imagination and wonder. The German students in the second half of the 1960s had formed a similar movement, characterised by cultural pessimism and a rejection of consumerism and commercialised culture. What the various counter-cultural groups had in common, according to Craig, was a retreat from reality into a self-created subculture and their lack of clear visions of what they wanted their new society to be like.

In his study on the relationship between social movements and literature, Alois Prinz argues that the romantic world view of the Student Movement had a profound influence on the literature representing it. It has the same aesthetics, the same political concepts, only the form of realisation is different. A romantic, utopian counter-world is created to convey the subjective 'Anspruch auf Glück' (Prinz 1990:96). But if the reality was not able to meet this need, how can literature?

I believe that we have to draw a distinction between the romantic impulse of writers to encapsulate an intense moment or experience, and the romantic need of readers to search for such moments to make them meaningful for their own lives. Writing between 'Radikalenerlaß' and 'Deutscher Herbst', authors like Uwe Timm, Peter Mosler, Hermann Kinder, Urs Jaeggi and Jochen Schimmang, much like the Romantics of the second generation, had to face a conservative backlash, and felt compelled to rescue the utopian dream of an egalitarian society by transporting it into the world of literature. Like their romantic predecessors, they had witnessed a revolution and experienced the disappointment of its eventual failure. They may have retreated from the ugly reality of politically motivated murder, intransigence of those in power and a generally unimaginative public, but they had also experienced personal liberation, brotherhood with their comrades, and the potential for a new political order, all of which they attempted to re-cast in literature.

The dual experience of exuberance and despair is central to the literary representation, and employed as the key moment which leads to the political awakening or radicalisation of the protagonist(s). Of course, an event like the attempted assassination of Rudi Dutschke is also central in the historical accounts and chronologies of the movement. Yet it is in the narrative that the collective experience gains real shape and weight. The literary representations do not treat this moment 'objectively', and it is precisely because of this that we can see what this moment meant to the people who made up the movement.

Let us now turn to the needs of the readers of this literature. The first readers of the books on, about or of the Student Movement were the '78ers', those who came of age ten years after the revolt. Although they had not lived through the 60s, they 'bought into' the romanticised view of the German Student Movement:

> Die 78er [...] waren fasziniert von der Entschlossenheit der Älteren, Schluß mit allem zu machen, was den Menschen unfrei machte, ungerecht und unerträglich

> war. Der Blick war nach vorn gerichtet, auf die unbegrenzten Möglichkeiten. In ihrem Widerschein wurde die Wirklichkeit wahrgenommen. (Mohr 1992:25)

We need to remember that there was no booming 'Erinnerungsmarkt' with coffee-table books picturing the protest in the late 1970s. It was its literary representation that fuelled the romantic imagination of the eager and young readership, telling them that change was possible because it had been possible in the past. Until the 78ers could find their own vision, the exciting 'moments' of the 'great revolt' were all they could aspire to.

Magic Moments

Heißer Sommer

Apart from Peter Schneider's *Lenz* (1973), which retains its position as the 'iconic text of the German Student Movement' (Riordan 1995:17), Uwe Timm's *Heißer Sommer* (1974) is the most cited and discussed novel on the Student Movement. The reason for this is partly because the narrative is embedded in a theoretical discussion about the social function of literature, but mainly because the events and protagonists are designed to be representative of the movement as a whole. The novel has recently been re-evaluated (Basker 1999), but there is still the question as to how far we can trust a utopian vision when it is undermined by the fact that the movement failed. Rhys Williams writes:

> Uwe Timm succeeds beyond doubt [...] in conveying the rage, the idealism, and the sheer creative disruptiveness, of the student movement [...] But the question remains whether the novels are more than merely a historical record. (In Basker 1999:62)

Ultimately, this question has to be answered by the reader. Timm cannot re-write history, but by providing us with a romanticised version of the essential experience of the Student Movement (the unity of 'Denken, Fühlen und Handeln'), he can ensure that it becomes part of our own utopian anticipation:

> Sie konnten unglaublich ernst und konzentriert miteinander diskutieren und im nächsten Moment wie Kinder herumalbern, um dann sogleich wieder genauso ernst wie vorher weiterzudiskutieren. Beides gehörte zusammen, das löste sich nicht ab, wie Ullrich zunächst gedacht hatte, sondern das eine ging aus dem anderen hervor. (Timm 1974:93)
>
> Er hatte sie untergehakt, er konnte lachen und reden mit ihnen, als kennten sie sich schon lange. Was er fühlt, ist eine Freude, die über ihn hinausgeht, die ihm ein Gefühl der Weite und Stärke gibt. Eine Freude, die vom Haß getragen wird, ein Haß, der verändert. (Timm 1974:142)

Was wir wollten, was wir wurden

Peter Mosler's *Was wir wollten, was wir wurden* (1977) is an attempt to take stock, 'damit wir uns einiger Stärken besinnen, die wir leichtfertig aufgegeben haben' (Mosler 1977:8). For this purpose, Mosler had visited members of the 68 generation up and down the country and described, in a collage of individual perspectives, their experiences and development. The result is a requiem to the movement, written in a deeply melancholic tone, but tempered with the diffuse hope: 'Geschlagen gehen wir nach Haus, die Enkel fechten's besser aus' (Mosler 1977:233).

Despite its underlying sadness, the book glows with the excitement of the collective experience, of 'making' the revolution. The time of the Student Movement emerges as 'eine Zeit, in der das trockene Stroh unseres Daseins lichterloh verbrannte' (Mosler 1977:2). Everybody is part of this collective, even those individuals who had embarked on the path of terrorism are integrated with staunch solidarity: 'wie in Amerika wurden aus [...] utopischen Romantikern Revolutionäre des bewaffneten Untergrunds' (Mosler 1977:24).

With hindsight, many trivial acts attain an extraordinary significance, and the literary pathos with which they are rendered borders on kitsch, but Mosler deliberately infuses them with the exuberance of the Zeitgeist: 'erst auf dem sonnenüberfluteten Kudamm [...] kam eine uferlose Ruhe über sie' (Mosler 1977:45), or: 'es gab die Atmosphäre einer Zärtlichkeit, auf die man rechnen konnte. Es gab ein Glück der Stille und Einsamkeit wie der lauten Abenteuer der Revolte' (Mosler 1977:64).

The deliberate romanticising and stylisation reaches its climax with a portrait of the 68ers as a romantically doomed generation which could easily be mistaken for that of their Romantic predecessors:

> Sie unterscheiden sich von ihren Vätern durch eine Sensibilität, die ihnen das unglückliche Bewußtsein an der Gesellschaft aufherrscht. Es ist ein Zustand, in dem das Alte ohne Kraft ist, aber das Neue noch ohne Konturen, selbst das Bewußtsein des Noch-Nicht ist selten, statt dessen lebt ein Bewußtsein des Nicht-Mehr, auch Trauer. (Mosler 1977:80)

Der Schleiftrog

Hermann Kinder's *Der Schleiftrog* (1977) shows no signs of sentimentality about the movement. His protagonist, a postgraduate in German philology, is in the throes of an identity crisis, his search for the promised concrete utopia is undermined by his repressive upbringing and the fact that the Student Movement simply did not happen in provincial Münster. Yet even he is granted his moment of vision. In a debate with Günter Grass before the national elections of 1972, he plucks up the courage to ask the great writer:

> Wie macht man denn das, die Dichtung und die Politik zu vereinen? Er zupfte sich einen Tabakkrümel von der Unterlippe: Eins sei ihm das, denn schließlich sei alles eine Realität.
> Das war ein Vorbild.
> Der Knoten war geplatzt. Keine Widerstände mehr. Nicht Trennen zwischen Drinnen und Draußen, das Ich und die Welt versöhnen, ohne die Seele zu kappen, einzufangen und stillzulegen, den Schmerz, die Sehnsucht nicht verbergen, bei sich anfangen und dem Allgemeinen zum Glück verhelfen: das war die Lösung, das ist das Glück. *Ohne die Zukunftsvision der Seher, der Dichter, der Künstler wird die Gattung Mensch nie zur Menschheit werden.* Du mußt, sagte ich mir, nur wollen, der Wille versetzt Berge. Noch in derselben Nacht füllte ich den Füllfederhalter und begann zu dichten. (Kinder 1977:143/4) [italics in original]

Though deeply ironic, this is a serious moment, and programmatic for a romantic solution to the dilemma of an intellectual's alienated existence after 1968. In a letter of 3 January 1979, Kinder elaborates on his intentions:

> Ich will den Kopf zeigen, sonst (fast) nichts. Die Mischung von Gedanken und Gefühlen, die eine kollektive Mentalität kennzeichnen. Mir ging es ja gar nicht um die paar 67er Jahre, sondern um die ganze Generation. [...] Der 'Schleiftrog' erzählt letzten Endes keine Entwicklung, sondern er stellt eine Frage zu einer Entwicklung, eine Frage genau aus der Situation, in der er endet und in der er anfängt: am Ende der Studentenbewegung.[1]

Der schöne Vogel Phönix

What makes Jochen Schimmang's *Der schöne Vogel Phönix* (1979) so irresistible to the reader is his insistence that he has had the time of his life:

> [...] dann der Mai 1968, jener kurze Moment, als alles möglich schien oder vielleicht auch alles möglich war, jener kurze Moment, der immerhin zwei Jahre dauerte. (Schimmang 1979:123)

For Schimmang's protagonist, the real achievement of the movement is the development of a collective identity which allowed the individual to endure the contradiction between romantic utopian vision and impervious reality:

> Daß es ihnen gelang, den Widerspruch zwischen den eigenen Aktionen, deren Intentionen und den Reaktionen der Bevölkerung auszuhalten, lag wesentlich an der intakten politischen Identität der Studentenrevolte, die die handelnden Subjekte in ihre Politik und Taktik miteinbezog, den Mut hatte, sich zu der eigenen, überdurchschnittlichen, politischen und moralischen Sensibilität und der daraus entspringenden, weitgehenden Isolation von der Masse der Bevölkerung zu bekennen, und diese nicht opportunistisch zu verleugnen versuchte. (Schimmang 1979:243)

Life after the movement is 'Leidensgeschichte', the bitter realisation of failure, a struggle for survival. The only comfort lies in comradeship, and the faint hope that the mythical Phoenix will one day rise out of the ashes again:

---

1 This letter is in my private collection, IC.

> Es ist nicht gesagt, daß noch einmal eine neue Flut kommt. Natürlich hoffen wir alle darauf, und mancher sieht in jedem kleinen Aufflackern gleich den Beginn einer neuen Bewegung. [...] Aber in Wahrheit versuchen wir vor allem zu überwintern, und der Winter kann ewig dauern. (Schimmang 1979:281)

Conclusion

So what should we make of the literary representation of the German Student Movement? Is it still worth reading, has it got anything to say to the modern reader? Do we see these texts differently because we see the Student Movement differently today? Do we see the Student Movement differently because of these texts?

More than three decades after the movement, 25 years after the debates about the 'death' of literature, and 10 years after the collapse of communism, the movement has become a 'Gegenstand der Geschichtswissenschaft' (Gilcher-Holtey 1998). We struggle to grasp the 'Lebensauffassung' of the 68ers. Their experiences and hopes have become unclear or the butt of cheap jokes. Only the 'Innenansicht' afforded by literary representation can help us to understand their motives and collective mentality.

A collage of texts emerges that recreates and sustains a breakthrough of consciousness, a feeling of awareness of others, both in moments of joy and great sadness. Following a romantic tradition, this literature preserves moments of intense 'Welterfahrung', not just 'Selbsterfahrung', set against a sobering reality.

I would argue that some of these 'moments' have to be understood as 'acts of memory', that they serve as the cultural memory of a generation. And this memory refuses to fade: the narrated experience of joy and exaltation is painted so exquisitely that it attains infinite desirability. And herein lies the subversive potential of these texts: the historical 'event' is romanticised so that the reader may wish for a similar experience. The unity of thought, feeling and action becomes reality for a moment, and as Schimmang's title implies, may become reality again.

The literary representation of the German Student Movement seeks to distill the intensive experience of youth, to hold on to collective advances in consciousness, and to convey and transcend what is hardest to convey: the experience of a 'konkrete Utopie'.

Bibliography

Basker, David (ed.) (1999) *Uwe Timm* (Contemporary German Writers), Cardiff: University of Wales Press

Becker, Thomas/Neumann, Ute (2000) *Quellenkunde zur Geschichte der Studentenproteste 1965–1970*, forthcoming

Bentz, Ralf, et.al. (1998) *Protest! Literatur um 1968* (Marbacher Kataloge 51), Marbach: Deutsche Schillergesellschaft

Beutin, Wolfgang, et.al. (1979) *Deutsche Literaturgeschichte*, Stuttgart: Metzler

Briegleb, Klaus/Weigel, Sigrid (1992) *Gegenwartsliteratur seit 1968* (Hansers Sozialgeschichte der deutschen Literatur Bd. 12), Munich: dtv

Briegleb, Klaus (1993) *1968. Literatur in der antiautoritären Bewegung*, Frankfurt am Main: Suhrkamp

Buhmann, Inga (1977/1998) *Ich habe mir eine Geschichte geschrieben*, Frankfurt: 2001 Verlag

Bullivant, Keith (ed.) (1989) *After the 'Death of Literature'*, Oxford: Berg

Bullivant, Keith (1994) *The Future of German Literature*, Oxford: Berg

Craig, Gordon (1982) *The Germans*, New York: Putnam's Sons

Dönhoff, Marion Gräfin (1968) 'Rebellion der Romantiker', *Die Zeit*, 23. Jahrgang, No.1, 1

Eichelberg, Ingrid (1986) *Mai '68 in der Literatur. Die Suche nach dem menschlichen Glück in der Gesellschaft*, Marburg: Hitzeroth

Enzensberger, Hans Magnus (1978) *Der Untergang der Titanic*, Frankfurt am Main: Suhrkamp

Enzensberger, Hans Magnus (1985) 'Erinnerungen an einen Tumult – Zu einem Tagebuch aus dem Jahr 1968', in: *Text und Kritik*, Heft 49, 2nd ed., 6–9

Gilcher-Holtey, Ingrid (ed.) (1998) *1968. Vom Ereignis zum Gegenstand der Geschichtswissenschaft*, Göttingen: Vandenhoeck & Ruprecht

Glaser, Hermann (1991) *Kleine Kulturgeschichte der Bundesrepublik Deutschland 1945–1989*, Bonn: Carl Hanser Verlag

Götze, Karl-Heinz (1981) 'Gedächtnis. Romane über die Studentenbewegung', in: *Das Argument*, No.23, 367–382

Habermas, Jürgen (1969) *Protest und Hochschulreform*, Frankfurt am Main: Suhrkamp

Hosfeld, Rolf/Peitsch, Helmut (1978) 'Weil uns diese Aktionen innerlich verändern, sind sie politisch. Bemerkungen zu vier Romanen über die Studentenbewegung', in: *Basis. Jahrbuch für deutsche Gegenwartsliteratur* 8, 92–126

Jaeggi, Urs (1978/1998) *Brandeis*, Hamburg: Rotbuch Verlag

Kinder, Hermann (1977) *Der Schleiftrog*, Zurich: Diogenes

Klinger, Cornelia (1995) *Flucht Trost Revolte. Die Moderne und ihre ästhetischen Gegenwelten*, Munich: Carl Hanser Verlag

Kluge, Alexander (1977) *Neue Geschichten.* Hefte 1–18 'Unheimlichkeit der Zeit', Frankfurt am Main: Suhrkamp

Kraushaar, Wolfgang (1998) 1968. Das Jahr, das alles verändert hat, München: Piper

Kraushaar, Wolfgang (1999) 'Der Aufschrei der Jugend', in: *Der SPIEGEL* 13/1999, 172–188

Löwenthal, Richard (1970) *Der romantische Rückfall*, Stuttgart: Kohlhammer

Ludwig, Volker/Michel, Detlef (1992) *Eine linke Geschichte* (Textbuch Fassung 1992), GRIPS Theater Berlin

Lüdke, W. Martin (1977) *Literatur und Studentenbewegung. Eine Zwischenbilanz*, Opladen: Westdeutscher Verlag

Lüdke, W. Martin (1979) *Nach dem Protest. Literatur im Umbruch*, Frankfurt am Main: Suhrkamp

Mohr, Reinhard (1992) *Zaungäste. Die Generation, die nach der Revolte kam*, Frankfurt am Main: Fischer

Mosler, Peter (1977) *Was wir wollten, was wir wurden. Studentenrevolte – zehn Jahre danach*, Reinbek: Rowohlt

Muschg, Adolf (1981) *Literatur als Therapie? Ein Exkurs über das Heilsame und das Unheilbare* (Frankfurter Vorlesungen), Frankfurt am Main: Suhrkamp

Offenbach, Judith (1980) *Sonja. Eine Melancholie für Fortgeschrittene*, Frankfurt am Main: Suhrkamp

Piwitt, Hermann Peter (1975) 'Rückblick auf heiße Tage. Die Studentenrevolte in der Literatur', in: Buch, Hans Christoph (ed.), *Literaturmagazin 4. Die Literatur nach dem Tod der Literatur*, Reinbek: Rowohlt

Plessen, Elisabeth (1976) *Mitteilung an den Adel*, Zurich: Benziger Verlag

Plowman, Andrew (1998) *The Radical Subject. Social Change and the Self in Recent German Autobiography*, Berne: Lang

Prinz, Alois (1990) *Der poetische Mensch im Schatten der Utopie. Zur politisch-weltanschaulichen Idee der 68er Studentenbewegung und deren Auswirkung auf die Literatur*, Würzburg: Königshausen&Neumann

Reich-Ranicki, Marcel (1999) *Mein Leben*, Stuttgart: Deutsche Verlags-Anstalt

Riordan, Colin (ed.) (1995) *Peter Schneider* (Contemporary German Writers), Cardiff: University of Wales Press

Schimmang, Jochen (1979) *Der schöne Vogel Phönix. Erinnerungen eines Dreißigjährigen*, Frankfurt am Main: Suhrkamp

Schneider, Peter (1973) *Lenz. Eine Erzählung*, Berlin: Rotbuch

Schnell, Ralf (1982) *Die Literarisierte Revolte. Erfahrungen mit der Literatur der Studentenbewegung*, WDR/NDR Radio production, broadcast on NDR III 9 March 1982

Schnell, Ralf (1993) *Geschichte der deutschsprachigen Literatur seit 1945*, Stuttgart: Metzler

Schwanitz, Dietrich (1995) *Der Campus*, Frankfurt am Main: Eichborn

Sonner, Franz-Maria (1996) *Als die Beatles Rudi Dutschke erschossen*, München: Kunstmann

Timm, Uwe (1974/1977) *Heißer Sommer*, Reinbek: Rowohlt
Zeller, Michael (1986) *Follens Erbe. Eine deutsche Geschichte*, Bad Homburg: Oberon

IAN FOSTER

Joseph Roth and *Der Neue Tag*

Klaus Westermann's 1989 edition of Joseph Roth's journalistic works revealed the scale and significance of Roth's writing for newspapers for the first time by making available many texts that had not previously been republished or were only obtainable with difficulty. The edition lacks, however, an appropriate critical apparatus and its transcriptions of some early texts are unreliable[1]. When one is dealing with journalistic texts, written to be read by a contemporary public, contextual reference points are vital to any attempt at understanding or analysis. With this in mind, this paper will examine those texts Roth published in the Viennese newspaper *Der Neue Tag*, which Roth worked for from shortly after its founding on 23 March 1919 until its demise on 30 April 1920[2].

Previously, Roth had published a number of poems and prose texts in various newspapers, among them the *Prager Tagblatt*, *Österreichs Illustrirte Zeitung*, the *Arbeiter-Zeitung* and the weekly *Der Friede*. The items in *Der Neue Tag*, however, represent the first significant body of work by the author for the same publication, some 158 articles in just over one year. This is where he learned his trade (Früh 1990:108).

Der Neue Tag itself was an unusual newspaper. Benno Karpeles, its editor and founder, was already well-known as the owner and editor of the provocatively-named *Der Friede*, founded in January 1918[3]. *Der Friede* was esteemed as a critical journal, with famous contributors like Alfred H. Fried, Adolf Loos, Oskar Maurus Fontana, Johannes Urzidil

1 Details of the edition appear in the bibliography under Roth (1989). I have used the abbreviation GW (=Gesammelte Werke) in the text together with the relevant volume number.

2 The date for the first issue of *Der Neue Tag* is given incorrectly in Bronsen (1993:104).

3 The flyer for *Der Friede* begins with the words: 'DER FRIEDE ist von seiner ersten bis zur letzten Zeile Protest gegen dieser Zeitläufte Roheit, Grausamkeit und Dummheit, wie sie sich in der Tatsache: Krieg am fürchterlichsten manifestieren.'

and Hermann Kesten. Its literary editor was Alfred Polgar, who went on to fulfil the same function at *Der Neue Tag* alongside a regular staff of journalists and feuilleton writers such as Richard A. Bermann, Rudolf Olden, Leo Perutz, Egon Wellesz, and Karl Tschuppik, who were also contributors to *Der Friede.* Little wonder, then, that Robert Musil referred to the editorial team at *Der Neue Tag* as an 'Elite-Redaktion' (Musil 1955:472).

Although the economic situtation was poor for launching a new newspaper, the collapse of the Habsburg regime and its highly developed mechanisms of both formal and informal censorship offered unprecedented freedom to editors and journalists. Significantly, 13 new titles were launched in 1919, replacing 13 newspapers that had closed down, compared with six closures and two new titles in the previous year (Melischek and Seethaler 1992:226–27). Initially, the popular press in particular benefited from the lifting of the 'Kolportageverbot', the ban on street-sellers. At the same time, the vacuum left by the disappearance of the quasi-official Habsburg press, with its impenetrable networks of sponsorship and subsidy, was filled by new politically-based newspapers, supported by parties and private interests (Sültemeyer 1976:46). In particular, the *Fremdenblatt*, a mainstay of the bourgeois press and the semi-official organ of the old 'k.u.k' Foreign Ministry, was now politically unacceptable. *Der Neue Tag* was designed to appeal to its former readers. After many years as a committed socialist and contributor to the *Arbeiter-Zeitung*, Benno Karpeles had left the Social Democratic Party after the death of Viktor Adler in November 1918. Karpeles's new publication *Der Neue Tag* belonged to the Elbemühl company, which also owned a number of other Austrian dailies. Its chief shareholder was Richard von Schoeller, owner of the Schoeller Bank. Karpeles had raised the idea of a privately-owned, but editorially independent newspaper modelled on the *Frankfurter Zeitung* in February 1918[4]. To this end he secured a contractual promise that he would have a free hand in editorial matters. He also promised that the paper would act as a forum for anyone 'der über ernste Dinge Neues und Beachtliches zu sagen hat'[5]. It was not

4 See 'Die Presse' in *Der Friede* (2 February 1918).

5 See *Der Friede* (59) 7 March 1919, where Karpeles writes: "Die 'Elbemühl'[...] hat mir vertragsmäßig zugesichert, daß ich bei der Führung der Redaktion freie Hand haben solle: die Redakteure werden von mir bestellt: der Administration steht

to support any one political party, but to secure the interests of the republic, social reform and the regeneration of public life, and aimed to mediate between bourgeois and worker. Despite these assurances, the newspaper was attacked as being in the pay of the capitalists, particularly when Schoeller sold his share of the company in October 1919, and Karpeles was denounced as an 'Überläufer'[6]. An acrimonious dispute ensued between *Der Neue Tag* and the *Arbeiter-Zeitung*, the official organ of the Social Democrats and owned outright by the party, culminating in personal attacks on Karpeles in the Austrian Parliament. Among other things, Karpeles suggested that the socialist leaders of the coalition government were behaving more like the ministers of the former monarchy than the representatives of the Republic. The Austrian Chancellor Karl Renner had chartered a train at a time of severe coal shortages in Vienna for what was in effect, despite repeated fierce denials, a private trip. This was revealed in the conservative daily the *Reichspost* and pursued in the pages of *Der Neue Tag*[7].

When it comes to Roth's views, the evidence suggests that he shared similar convictions to Karpeles. There is little that can be said to improve on David Bronsen's description of the author in this period as 'ein skeptischer und dennoch zukunfstfreudiger linksorientierter junger Mann, der eindeutig gegen den Klerikalismus und den Monarchismus Stellung nimmt' (Bronsen 1993:108). Certainly, the much-cited sentence from a letter of 17 September 1922 to Herbert Ihering – 'Ich kann wahrhaftig nicht mehr die Rücksichten auf ein bürgerliches Publikum teilen und dessen Sonntagsgeplauder bleiben, wenn ich nicht meinen Sozialismus leugnen will' (Roth 1970:40) – can be read as rhetorical exaggeration. As Eckart Früh points out, Roth was asking for more money from the *Berliner Börsen-Courier* at the time.

Roth's articles for *Der Neue Tag* are critical of the socialists in power where he sees abuses of privilege and compromises forced upon them by the post-war coalition government. In 'Der neue Hofpark' (GW I:155–

---

keinerlei Einfluß auf die Redaktion zu; ohne meine Zustimmung dürfen Inseratenverträge nicht abgeschlossen, Inserate nicht angenommen werden; zwischen den anderen Blättern, die im Verlag der 'Elbemühl' erscheinen, und dem 'Neuen Tag' gibt es keine Verbindung [...]".

6 See 'Die Arbeiter-Zeitung und Der Neue Tag' in *Der Neue Tag* (18 October 1919).

7 *Die Reichspost* (30 November 1919), *Der Neue Tag* (4 December 1919).

156), Roth comments on the significance of the fencing in of a previously open lawn between the chancellor's residence and the Foreign Ministry at a reported cost of 160 000 Kronen, suggesting that this is being done out of sheer political vanity:

> Ein Staatskanzler, der in einem Büro arbeitet – wodurch unterscheidet er sich von einem simplen Diener des Staates? Aber ein Staatskanzler in einem Park – den nenn' ich einen Staatskanzler. (GW I:155)

The article caricatures Renner and his government as would-be royalty and offers thc motto 'Odi profanum vulgus' to hang on a sign above the new park. Similarly, in an article entitled 'Die Freikarten – Zehn Millionen', amid the criticism of the cost of providing free public transport for among others members of the fire brigade and 7000 soldiers of the Volkswehr, Roth singles out the hypocrisy of workers' council representatives for attack. Having applied for free public transport for themselves, only to have their application turned down, the 'Arbeiterräte' had then complained about the extent of the practice of providing free tickets. One does not find warm words for the ameliorative programme of Austromarxism in *Der Neue Tag*. For example, one might cite the abolition of child labour, the introduction of the 8-hour working day and regulation of opening hours as significant achievements of the first year of the Austrian Republic, none of which receive any substantial mention in the newspaper (Früh 1993:110–111).

In Roth's articles runs a common thread: he pokes fun at those unwilling to grant privileges and benefits to the poor and disadvantaged, but all too ready to feather their own nests. Perhaps the best description of Roth's political stance is to be found in a recently republished article from *Der Neue Tag* entitled 'Minister Moissi'[8]. The pretext for the article is an interview following up on a report that the German actor Moissi has been named by the Sparticists as a potential ministerial candidate. Moissi immediately denies this rumour and goes on to describe himself as a Christian attracted to Communist ideas because of their similarity to Christian charity towards the poor and oppressed. Roth as interviewer concludes:

---

8 *Der Neue Tag* (7 July 1919), reprinted in Roth (1994:33–36).

> Nein, 'Minister' Moissi ist kein Bombenschmeißer und Putschist, kein ungarisch besoldeter Agitator und Revolverheld. Er ist auch nicht, wie ihn ein Wiener Schriftsteller in einem jüngst erschienenen Feuilleton ungefähr genannt hat, ein Instrument, das unbewußt kommunistisch klingt, weil der Zeitgeist ihm diese Töne entlockte. Er ist nichts anderes als ein Künstler, der Herz und Sinn hat für den leidenden Teil der Menschheit, der den Spießbürger haßt, wie ihn die Künstler *aller* Zeiten gehaßt haben, und der die graue Nivellierung der Menschheit ebenso fürchtet wie jeder andere Nicht-Kommunist. Der prinzipielle Unterschied liegt nur in der göttlichen Ungenauigkeit des Künstlerwesens, das keine scharfen politischen Grenzen kennt und dem die Nuancierung der Parteien Hekuba ist.

These words offer a clue to understanding the indeterminate nature of their author's own political allegiances. Attempting to tie Roth to a particular label is certainly a mistake. Roth's extraordinary sympathy for the casualties of history, that combination of remorselessness and compassion, to borrow Reich-Ranitzki's phrase from another context, is the touchstone of his journalism (Reich-Ranitzki 1984:247). A fundamentally religious and ethical sensibility lies at the heart of his perceptions and informs his journalistic writing. A good example is the use of the term 'Ebenbild Gottes' in this formative period. In a text entitled 'Der Zeitgenosse', published in the *Prager Tagblatt* on 17 April 1919 with another piece under the title 'Menschliche Fragmente', one finds a description of a disabled shell-shocked war veteran with a broken back:

> Das war einmal Mensch. Nannte sich Ebenbild Gottes, Krone der Schöpfung, und wandelte aufrecht und mit den Füßen durch den Staub, aus dem er gemacht war. (GW I:21)

The reference is presumably to Genesis 1 verse 27[9]. Now this 'Zeitgenosse' resembles an exotic animal that looks as if it should be kept on a leash. And yet the text insists: 'Es ist Mensch! Mensch mit menschlichem Antlitz, mit einem Hirn, das denken, phantasieren, erfinden, träumen, arbeiten, wagen, schaffen kann' (GW I:22). His zig-zag gait and physical infirmity are an image of the society that he has returned to and a constant reminder of the barbarity that that same society engendered. The phrase 'Ebenbild Gottes' is repeated in four further articles published by Roth in *Der Neue Tag* over the succeeding six

9 'Und Gott schuf den Menschen ihm zum Bilde, zum Bilde Gottes schuf er ihn.'

months and recurs in early articles written after his move to Berlin in 1920[10]. In each case, the term is ironic, as in another description of a war veteran in 'Schuhriemen Bitte!' (15 June 1919), who is introduced as 'Sinnbild und Überrest einer großen Zeit' (GW I:35). At the same time, the term also signals a protest against the degradations imposed by the post-war era. Roth rejects in numerous articles what he refers to as the materialism of the new age. In 'Die Auferstehung des Geistes' (11 April 1920) he characterizes human development as retrograde, modernity as filled with 'Ellenbogenmenschen' and 'Unterleibsmenschen' and lacking in spirituality: 'Der Geist fehlt, der allein Bestand verleiht, und Gottes Atem, der den Erscheinungen ein Stückchen Ewigkeit einhaucht' (GW I:278).

Roth's early texts display a profound concern for the autonomy and dignity of the individual. Examining his work for *Der Neue Tag,* it is remarkable how many portraits of individuals there are to be found here: from what, in lesser hands, would be a banal or sentimental feature on a 100 year-old Viennese lady (GW I:223–225) to the short-story-like tale of the returned peasant emigré Petro Fedorak (GW I:215–217).

Yet while it is possible to chart Roth's political affiliations as exhibited in his journalistic writing with some precision, it is far harder to categorise the material itself. Furthermore, there is an inherent danger in sifting out the contributions of one individual journalist to a publication and treating them according to established literary criteria. When it comes to 'Feuilleton' texts the problem is acute. As Almuth Todorow has noted: 'Feuilleton – das ist bis heute eine publizistische Fundgrube, ein Steinbruch, aus dem jeder sich bedienen kann und Einzelteile ohne Kenntnis ihrer tektonischen Verbindungen herausgebrochen werden' (Todorow 1988:701).

It is important to remember that Austrian newspapers of 1919 that understandably aspired to a degree of political independence formed self-consciously collective projects. Newspapers in the German-speaking countries have always spoken of themselves in the first-person plural, hence Karl Kraus's famous parodic inflection of a newspaper's manifesto: 'Kein tönendes "Was wir bringen", sondern ein ehrliches "Was wir um-

10 See for example 'Lebende Kriegsdenkmäler', first published in *Neue Berliner Zeitung* (31 August 1920), or 'Der Wiederaufbau des Menschen', first published *Neue Berliner Zeitung* (6 June 1921).

bringen"'. Editorial comment was always signed 'Die Redaktion'. The distinction between this and the English 'the editor' may be a fine one, but it is nonetheless significant. Within the collective identity of a newspaper's editorial team, it may be the case that the Feuilleton writer enjoyed a special position, not exactly 'Narrenfreiheit', but a relative degree of freedom to comment on events and cultural phenomena. However, this should not permit us to consider those texts we designate 'feuilletons' in isolation from the rest of a newspaper's content.

Roth's contributions to *Der Neue Tag* can be classified in a number of ways. There were pieces of political reportage, as, for example, when he was sent as a special correspondent to the territory that would subsequently become the Burgenland[11]. He also wrote similar pieces of reportage on local subjects, for example, 'Die Wanderung des amerikanischen Mehls' (GW I:70–72) or 'Der Marktplatz der Kettenhändler' (GW I:65–67). His versatility showed in his review articles like 'Die Muse der Blinden' (GW I:62–63) and in his features, like the description of the newly-opened former Imperial apartments at Schönbrunn (GW I:165–166). To describe all of these texts as 'feuilletons' is both misleading and unhelpful. There are *some* which more closely fit conventional definitions of the feuilleton and it should come as no surprise that these have received more attention than other more intractable texts.

A particular case in point are those articles that appeared under the rubric 'Wiener Symptome'. According to Rainer-Joachim Siegel's Joseph Roth bibliography, Roth contributed 33 items to this column (Siegel 1995:79–106). In five cases, I believe the attribution to Roth to be uncertain. My arguments are as follows: 158 texts from *Der Neue Tag* have been attributed to Joseph Roth. Of these 83 were signed 'Josephus' and a further 36 with Roth's full name. Among the remainder, the largest group are 18 articles signed 'R.' (five of which appeared under the 'Wiener Symptome' rubric). These are stylistically some of the weakest and least interesting texts. None was ever republished by Roth, who later became adept at recycling articles from his Viennese days in Berlin newspapers. During Roth's time at *Der Neue Tag* another journalist

11 Not all of Roth's texts about the Burgenland are included in Westermann's 1989 edition. Some may be found in GW I:100–116; the remainder in Siegel's collection *Unter dem Bülowbogen* (Roth 1994:39–52).

signed articles with the name Oscar Retzer. When it comes to a discussion of the 'Wiener Symptome', I would therefore exclude from consideration the texts entitled 'Kunstpflege' (30 November 1919), 'Das Postbüchel' (4 January 1920), 'Das Unwahrzeichen' (15 February 1920), 'Ein Stern ist aufgegangen…' (29 February 1920) and 'A jour' (14 March 1920)[12]. It should also be noted that the last four of these appear as the last 'Wiener Symptome' attributed to Roth.

Westermann presents the texts in his edition separately from the rest of Roth's writing in this period under the heading 'Wiener Symptome'[13] (GW I:30–57). Indeed, the critical reception of their republication has already elevated them to the status of 'Feuilleton-Zyklus', which conveniently overlooks the fact that the rubric was not Roth's own invention and that other writers contributed to the same section (Wirtz 1997:44). Chief among them was Richard A. Bermann, writing under his pseudonym Arnold Höllriegel. Viewing texts as a 'cycle' imbues them with an intentionality that may be attractive and even justified at times when, as in Wirtz's analysis of Roth's techniques of character portrayal, literary aspects are being stressed, but it does tend to distort our understanding of the relationship these kind of texts may have had with the contemporary readership. In order to understand that relationship better, it is necessary to examine in greater detail the communicative context in which the texts first appeared and to look therefore at the overall make-up of *Der Neue Tag* as a newspaper.

Der Neue Tag was, as its name suggests, a daily. From Tuesdays to Saturdays there was a separate evening issue as well, on Sundays a morning edition only, and on Mondays an evening edition only. A weekday morning issue would run to 10 to 12 pages, an evening paper between 4 and 6 pages. On Sundays, the length would increase to 16 to

12 Westermann includes 'A jour' incorrectly as being signed 'Josephus' where it was signed 'R.', see GW I:57. Unfortunately, Westermann also groups together 'Wiener Symptome' texts which appeared under separate titles. This was presumably done to emphasize those texts which appeared in the same issue, but it has the unfortunate side effect of making the title of one text appear as if it is an overall title for others from the same issue. The other texts whose attribution I consider doubtful may all be found in Roth (1994:57–62).

13 The 'Wiener Symptome' texts not included by Westermann which I believe can be safely attributed to Roth are 'Das Fünffrankstück' (14 September 1919) and 'Selbständig' (9 November 1919), republished in Roth 1994:55–57.

18 pages. The price of 30 Heller on weekdays made the newspaper dearer than its direct competitor, the *Arbeiter-Zeitung*. Text was in gothic type, appearing in four full-height columns. Major stories would sometimes divide up the page by occupying the central two columns. There was no horizontal line demarcating 'feuilleton' from 'news'. However, that does not imply that one can simply assume that news and comment, supposedly 'subjective' and 'objective', were somehow mixed up in a cavalier fashion. *Der Neue Tag* exhibits a hierarchy typical of its time in the order in which it presents individual items, beginning on the front page with chief political stories, the left-hand column typically containing an editorial piece relating to these stories. Pages 2 and 3 would continue with further foreign news and major domestic stories. In most cases, the contributions of individual correspondents are clearly attributed. Though there is frequent use of 'Siglen' or ciphers, these are often obvious abbreviations of names that appear in full under other contributions and may have served principally to obscure the small number of staff responsible for most of the content. Shorter domestic news reports then followed, usually alongside a review of the local press ('Die Blätter von heute'), followed by local news reports (police, courts), then theatre, lectures, auctions, personal news. Sport and business articles would usually come last, and the paper was rounded off by small ads and advertising for local entertainment venues.

The feuilletons, which tended to appear only in mid-week issues of the newspaper and always and in greater numbers in the Sunday edition, were normally placed in the middle of this order, between domestic and local news. In other words, feuilleton texts were positioned in such a way that they could absorb and reflect both 'high' and 'low' content of the paper itself.

The section in which feuilleton texts appeared in *Der Neue Tag* was never labelled 'Feuilleton' in the modern usage at all. Leaving aside the question of whether it is possible to define the term 'feuilleton' more precisely, it is more important to observe how 'feuilleton texts' fitted into the structure of information in the newspaper as a whole. They form part of a continuum of informative, discursive writing. In terms of communication theory, literary scholars tend to accord the feuilleton too privileged a place. No newspaper has ever offered a uniform scheme of news writing that could be construed in simple binary opposition to a subversive feuilleton. At the factual end, there are news stories which are reported as fact, where narrative structures and strategies may be evident, but there is no overt narratorial presence. Somewhere in the middle of the range are interpretative texts like editorials, correspondents' reports and critical reviews. At the same time, Austrian newspapers had always published purely fictional texts as well. Indeed, some of Roth's contributions to *Der Neue Tag* could easily have appeared among the prose texts that form the other three volumes of the six volume collected works. The feuilleton text usually draws its inspiration from factual elements, be they events reported elsewhere in the paper or scenes or events from daily life presented by the narrator. As Irmgard Wirtz puts it, the feuilleton draws on the characteristics of both news reports and literary tradition (Wirtz 1997:22). It is a 'Zeitzeichen' in a double sense: it both represents the era in a documentary fashion and offers a counterfactual opposition. Yet the feuilleton was not the only discursive form that mediated between news events and the cultural consciousness of the newspaper readers, and should not be seen in isolation from other forms which performed a similar function. In particular, two well-established forms, political cartoons and jokes, commented upon and dramatised events in a similarly self-conscious and structured manner.

To illustrate this mediating role one can examine a major news theme and how it is presented under different rubrics in *Der Neue Tag*. The running story with the greatest immediate significance for the readers of a Viennese newspaper in 1919 was the issue of food shortages and rationing. The collapse of the Habsburg Empire produced a trade war between Deutschösterreich and Hungary in the winter of 1918–19, followed by conflicts with the other successor states over tariffs and customs. Even the German-Austrian *Länder* refused to supply food to the former Imperial capital. While the entente governments attempted to organize relief, food rations for adults in the city of Vienna fell to half the daily recommended calorie intake, and bread, milk and potatoes were in short supply (Wirtz 1997:44–45).

The immediate threat of starvation appeared on the front page of the very first issue of *Der Neue Tag* (23 March 1919) in a political cartoon depicting a starving mother and her children waiting in vain for a decision from the Paris conference table. In the cartoon, a group of bald, cigar-smoking politicians are seated at a table. The emaciated mother stands to the right. The caption reads: 'Die Friedenskonferenzler: "Das Volk Deutschösterreichs will..." – Eine Stimme "Brot!!"' On p. 11 of the same issue is a feature that ran throughout the life of the newspaper under the title 'Unser tägliches Brot'. Some typical headlines from this rubric included: 'Milchbeschlagnahme durch das ungarische Ernährungsamt'; 'Die Großmarkthalle heute geschlossen'; 'Neue Brotmischung'; 'Erhöhung der Zuckerpreise'. Food, or rather the lack of it, was the source of a rich vein of black humour. A cartoon published on 26 March 1919 depicts a waiter offering to fry a goldfish to go with the restaurant's copious supply of salt, pepper and mustard. In its Sunday issue of 30 March 1919, the paper published a short story translated from the English with the telling title 'Fleisch' – about a group of starving explorers awaiting rescue in Greenland. In the grim post-war months, even the fact that rations were not to be cut could be regarded as newsworthy: a headline on 1 April read 'Die Brot- und Mehlquote wird nicht gekürzt'. Absurdist jokes are typical. For example:

> "Nun," sagte Alfred, "was für ein Aprilscherz ersinnen wir heute?"
> "Wir wollen den Leuten einreden, daß Krieg war," schlug Edouard vor, "und daß Hungersnot herrscht und Haß und Ungeist und Schmutz und Erbärmlichkeit."
> "Und wenn die Narren uns das glauben," sagte Alfred, "Dann rufen wir fröhlich: April! April! Alles nicht wahr!" (1 April 1919)

Through these early months of the new newspaper, the theme of starvation is ever-present and connected in its feuilletons, in caricatures and jokes with the political impasse in Paris. In a cartoon of 20 May 1919 entitled 'Die 14 Punkte Wilsons', Woodrow Wilson appears as an apologetic waiter with the words 'Bedauere, schon alles gestrichen! '.

It comes as no surprise, therefore, that Roth's very first contribution to the rubric 'Wiener Symptome' – a column devoted to the various manifestations of post-war Vienna's crisis – consisted of two short texts with words referring to food in the their titles: 'Mai und Mais' and 'Schokolade' (18 May 1919). 'Mai und Mais' takes its cue from an item in the official 'Verordnungsblatt' and the coincidental pun between the return of the month of May and the return of maize meal as part of the food ration, a staple scarce in wartime. The text transposes the physical sensations of hunger and pleasure in satiating it to the associations that maize bread calls forth:

> Als der Mai trotz Abschaffung der Sommerzeit doch über die Welt kam und das Maisbrot auch noch auf den Tisch, kostete ich noch einmal das erhebende Gefühl des Durchhaltens in vollen Zügen und würzenden Bissen, schwamm in goldgelben Reminiszenzen aus der Zeit, in der man Gold für Maisbrot gab, das schwer verdaulich war wie ein Kriegsbericht und zwerchfellblähend wie ein A-Befund [....]

An explicit contrast is made with the previous May, the month of the final summer offensive, when maize bread was still 'Volksnahrungsmittel'. The writer wonders about the origin of the maize – whether it comes from those Ukrainian fields trampled by war, conflating the hollow phrase of an honourable death for the fatherland and the German for ears of corn: 'Drischt man ihn aus den Ehren jener Felder, deren Aehren man zerstampft?'[14] The text concludes by questioning whether this unexpected return of maize is a sign of good things to come from the Paris Peace Conference, whether it is 'Punkt und Pause hinter der ganz ungenügend ausgefallenen Hausarbeit über die große Zeit [...] Alles in allem: ein Wiener Symptom'. Where the first half of Roth's contribution to the column springs from an official announcement and connects the public decisions of governments with the privations of the personal sphere, the second text, 'Schokolade' opens with a street scene: a child stands before a shop window staring at chocolate bars on display. This would be unremarkable at any other time, but in the context of Vienna's starvation diet in the summer of 1919 the scene represents a slight return to normality: 'Dem Kinde neben mir ist die Rippe die Schwelle zum Himmelreich. Mir – Schwelle am Tor der Zukunft.'[15]

It is clear that, as a journalist who was also a writer of fiction, Roth's strengths were best displayed in his feuilleton texts, where he was free to choose and explore his subjects in the manner he felt most appropriate. At the same time, the strengths of feuilletons emerge best when they are considered in relation to the context in which they were originally produced. Reconstructing them as a polished prose cycle does a disservice both to the creative imagination of their author and his engagement with the issues of the day.

---

14 Unfortunately Westermann's edition gives the the spelling of the first 'Ehren' as 'Aehren', which ruins the intended pun. See GW I:30–32.

15 Again, this part of the text is defective in Westermann's edition, which gives the word 'Kinde' as 'Feinde'. See GW I:32.

Bibliography

Primary Sources

Der Friede 1918–1919

Der Neue Tag 1919–1920

Karl Kraus (1968–) *Die Fackel 1899–1936. 922 Nummern in 37 Jahrgängen* München: Kösel

Musil, Robert (1955) *Tagebücher, Aphorismen, Essays und Reden*, Hamburg

Roth, Joseph (1970) *Briefe 1911–1939*, ed. Hermann Kesten, Köln:Kiepenheuer und Witsch

Roth, Joseph (1989) *Das journalistische Werk* 3 vols., ed. Klaus Westermann, Köln: Kiepenheuer und Witsch

Roth, Joseph (1994) *Unter dem Bülowbogen Prosa zur Zeit,* Köln: Kiepenheuer und Witsch

Secondary Literature

Bronsen, David (1974) *Joseph Roth. Eine Biographie*, Köln: Kiepenheuer und Witsch

Bronsen, David (1993) *Joseph Roth. Eine Biographie. Gekürzte Fassung*, Köln: Kiepenheuer und Witsch

Früh, Eckart (1990) 'Joseph Roth im Spiegel österreichischer Arbeiterzeitungen' in Michael Kessler and Fritz Hackert (eds) *Joseph Roth. Interpretation – Rezeption – Kritik*, Tübingen: Stauffenberg 107–126

Melischek, Gabriele and Seethaler, Josef (1992), *Die Wiener Tageszeitungen. Eine Dokumentation. Band 3 1918–1938*, Bern: Peter Lang

Reich-Ranitzki, Marcel (1984) *Nachprüfung* München: dtv

Siegel, Rainer-Joachim (1995) *Joseph Roth-Bibliographie* Morsum/Sylt: Cicero Presse

Sültemeyer, Ingeborg (1976) *Das Frühwerk Joseph Roths 1915–1926*, Wien: Herder

Todorow, Almuth (1988) '"Wollten die Eintagsfliegen in den Rang höherer Insekten aufsteigen?" Die Feuilletonkonzeption der *Frankfurter Zeitung* während der Weimarer Republik im redaktionellen Selbstverständnis', *Deutsche Vierteljahres-schrift*, 62, 697–740

Vala, Heimo (1996) *Joseph Roth – journalistische Verfahrens- und Schreibweise am Beispiel von Personenporträts*, MA Thesis Salzburg

Wirtz, Irmgard (1997) Joseph Roths Fiktionen des Faktischen. Das Feuilleton der 20er Jahre und die Geschichte der 1002. Nacht im historischen Kontext, Berlin: Erich Schmidt

PETER DAVIES

Utopia Incorporated: The Lives of Stephan Hermlin in the GDR

Stephan Hermlin's autobiographical work *Abendlicht* was published in the GDR in 1979, to rave reviews on both sides of the Wall. The text seemed to be a summing up of the life's work of one of the iconic figures of GDR literature, a committed communist and antifascist who nevertheless took a principled stand against the repressive nature of SED cultural policy, including signing the petition against the expulsion of Wolf Biermann in 1976. Hermlin seemed to many to embody the potential of 'Geist' to stand up to 'Macht', without rejecting the utopian ideals of socialism, and *Abendlicht* was his statement of faith both in the cause and in the ability of art to redeem the communist party from its own faults. This all changed in 1996, a year before Hermlin died. Karl Corino published an article in *Die Zeit* in which he carefully picked apart the aura around Hermlin using the simple method of comparing aspects of *Abendlicht* and Hermlin's public biography with the facts as Corino could establish them.

The substance of Corino's accusations was as follows: that Hermlin, in *Abendlicht* and in other works, as well as in statements in public and private, had falsified aspects of his biography in order to establish his credentials as the senior writer-intellectual in the GDR. His curriculum vitae – fighter in the Spanish Civil War and with the resistance in Germany and France, close connections with Erich Honecker dating from their association in an illegal communist cell in Berlin after 1933 – together with his independence of mind and commitment to a socialism based on openness and acceptance of modernist cultural influences, had given Hermlin an iconic status in both East and West.

This status resulted from the peculiarities of the interlocking public spheres of East and West Germany: the figure of the writer-tribune can only emerge in a society with a highly restricted public sphere, and where literary language is accorded a truth-telling function denied it in more pluralist societies. Similarly, writers in the West, chafing at their perceived marginalisation, were willing to go along with the creation of this image as a projection of their own fantasies about the importance of literature. Corino calls Hermlin's mythical image a 'Gesamtkunstwerk', a 'sorgfältig kalkuliertes System' (Corino 1996:190) of literary texts and public statements which allowed him to justify his conformism while collecting admirers and pet academics around him.

The following is the substance of Corino's allegations: Hermlin's credentials as a resistance fighter are spurious. He was never in Spain, nor did he know Honecker in Berlin, and he had little or no contact with the French Resistance. It is likely that, as a member of the KPD since 1931, he carried out some small-scale anti-Nazi agitation for a few months after January 1933, but he did not live in hiding in Berlin in this period, but with his parents. He was certainly never arrested, as he claimed, nor was he interned in a concentration camp. Stranger still, and more important for our purposes, are the myths which grew up around Hermlin's family. Hermlin makes much of his high bourgeois background, his liberal Jewish upbringing and his father's connections with painters like Max Liebermann and Lovis Corinth. So much is true, although Hermlin does exaggerate the family's wealth and connections, painting an idealised picture of servants and nurses, and a childhood filled with music. As we shall see, it is the figure of his father which Hermlin returns to constantly in later years in order to support his views on culture and tolerance. However, in doing so, he allows the legend to arise that his father had died in Sachsenhausen, whereas in fact he had been interned there briefly after the *Kristallnacht*, was released, and had left Germany for London, where he died of cancer in 1947. In fact, he had broken off contact with his son in 1946, since Hermlin had given his second daughter a Christian baptism.

Hermlin had always made a secret of his family's staunch zionism, partly because of his own disillusionment after a visit to Palestine in 1937, and partly because of the atmosphere in the GDR in the early 1950s, when Jewish communists were often held under suspicion of disloyalty to the SED. This may help to explain his lifelong silence about the existence of a sister, Ruth, who emigrated to Israel, and with whom he had no contact. Similarly, Hermlin denied his mother's origins, preferring to claim that he grew up in a mixed Jewish-Christian family. His mother, though, was not the blonde English beauty into which she is transfigured in *Abendlicht*, but a Galician Jew, whose Eastern origins did not seems to be a problem for his father, at least.

The final person to mention is Hermlin's brother, Alfred, who, Hermlin claimed, had been an RAF fighter pilot shot down over the Channel at some unspecified time in the 1940s. In fact, Alfred had been training to be a pilot in Canada, but had died a far less romantic death in a collision between two training aircraft in 1943.

So much for the specifics of Corino's allegations, to which I will return when I consider *Abendlicht* in more detail later. What I intend to do first is to set out where Corino left off by looking at the way in which Hermlin's biography is constructed, in order to show how he developed an identity as an intellectual in the GDR. The concept of a moral voice will become important here; what I mean by this is related to the position occupied by the intellectual within the structures of power, from which he/she can make interventions in the political or cultural life of the state. Moral claims are made for this voice, which, in Hermlin's case, are made on the basis of an exemplary biography, which follows certain well-defined lines. The story which he writes for his life is a version of one of the standard plots of Marxist-Leninist biography, that is, the story of the bourgeois intellectual who shrugs off the influences of his past and finds his way to the communist party.

In *Abendlicht*, Hermlin takes up this model and changes it, turning it into something more fragmentary and elusive, while retaining the basic structure of the master plot. In this way, he creates a structure for his life-story which supports the moral voice which he had begun to develop in the 1960s against the cultural-political line of the regime. But this voice is not first and foremost the creation of the individual, but is in many ways created by others in ways which are conditioned by aspects of the public sphere in the GDR; Hermlin seems, in fact, to step into a role which was already prepared for him.

'Stephan Hermlin' as a public figure

It is noticeable that most assessments of Hermlin's work begin with a list of his credentials as a resistance fighter. The purpose of these lists of credentials is primarily an aesthetic one, namely, to give a sense of authenticity to Hermlin's literary voice and his stance in the cultural-political debates of his time. He is presented in many accounts as the embodiment of the unity of art and life, and it is noticeable that this claim is often made for Hermlin as a person, rather than simply for his work. This image of the writer as personifying some putative unity of 'Geist' and 'Macht' has a long tradition in German culture, a tradition which fed into the GDR largely through the influence of Johannes R. Becher, and has its obverse in the equally dubious Western view of Hermlin as *Staatsdichter*, that is, of 'Geist' prostituting itself in the service of 'Macht'. Such personifications are, on both sides of the spectrum, thoroughly unproductive in terms of a fuller understanding of Hermlin's life and work. Therefore, our first task must be to look at the various literary-historical narratives which have found a place for Hermlin and *Abendlicht*, before moving on to pay more attention to the text itself.

I will start with the story told by Hermlin's biographer in the GDR, Silvia Schlenstedt (1985), an account which corresponds broadly with the lines which emerge in *Abendlicht* itself. Though it would be an overstatement to say that there was anything like an 'orthodox' GDR account of Hermlin or of *Abendlicht*, Schlenstedt's narrative follows many of the contours of the GDR's legitimising narratives of antifascism. In Schlenstedt's account, Hermlin's development as an artist runs parallel to the development of the cultural life of the GDR (naturally, in a considerably sanitised account). Schlenstedt tries to show that Hermlin embodies the dialectical unity of 'Geist' and 'Macht' which the GDR claimed for itself, and which, thanks to Hermlin's public interventions in artistic debates, is coming closer: explicit parallels are made between what she calls the 'wachsende Souveränität der sozialistischen Gesellschaft im Umgang mit ihren Traditionen' and Hermlin's own 'gewachsene Souveränität' (Schlenstedt 1985:139–40). The rhetorical character of such juxtapositions is clear, for the description of processes of reform occurring within the Soviet Bloc contains a programme: the

GDR will gain new creative energies through the unity of the workers' movement with the Art of Modernism.

Schlenstedt stresses the 'innersozialistischen Charakter' of the artistic debates in which Hermlin takes up his sword against the dogmatics in the SED (Schlenstedt 1985:138). The idea of the workers' movement evolving and progressing out of its own productive inner contradictions is central to the role which is created for Hermlin in this text, and, for example, it leads the author to quote approvingly Hermlin's support for the intervention in Hungary in 1956, since this 'peaceful' process was being threatened by outside influences (Schlenstedt 1985:139–40). Statements like this, and many others, make very clear that the public personality of Hermlin as embodiment of a liberal, socialist cultural policy was nevertheless dependent on the existence and continued legitimacy of the GDR.

Schlenstedt constantly stresses the 'subjectivity' of Hermlin's work, which guarantees its authenticity as an expression of the artist's role in the dialectic of history. His work is 'bewegt von einer durchgreifenden Subjektivität, die auf die Aufhebung der erlittenen und erfahrenen Widersprüchlichkeit der Welt dringt' (Schlenstedt 1985:68), or is characterised by a 'Subjektivität der Weltsicht, die Äußerungsform eines aktiven Ergreifens von Welt ist' (Schlenstedt 1985:97).

These statements are polemical rather than analytical, reflecting the rhetorical structure of Schlenstedt's biography, which aims to justify Hermlin's interventions in the literary life of the GDR, and to present GDR cultural policy as a gradual (dialectical) process of debate, negotiation and liberalisation; to this end, Hermlin's conflicts with Ulbricht-era dogmatists in the 1960s are commented on, whereas Hermlin's role in the petition against the expulsion of Wolf Biermann is not. The special emphasis on Hermlin's committed, authentic subjectivity is in itself an intervention in cultural debates in the GDR, and reflects the rhetorical patterning of *Abendlicht* and of Hermlin's public persona: the writer's relationship with the mass movement is seen as a dialectical one, loosening the dogmatic politics of the present with reminders of the movement's utopian goal. In a piece on Attila József in the volume *Lektüre*, Hermlin states that 'Dichtung [...] immer und überall ein Stück vorweggenommener Zukunft ist, dass ihre Heimatlosigkeit erst in der

Begründung der großen Menschenheimat ihr Ende findet' (Hermlin, 1997:12).

This is a utopia bound into the processes of the GDR, dependent on a system which grants writers unique access to a limited public sphere where their public persona is constructed, negotiated and 'performed'. A writer like Hermlin comes, through his work and public statements, but above all through the statements of others, to embody a unity of opposites, an overcoming of the supposed conflict between *Geist* and *Macht*. The stories which critics like Schlenstedt tell about their subjects can thus tell us something about the narratives and counter-narratives of power in the GDR. In Schlenstedt's biography, the figure of Hermlin is constructed as a unity of opposing principles, the authenticity of the literary voice guaranteed by the experience of active antifascist resistance.

Examples like this may serve to make clear the emotional investment placed in sustaining figures such as Hermlin as representatives of an 'alternative' (rather than 'oppositional') cultural-political discourse in the Eastern Bloc which projected utopian longings towards a desired future synthesis. It is at this point that it becomes difficult to talk about the 'truth'or 'falsehood' of the claims made for Hermlin's life, because this 'Hermlin', as a fictional figure performed in the public sphere, represented a real aspiration shared by a large number of people. Hermlin's rarity value in the German context lies in the necessity for alternative discourses to deal with the problem of antifascism. Since unashamedly nationalist positions were unavailable to high-profile writers in the GDR, the temptation to latch onto Hermlin's resistance credentials as an authentic alternative to the dead hand of official antifascist discourse was overwhelming. The details which Corino's research has revealed cannot demonstrate some supposed 'truth' or 'falsehood' of this alternative discourse of antifascism but can help us to understand what its foundations were and why it was tied to the existence of the GDR.

After 1996, the lines of battle shift, but both Hermlin's defenders and his accusers still refer to him as a guarantor of the integrity of the alternative discourse of socialist antifascism: the integrity of the personality is still confused with the integrity of the idea. In his defence of Hermlin against Corino's 'Enthüllungsjournalismus', Klaus Völker sets Hermlin's work in the context of his campaigns against oppressive SED cultural practices, which tried to throttle 'die bewusstseinsverändernde

Kraft von Literatur und Kunst' (Völker 1997:20). This is the story which Hermlin himself tells about the power of art, and Völker makes a similar connection between artistic and political practice by making the renewal of art a precondition for the renewal of Socialism. This aspiration, where it occurs in the work of GDR authors, tends to be connected with the desire to bring the moral voice of authentic subjectivity to bear on the 'objective' processes of history. In Hermlin's case, the claim to authenticity is made for his work on the basis of a presumed unity of art and life *in his person*; this can then be applied to the voice or voices which speak in the texts in an operation which blurs the boundaries between author and text.

To the objection that this is in any case a characteristic of human memory, or a tendency we all have to create a 'true' life-story for ourselves – as Völker puts it, 'seinen Lebensstoff wahrzulügen' (Völker 1997:5) – one might answer that moral claims are made for the voice of the writer/intellectual in the GDR, and that it is therefore of legitimate interest to investigate the basis upon which these claims are made. In this case, Hermlin's fictionalised life-story is explicitly linked with the high and low points of German history, whether through his own reworkings of the key incidents of his life or in the clichéd language handed on by others on his behalf, where his life becomes, in the words of Denise Daun, 'une histoire individuelle intimement liée à l'histoire allemande' (Daun 1982:77). This attempt to write oneself into history is a characteristic of the committed intellectual, and once a figure like Hermlin has been committed irrevocably to the public sphere, then conflicts about the 'truth' or 'falsehood' of his biography are in reality disagreements over stories told about German history and about the role and voice of the intellectual in it. Hermlin's notorious reticence about his personal history allowed both supporters and enemies to 'fill in the blanks' according to the meanings which they themselves wished to read into this biography.

'Late-bourgeois writer' and mass party

The role of poet-tribune, to which Hermlin aspired in the GDR, sprang from the obligation constantly to document one's own life in the public sphere, where the authenticity of the voice was dependent on the construction of the life-story. In a public sphere which was severely restricted, and yet which simultaneously privileged the voice of the literary intellectual, such subjective self-documentation took on an aura of truth-telling, whether the individual writer was for or against the regime. Literary dissidents shared with their loyal counterparts the conviction that 'truth' was embodied in the figure of the writer as a personality shaped through his/her work as a public act.

The positions which Hermlin took up in semi-public institutions like the Academy of Arts from the 1950s onwards show very clearly the task which he had set himself, namely to criticise the cultural policy of the SED without questioning the fundamentals of communist rule. This was a difficult trick to pull off, as he had to fight off attacks from dogmatists without making the decisive connection between Socialist Realist dogma and the nature of Marxism-Leninism. Hermlin began in the 1960s to stress his bourgeois background not as something which had to be overcome in order to gain acceptance by the party, but as something positive which he could bring to the party as a utopian claim on the future. By 1978, at the time that *Abendlicht* was appearing, he could tell the Writers' Congress: 'Ich bin ein spätbürgerlicher Schriftsteller. [...] Wenn ich diese Herkunft verleugnen oder verdrängen würde, müßte ich mich selbst verlieren und könnte demnach für etwas Anderes, Neues gar nicht nachhaltig eintreten' (Hermlin 1995:22–3).

The family background of the narrator in *Abendlicht* is supplied by brother, father and almost absent mother. The brother is stylised from the beginning as Icarus, the wild, headstrong, beautiful boy who flies too near to the sun. Hermlin had already used this image for his brother in 1944, in a poem written to commemorate his death, 'Ballade vom Gefährten Ikarus' (Hermlin 1990:65). The brother can no longer be shown to have died in a training flight; Icarus didn't go through basic training, he made a bold, doomed leap into the unknown, just as the brother in *Abendlicht* behaves as an RAF fighter pilot: 'Seine Staffel hatte ihn geliebt, er flog gut und ging ungestüm auf den Feind los, man hatte ihn "Starlet" geheißen' (Hermlin 1987:53). The brother embodies a promise of utopian physical perfection: an active, militant struggle against fascism which echoes orthodox descriptions of communist antifascists, and to which the narrator can never hope to aspire. The preservation of the brother in art might have served to demonstrate that children of bourgeois families could also oppose fascism, but the extraordinary stylisation of the description (for example, he is referred to as 'hochgemut') seems to indicate that Hermlin is more concerned with the utopian function of art (and by extension of his own role in the party) than with creating a true memorial. This suspicion seems to be confirmed in the final section of *Abendlicht*, where the Icarus motif is resolved by inserting the brother's dramatic death in a description of the painting *The Fall of Icarus* by Pieter Breughel the Elder, where it can be preserved for posterity.

The father is a more complex, problematic figure, presumably because Hermlin's relationship with his own father was so much more difficult. To replace the real father, who had broken so painfully with him, Hermlin creates a figure who is the personification of those attitudes to culture which he himself wishes to represent in the GDR: 'Heute weiß ich, daß seine wenigen Worte [...] Wichtigeres für mich enthielten als die Sophismen, mit denen ich mich später allzu lange herumschlug. Sein Schweigen lehrte mich Toleranz. Aber wir lebten in intoleranten Zeiten' (Hermlin 1987:36). Here, Hermlin plays his father's tolerance off against the inadequacy of the artistic theories of the workers' movement:

> Die Kunst des Jahrhunderts wurde mehr und mehr zu einem Pfuhl der Verdammnis, die großen Namen der Literatur, der Musik, der Malerei stellten personifizierte Übel dar, drittrangige akademische Epigonen wurden zu Genies befördert. (Hermlin 1987:34)

His strategy here is quite clear: he is trying to carve out a niche for himself as the representative of a synthesis of the values of high culture with those of the workers' movement. After the failure of the Stalinist experiment, where 'bourgeois' intellectuals tried to merge with the mass of the party, the recreation of a semi-autonomous public persona, a moral voice which nudges the party in the right direction, is the only possible way forward for Hermlin, who has invested too much in his own myth to be able to break with the movement. Referring to his efforts to liberalise the party's cultural line, he states: 'Was mich noch einsam machte, würde Spätere zusammenschließen' (Hermlin 1987: 34–5). Hermlin breaks with the orthodoxies of Socialist Realism, which had cost him so much effort, but stylises himself as an early prophet of better things to come.

In order to do this, Hermlin creates in *Abendlicht*, and in other public statements, an idealised family constellation which he can use to support his own position, something which is also a commonplace in the models of Socialist Realism, except that in this case it is the high bourgeois family which is raised onto a pedestal instead of the proletarian background. After a section which strongly hints, but never states outright, that the father died in the camp, the last sight of him which is granted us in *Abendlicht* is a childhood memory of the narrator's, in which the father's distance to his son is stylised, as with the brother, into a romantic-medieval picture of nobility and perfection. For all the stylised distancing which Hermlin practises in these descriptions, the act of replacing the real father and brother with mythological figures is simply a way of erasing and annexing their deaths for his own needs.

In *Abendlicht*, Hermlin imagines the relationship between individual and collective in terms of setting his signature on the party. He describes the scene in a Berlin street in 1931, where the seventeen-year-old narrator stands on the outside of a group of workers debating politics. He feels himself drawn to the communists in the group, and one of them turns to him and offers him membership on the spot:

> Gleichzeitig empfand ich, daß ich das Beste in mir aufgeben mußte, wenn ich je meine Unterschrift, die ich um die Mittagszeit eines beliebigen Tages in einer beliebigen Straße geleistet hatte, als nicht mehr gültig betrachten würde. (Hermlin 1987:27–8)

In 1952, Hermlin had provided an account of his first joining the party which is similar, apart from the crucial detail that the communist worker simply invites him along to the next meeting of the *Kommunistischer Jugendverband* (Hermlin 1983:135). The version which Corino had from Hermlin's sister is more banal: she claims that she had persuaded her two brothers to come along to the *Sozialistischer Schüler-Bund* because her current boyfriend was a member (Corino 1996:66).

The 'truth' here, whatever it is, is really not important, but what Hermlin made of the event is. The stress which he places on his signature emphasises an ambiguity which characterised his relationship with the party of which he had become a member; the signature represents on the one hand a commitment to becoming part of a mass movement, which it would be an act of self-betrayal to revoke, but on the other hand it stands for an assertion of an *individual* choice. In a nutshell, putting one's personality at the service of an idea or movement is an assertion of that personality.

Hermlin's narrator seeks, and fails, to establish a consistent self-image to set against the mass movement which he simlutaneously desires and fears. In order to do this, Hermlin must perform an impossible balancing act, attempting to assert the narrating voice without creating the heroic, individual self which characterises the work of 'renegade' authors, such as Arthur Koestler, since the logic of self-assertion is, finally, the break with the party. The text itself is structured around conflicting images of acceptance and isolation, both of which the narrator fears and desires; he is often depicted as standing on the outside of a group, whose speech he only incompletely understands. Joining the party is portrayed as the key to overcoming this isolation. His satisfaction at this success is contrasted with dream-images which express a panicky fear of being overwhelmed by the movement of which he is a part.

This conflict is never resolved in *Abendlicht*, but this is a self-conscious depiction of failure which is on a very different plane from the tragic, existential conflicts of the previous generation of communist intellectuals. Hermlin manipulates the forms of the traditional Stalinist autobiography in order to demonstrate his awareness of the impossibility of achieving unity with the movement, and yet he must propose some kind of solution which allows him to draw back from the final act of creation of the consistent, and thus potentially renegade, self.

Hermlin's awareness of this problem helps explain the fragmentary nature of the text, in which contrasting voices and episodes with no strict chronological ordering question and undermine each other. Scenes from the narrator's childhood are juxtaposed with artistic meditations and political commentary, and the voice can switch rapidly between narration and reflection, denunciation and reverie, sober analysis and the evocation of dream states. Yet, once one has taken the trouble to piece together the fragments, this stylistic virtuosity reveals a fearful oscillation between the narrative of party orthodoxy and the narrative of the renegade.

The solution proposed in *Abendlicht* is simple: the dilemma of the communist intellectual is simply set aside in favour of abandoning the individual self in the utopian community of art. The text is structured around visions of stillness and peace which hark back to childhood experiences of unity and timelessness. '*Und der Himmel da oben, wie ist er so weit*, wie still konnte er damals sein [...] nirgendwo war [die Stille] tiefer als im Blau da oben, in das ich hinaufschwebte, in das ich niedersank' (Hermlin 1987:8). References in this section to the deep blue of the sky and to the final song of Schubert's cycle *Die schöne Müllerin*, which describes the gentle rocking motion of the stream which cradles the drowned body of the young miller, are resolved in the final two sections of the text; for the moment, they hint at the presence of a utopian alternative to the cacophony of politics. I have already quoted the narrator's comments about the profundity and tolerance of his father's silence; contrasting images are found in the narrator's descriptions of communist mass meetings and Nazi parades. At the narrator's first demonstration, it is the music which strikes him most strongly, particularly the appalling racket made by the playing of the shawm to accompany the singing:

> In seiner unverhüllten Häßlichkeit wurden Qual und Not hörbar und das unartikulierte Drängen nach Würde und Schönheit, die für alle da sein sollten [...] für diese in Nebel gehüllten Massen hatten Bach und Mozart, was immer sie auch beabsichtigt haben mochten, ihre Architekturen entworfen. (Hermlin, 1987:41–2)

This straining of the uneducated workers after an elusive beauty which the narrator can take for granted through his upbringing is contrasted with the brutality of Nazi singing in their torchlit parades, which the true Germany, in its art, silently resists:

> Hinter der dröhnenden Dunkelheit spürte ich die stille Duldsamkeit des Landes, lautlos die unüberwindliche Melancholie seiner Musik, die unhörbaren Verse seiner Dichter. (Hermlin, 1987:43)

Music holds the key to *Abendlicht*. The text opens with a section describing the narrator's response to Bach's cantata *Bleibe bei uns*. By setting the words of the disciple Kleophas to a stranger whom he has not yet recognised as the risen Christ – 'Bleibe bei uns, denn es will Abend werden, und der Tag hat sich geneiget' – for the chorus, instead of for a soloist, Bach makes of this small gesture of humanity a plea on behalf of the inward-looking congregation for the return of the lost saviour. With this reference, Hermlin sets up the complex series of oppositions – stillness-tumult, inclusion-exclusion – around which the text is structured:

the sense of belonging offered by this music, with which he has been familiar since childhood, is the only 'Gemeinschaft' truly available to the narrator, who has never overcome his alienated status in the workers' movement. By figuring these deeply-felt artistic experiences as utopian, in other words, by universalising his own artistic tastes, Hermlin reinforces his system of support for the role he conceives for himself as 'spätbürgerlicher Schriftsteller'; to put it crudely, he represents in his public persona the utopian aspirations of the workers' movement.

The contrasting moods of exclusion and inclusion which Hermlin has set up with such references are treated at the end of the text to the kind of resolution which is possible in literature, but not in life. In the final two sections, the narrator moves through a utopian landscape surrounded by music and voices from his past. The penultimate section is structured around musical motifs from Beethoven and Schubert, and resolves the reference to *Die schöne Müllerin* from the beginning of the text. Hermlin picks up Romantic motifs of death-longing and dissolution, imagining himself returning to the lost childhood paradise of silence and timelessness:

> [...] das Schweigen, das das leere Gelärm überwächst, und das machtvolle, das unaufhaltsame Wiegen, und der Blick aufwärts, der sich nicht mehr abwendet, *und der Himmel da oben, wie ist er so weit.* (Hermlin 1987:89)

The death which is imagined in these pages is no longer the death of the bourgeois self which the previous generation had proclaimed, but is the resolution of the narrator's conflicts in the utopia of art. This aesthetic resolution of very practical problems of the individual's relationship to the collective is not as far removed from Socialist Realism as the author would like us to believe.

Looked at in this way, we can reconstruct the basic structure of the text which has been concealed by its complex narrative patterning. The text seems to operate on the Hegelian principle of *Aufhebung*, exploring for its utopian rhetorical effects the rich ambiguities of the term. Hermlin's narrative combines notions of cyclical and linear time in both the personal time of the narrator and the historical time of the events through which he lives. Thus, the childhood visions of stillness and peace – not yet understood as utopian by the narrator's young self – return at the end, raised to a higher level, once the conflict of exclusion and inclusion has been worked through in the narrator's life. The effect of all this is the explicit conclusion that the narrator's life should be read as a narrative inseparable from the history of the workers' movement, perhaps as one term of the productive contradiction between *Geist* and *Macht* which is on its way to being resolved in the GDR. The movement of historical time is forcibly given the same dialectical patterning as the narrator's personal time, so that a work which is ostensibly about the mutually agreeable resolution of the party's relationship with its intellectuals actually simply absorbs history into the story of the development of the narrator's self and the justification of his life's work. History vanishes into the text – is *aufgehoben* – in the same way that the lives and deaths of the father and brother are annexed, erased and recreated to form part of the structure of a public personality.

The form and content of *Abendlicht* are intimately intertwined with the form and content of the public persona which Hermlin was able to establish in the GDR, and through which he was able to make effective interventions in the cultural life of the GDR. By exploring the text in this way, we can move beyond the somewhat sterile arguments about whether we should regard *Abendlicht* as 'autobiographical', and whether this matters or not. The text's structure reflects and reproduces the structure and contradictions of the public persona created by and for Hermlin in the GDR, whose voice can be used to criticise the cultural policy of the SED without questioning the legitimacy of the party's rule. Even after 1989, it is the party, which gave such prominence to writers, and thus a meaningful role for the 'spätbürgerlicher Schriftsteller', which earns his continued loyalty: 'Ich war dieser Partei treu, trotz ihrer entsetzlichen Mängel, weil sie eine Vorform von Utopie realisieren konnte' (Hermlin 1995:96).

Bibliography

Corino, Karl (1996) Außen Marmor, Innen Gips. Die Legenden des Stephan Hermlin, Düsseldorf: ECON

Daun, Denise (1982) 'Dans les traces de *Abendlicht*', *Connaissance de la RDA*, 15, 76–98

Hermlin, Stephan (1997) *Lektüre*, Berlin: Wagenbach

Hermlin, Stephan (1995) *In den Kämpfen dieser Zeit*, Berlin: Wagenbach

Hermlin, Stephan (1990) *Gesammelte Gedichte*, Munich: Hanser

Hermlin, Stephan (1987) *Abendlicht*, Berlin: Wagenbach

Hermlin, Stephan (1983) 'Begegnung mit der Partei', *Äußerungen*, Berlin and Weimar: Aufbau, 134–38

Schlenstedt, Silvia (1985) *Stephan Hermlin: Leben und Werk*, Berlin: verlag das europäische buch.

Völker, Klaus (1997) 'Wir sind ganz das Werk der Zeit', *Neue Deutsche Literatur*, 5/6, 5–26

TANJA NAUSE

Post-*Wende* Literature and Cultural Memory: Moments of Recollection in Thomas Brussig's Novel *Helden wie wir*

> Imagination, he realized, came harder than memory.
> (Irving 1990:124)

Introduction

When the German border opened in November 1989, the GDR protest movements of the summer and autumn had found their dramatic climax. At the same time, the event indicated that the somewhat utopian ideas of a future 'democratic' socialism would soon end and it was hardly surprising that intellectuals began to forewarn of the consequences and costs that an accelerated unification would impose upon the two countries. But their warnings went unheeded. The social impact of unification was quickly reflected in the literary scene. Pamphlets, papers, essays and all sorts of other statements appeared in newspapers, journals, and only a little later as books. The mutual accusations among the writers culminated in the German–German *Literaturstreit*. It is interesting to note that, of all genres, it was an autobiographical work that stood at the centre of the furore. But Christa Wolf's *Was bleibt* was not a lone example of the genre; other memoirs, autobiographies and diaries began to appear in large numbers. Fröhling's bibliography *Wende-Literatur* (1996) lists more than a thousand autobiographical works which appeared in no more than five years after 1989, a fact that, according to Julian Preece, is already a 'publishing phenomenon' (Preece 1995:349). Or, as the main character in Jens Sparschuh's *Der Zimmerspringbrunnen* puts it:

> Einmal [...] verwunderte sich Strüver darüber, daß im Schaufenster so zahlreich Memoirenbände aufgebaut waren. So viel, wie da geschrieben stand, meinte er,

> könne ja niemals wirklich mit rechten Dingen erlebt worden sein. (Sparschuh 1995:123)

There appears to be a particular need for autobiographical writing in times of cultural change. Why is this? Some preliminary assumptions can be made. Firstly, memoirs can be, to a certain degree, a way of taking revenge. The advantage is that the 'coming-to-terms' with the past takes place in a private sphere and, in this way, possible interference can be avoided until the date of publication.

By contrast, Jost Hermand pointed out that this phenomenon could also be seen as a post-modern retreat into the private sphere where all forms of social commitment are 'out' and nothing is left but 'Ideologie-, Staats- und Systemverdrossenheit' (Hermand 1993:255). Hermand's example for this thesis is Heiner Müller's autobiography *Krieg ohne Schlacht* (1992). According to Hermand, Müller had consciously used the opportunity to write a new version of all of his former commitment to the GDR and its socialist ideas.

Another hypothesis is formulated by Kornelia Hauser. Referring to a common GDR slogan that went 'Vom Ich zum Wir', she puts it concisely: 'Wo wir war, muß ich werden' (Hauser 1992:248). Hauser remarks that GDR citizens have to come to terms particularly with their previous experiences of the all-embracing social 'we'. Günter de Bruyn even begins his autobiography *Zwischenbilanz* with the hopeful remark that his book could be 'ein Training im Ich-Sagen' (de Bruyn 1996:7).

Lastly, East German writers, of course, want to pit their experiences against the old official statements about life in the GDR. In Hans Mayer's words: 'Es war alles *ganz* anders' (1993:8, my italics). Writers want to remember how the story 'really' was, reacting to the commonly expressed fear of forgetting everything related to the GDR too fast.

However, as literary theory has it, it became increasingly difficult to maintain an idea of 'authentic' memories[1]. An autobiography is just another text; it cannot reveal more than any other book. The most typical feature of autobiography is thus not its content but its

1 In a German-language context see Wellershof (1991), Sill (1991), Muschg (1984), Jurgensen (1979), Müller (1976).

perspective: 'Wer "Ich" sagt, sagt [...] nicht die Wahrheit, er hat eine Form der Erzählung gewählt' (Muschg 1984:33). In this context, Philipp Lejeune's theory about the 'autobiographical pact' is a pragmatic tool which helps the critic to decide about the author's intention (see Lejeune 1975). Yet, since it is an external device, it tells more about how we *read* a text than about how it is written. The critic Paul de Man stated that 'autobiography' is nothing more than the name for a pattern of understanding which, to a certain degree, can be found in all texts. With statements like these, genre-borders have become vitally blurred. Not only is autobiography to a large extent fiction, all fiction is also partly autobiographical:

> Als Proust zu André Gide sagte: 'Man kann alles erzählen, aber unter der Bedingung, daß man nie "Ich" sagt', hat er zu der verbreiteten Vermutung, daß auch alles fiktionale Schreiben im Grunde Autobiographie sei, eine wichtige Ergänzung beigetragen. (Wellershof 1991:3)

If we apply these considerations to autobiographical writing after 1989, we can naturally find quite diverse attempts to recall life in the GDR. There are many autobiographies that want to set the record straight, as Preece showed in his article (1995). But there are also attempts at serious self-inquisition (e.g. de Bruyn 1994). And there are other texts that are written from a first-person perspective but do not establish the 'autobiographical pact' (e.g. Hensel 1997) – at which point the extent of actual autobiographical experience becomes hard to judge. Lastly, there are also invented memories – a step that finally leaves behind the classic genre 'autobiography' for another one, showing elements of the 'picaresque novel' (e.g. Fries 1999).

These two genres are closely related, not least because they are both dominated by the first-person narrative. One can hardly imagine a 'picaresque' novel that does not remember life in an autobiographical retrospect. And *vice versa* – the autobiographical genre always has examples of 'picaresque' memoirs:

> Daß auch manche literarische Selbstdarstellungen sich pikareskem Fahrwasser nähern, belegen auf je unterschiedliche Weise Benvenutto Cellini, Giacomo Casanova und überhaupt die Autobiographien vom Typus der 'abenteuerlichen Lebensgeschichte', die sich bis ins 16. Jahrhundert zurückverfolgen lassen. (Jacobs 1983:91)

However, the picaresque novel is not traditional autobiographical writing; it is a fictional lifestory of an 'outcast' (Neumann 1970:168). Therefore, critics have assumed that the picaresque flourishes in times of social crisis[2]. Consequently, regarding the intricate economic and social situation after the *Wende* in East Germany it seems logical to suspect the long awaited *Wenderoman* of being a *Schelmenroman*: 'Daß eines Tages jemand kommen und schreiben würde: "Ich habe die Berliner Mauer umgeschmissen" – das war klar, auch, daß dieses Ich ein Simplicissimus sein würde' (Franke 1995). And, indeed, many critics jumped on this bandwagon. At the moment, a lot of writing from the East or with a specific East German viewpoint tends to be referred to as 'picaresque' – above all Thomas Brussig's novel *Helden wie wir* (1995)[3]. Fashionable though these statements might be, there is some truth in them. *Helden wie wir* is not a genuine *Schelmenroman* but it is an invented lifestory told from an 'I'-perspective. Thus, from Hermann Kant's *Abspann* (1991) and Günter de Bruyn's *Vierzig Jahre* (1996) to Thomas Brussig's *Helden wie wir*, there is one common feature that crystallizes in post-*Wende* writing which could be described as an 'autobiographical discourse'.

It would appear in general terms, whatever the superficial genre characteristics, that people want to preserve their memories and to maintain a knowledge of their past. In this sense, it is possible to argue that what they are seeking is to be represented in a sphere that the theorist Jan Assmann calls 'cultural memory' (Assmann 1997). Assmann's theory about different types of the 'collective memory' sheds a distinct light on post-*Wende* first-person narratives. On the one hand, it stresses the necessity of remembrance in times of cultural change. On the other, it provides an analytical base for a comparative look at post-*Wende* autobiographical writing and other fictional texts. Assmann's theory explains why memory finally shifts from the short-term memory to either oblivion or 'cultural memory'. In this framework, the textual analysis of *Helden wie wir* below attempts to answer the question about the capability of a so-called 'picaresque'

---

2 See, for example, Jacobs (1983) and Marckwort (1984).

3 *Helden wie wir* was called a 'Schelmenroman' (Löhndorf 1995, Biermann 1996, Zachau 1997, Krause 1998), 'Bildungs- und Schelmenroman' (Wille 1996), the main character a 'Simplici(ssim)us' (Löhndorf 1995, Kraft 1995), or a 'spätgeborener Bruder von Oskar Matzerath' (Krause 1996).

text to survive this major transition. But before proceeding with the analysis of the text, it will be context-widening to establish the main aspects of Assmann's theory.

Cultural memory

Assmann's book *Das kulturelle Gedächtnis. Schrift, Erinnerung und politische Identität in frühen Hochkulturen* (1997) provides interesting insights into the processes of cultural change. The author, originally an archaeologist, wants to contribute 'zur allgemeinen Kulturtheorie' (Assmann 1997:19) with the theoretical part of his book. He wants to approach, if not answer, questions like: How do societies remember? How do communities imagine themselves through memory?

Memory, according to Assmann, is a phenomenon that is still widely imagined as something inside people: located in the brain. But what sorts of things make their way into memory? How is memory organised? How long does something stay in memory? These are mainly questions of cultural conditions. Assmann chose the term 'collective memory' as the starting point for his own argumentation, for which he draws on the work of the French sociologist Maurice Halbwachs (Assmann 1997:34–48). According to Assmann, Halbwachs developed the term 'mémoire collective' as an attempt to interpret memory as a social phenomenon. One of Halbwachs's central assumptions is that people develop the ability to remember only within the process of their socialisation. Somebody who grows up in complete solitude would, in theory, have no memory. Hence, memory is acquired and formed only because people live in societies and take part in everyday communication.

Other important assumptions which had a crucial influence on Assmann are also related to the social character of memory. Memories, for example, are always concrete in terms of space and time and belong to individuals. Memories do not exist independent of people. In fact, memories do not have an 'existence' as such at all; they are necessarily re-constructions. Memories only exist when and only while someone makes reference to them. For this to happen, two conditions have to be fulfilled. First, there have to be some records of the past. Second, these records have to show crucial differences to the life of the present. They can then become triggers for memory.

According to Assmann, there are four different dimensions of the human 'collective' memory. First, there is 'mimetisches Gedächtnis' (1997:20). This is the sphere of gestures and actions: people learn by watching and copying, by mimicry. Secondly, there is 'Gedächtnis der Dinge' (1997:20). The everyday things that surround people are all created and designed according to people's tastes in appropriateness, comfort and beauty. Everything has its own 'date stamp' and its own 'history'. Thirdly, there is 'kommunikatives Gedächtnis' (1997:20). This is the sphere of everyday communication and 'living' memory, that is, memory that belongs to the individual. It is largely shared by contemporaries and includes things that people have experienced themselves or that they know from hearsay. Communicative memory has a 'life' of three to four generations, 80 to 100 years.

And, finally, there is the sphere of 'kulturelles Gedächtnis' (1997:21). This is the sphere where the meaning and values of a society are created. It is the accumulated knowledge of a society that shapes its identity. Assmann stresses that it is not facts that are stored here, rather it is myths that are remembered (re-constructed) again and again. Cultural memory transcends individuals. It is formal and exists in *repeatable* images, words, actions, etc.

It is interesting to note that there is an important difference between the first three types of memory and 'cultural memory', because everything from the first three spheres can become part of cultural memory as soon as it loses its 'everyday' character. Actions and things can gain a ritual meaning. These particular processes are excluded from Assmann's book; he is more interested in the third transition: between communicative and cultural memory. Most importantly, these two spheres of memory do not oppose one another nor do they follow each other. Rather we have to imagine both existing at the same time. Assmann stresses that one could understand them like two ends of the same scale (1997:55). The things people remember move up and down on this scale. But there is also such a thing as a 'final' transition. Since communicative memory does not exist in perpetuity, it eventually tends to move towards the other end of the scale, to cultural memory.

Some interesting questions arise from Assmann's theory in the case of the vanished GDR. In 1989 a whole chapter of German history came to an end. A decade later, the GDR is still present within German communicative memory, most vividly in the memory of those who spent some time of their lives in that society, but people are afraid that soon these memories might be lost and that nothing of their experiences will be preserved in the sphere of cultural memory. At the same time, it is the clear wish of East Germans to see something of their past lives fixed in the cultural memory of a unified Germany. If one considers again the amount and different forms of autobiographical writing after 1989, it becomes conceivable that these works intend to preserve the GDR 'in memory'. Having said this, perhaps the most interesting question to ask is what kind of texts might succeed in this mission of recollecting the GDR appropriately. I would like to take as an example Thomas Brussig's well-known novel *Helden wie wir*.

The fabulous memories of *Helden wie wir*

Helden wie wir (1995)[4] sets out like a 'real' autobiography – with the description of the narrator's birth, only to stop again after the first four sentences. The main character, Klaus Uhltzscht, abandons the written form of autobiography because, as he tells us later, there were numerous things in his (fictional) life that he would not dare to write about. So he turns to a curious American journalist from the *New York Times* who appears in Berlin because he has seen some videos about the *Wende*. Klaus Uhltzscht emerges on these videotapes in a way that has captured the journalist's interest. Now, he wants to interview Uhltzscht about the events; this gives Uhltzscht the opportunity to 'confess' – and affords Brussig a fascinating narrative scenario.

Kitzelstein is a complete stranger to the GDR. What is more, during the whole of the novel he does not say a single word, and yet he is always present, in particular in Uhltzscht's addresses and

4 English translation: *Heroes like us*, translated from the German by John Brownjohn, London: The Harvill Press 1997. The page references which follow are to Brussig (1995).

comments ('Ja, es ist eklig, verziehen Sie bloß nicht so billig Ihr Gesicht, 85). The character of Kitzelstein allows Brussig to explain things that are closely linked with the GDR to a wider audience:

> Meinen ersten Steifen hatte ich bei Dagmar Frederic! Um mich Ihren amerikanischen Lesern verständlich zu machen: Dagmar Frederic ist eine Fernsehshow-Moderatorin, ungefähr so apart wie Nancy Reagan. (67)

Moreover, Uhltzscht can comment without inhibition on various things in front of his listener. This, inevitably, gives the speech of Uhltzscht the character of a confession: 'Oh, Mr. Kitzelstein, so leicht läßt sich das heute alles durchschauen, aber damals, als ich ein kleiner Schuljunge war' (100). Apart from the confessional elements, these comments also enable the author to highlight his own ironic distance towards his anti-hero by means of Uhltzscht's apparently sovereign control of the situation: 'Meine Ironie ist unüberhörbar? Ich bin beruhigt' (26).

This leads to the second dazzling feature of Brussig's idea. It is related to the technical device that is used here: a tape recorder. The use of tapes for autobiographical writing is nothing new. The most prominent example of this technique is Heiner Müller's *Krieg ohne Schlacht*, which was based on tapes. Müller himself stated that he never had enough interest in his own person to actually *write* an autobiography. Klaus Uhltzscht has enough interest, but he is too scared to write about his obsessions. Therefore, he is happy to talk as long as Mr. Kitzelstein leaves him the illusion that it is only a voice test: 'Ich darf alles sagen, was mir in den Sinn kommt, ohne daß ich dafür festgenagelt werden kann – ist ja nur eine Sprechprobe' (18). To 'tape' an autobiography leads eventually to the same flood of 'authentic' records that emerged after the *Wende*. As Klaus Uhltzscht puts it, highlighting an element of such analysis:

> Nach all den 'Wortmeldungen', 'Zwischenrufen', 'Protokollen' und 'Befragungen' droht uns eine Verbreitung des Materials unter dem Titel 'Sprechprobe'. Vermutlich gibt es ohnehin schon ein halbes Dutzend Entwicklungsromane, die so heißen. (18)

But the feature 'tape recorder' has yet another dimension – at least for GDR citizens: to tape or to be taped was always associated with the methods of the *Ministerium für Staatssicherheit* (*MfS*), the 'Stasi'. Manfred Krug's book *Abgehauen* (1996) provides a fine example of this. Here, we find the authentic script of a tape Krug secretly recorded in his house in Berlin-Pankow back in 1976. The object of his record was a dialogue between various GDR artists and some GDR politicians that took place there. Krug was quite sure that the men from Erich Mielke's ministry also taped the discussion. Thus, Krug gave the situation a crazy twist and 'taped the Stasi'.

And another taped statement became very famous after the *Wende*. This was Günter Schabowski's declaration of the freedom to travel for all GDR citizens. At a press-conference on the eve of 9 November 1989, a journalist asked: 'Wann tritt das in Kraft?' (Groth:CD), and Schabowski spontaneously decided: 'Das tritt nach meiner Kenntnis ... ist das sofort ... unverzüglich'. Schabowski was wrong. He had ignored the blocking period on the declaration until 10 November. This event became the starting point for various jokes about the *Wende* being only a 'slip of the tongue'. *Helden wie wir* originates in this joke: it is precisely Schabowski's lapse that gives Klaus Uhltzscht the opportunity to open the Berlin Wall. And Uhltzscht did not do so with words, but with a very different part of his body, namely his genitals. As shown, the mere technique of using a tape recorder in the novel evokes various memories related to the GDR and its end. And while talking, Uhltzscht's confessions parody both autobiographical writing and 'oral history' at the same time.

Symptoms

One of the main characteristics of the protagonist Klaus Uhltzscht is that he never has any idea of the things that are going on around him. He sees himself as the 'most ill-informed person' in the world. Hence, there are numerous cries of anguish in his 'confessions' to Mr Kitzelstein: 'Daß die anderen immer alles wußten und ich nie die geringste Ahnung hatte! Wenn ich überhaupt von einer Sache erfuhr, dann garantiert als letzter' (78). As a child, the main source for Klaus's information was the annual summer camp. The other boys were invariably better informed than Klaus, which led him to the conclusion that they were more trustworthy than anybody else in his life at that time. Thus, after having learned about the way children are made and having seen his camp-mates masturbate, Klaus has no hesitation in believing the third big revelation: 'Dein Vater ist doch auch bei der Stasi' (83). Suddenly, at the age of fourteen, Klaus has to accept that his father does not work for the Ministry of Foreign Trade, as he had been told. This constant lack of knowledge, of course, leads to tragicomic misunderstandings. But Klaus's misjudgements are not all innocent. As soon as they relate to his job, they become seriously bizarre. Klaus's father arranges for him to work for the Stasi, but Klaus mistakes the whole situation for something highly adventurous. He dreams about a mission that would send him to the United States, or at least to West Berlin, where he hopes to meet the genuinely beautiful women of the West. On orders from the Stasi, Uhltzscht breaks into a flat, kidnaps a child for an afternoon, and observes people – and still he thinks of himself as a wicked outlaw who could soon be captured by the police.

The situation culminates in Klaus's last big confusion. On 4 November 1989 he takes part in the famous demonstration at the *Alexanderplatz* where he listens to a speech. Uhltzscht approaches the platform and recognises the person making the address: Jutta Müller, the prominent GDR ice-skating trainer. Puzzled because he had once seen Müller on television and had had sexual feelings about her, Klaus stumbles over a cardboard placard and severely hurts his genitals. Later, in hospital, he realises his mistake: the speaker was not Jutta Müller, but Christa Wolf.

Uhltzscht's pivotal ignorance turns him into a very artificial character. He seems like a proto-type of *the* young man in the GDR, or rather its staggering parody. Uhltzscht is not an individual, but a symptom. His lifestory contains elements of millions of other lifestories, each with its own portion of repression. Yet it is not only Uhltzscht who is constructed by means of parody. Everything and everybody in the novel seems so *typical* of the GDR that one can read it as a modern tale: a comic, full of caricatures.

Uhltzscht's parents, for example, are a parody of the typical GDR petty bourgeois. Klaus's mother is a 'Muster an Rechtschaffenheit' (21). She is 'Hygieneinspektorin' and treats her family like the children for whom she used to be the nit-nurse. Klaus's hypochondriac behaviour is only a stone's throw from his mother's hygienic obsessions. Later, his mother is associated with the Jutta Müller of his sexual stirrings. The trinity of Müller, Christa Wolf, and his mother, women of the same age, stands for a whole generation of mothers who greatly shaped Uhltzscht's childhood and adolescence with the sense of (false) harmony they imposed on him. Brussig reveals how 'gnadenlos un-ta-de-lig' (311) 'our mothers' were, and he shows with great humour that this generation will be remembered for their hypocritical attitudes.

As for Uhltzscht's authoritarian father, he thinks his son is a complete failure and never speaks to Klaus personally. No wonder that Klaus's statement about him consists of the telling sentence: 'Ich liebte ihn, aber ich konnte ihn nicht leiden' (37). Because he works for the 'Stasi', his father is suspicious of everything. Doors have to be closed and locked, wallets have to be in a safe place, and the first thing he teaches Klaus about summer camps is how to open suitcases so that no other child can catch a glimpse of the contents. Klaus: 'ich werde trainiert, als ob ich in der Unterwelt bestehen müßte, als ob ich mein Hab und Gut zu verteidigen hätte' (48).

And how do they get Uhltzscht to work for the Stasi, although he hates what his father is doing? 'Er traf mich an meiner verwundbarsten Stelle, *Wir brauchen dich, du gehörst zu uns*' (109/110). This argument was widely used in the GDR, as can be seen in other post-*Wende* writing. The main character in Christoph Brumme's second novel *Tausend Tage*, for example, is caught by the army under the same pretext: 'Es hatte ihm geschmeichelt, dass man ihn brauchte' (Brumme 1997:21). A different element of persuasion is the fact that nobody ever mentions the word 'Stasi': 'Von *Stasi* war nie die Rede!' (112), and: 'Ich hätte es ungemein beruhigend gefunden, wenn einer nur ein einziges Mal erwähnt hätte, daß ich bei der Stasi bin. Nur um der Gewißheit willen' (113). These remarks also prepare the way for the sort of characters we find inside this 'Stasi': Uhltzscht's colleagues are three caricatures of Stasi–employees, a 'Monty-Python-Showtruppe minderer Güte' (Kraft 1995). There is Eulert, an 'Attrappe von einem Geheimdienstmann' (158), who speaks continually about the principle of 'Negation der Negation', which he has not really understood. There is Grabs, a man who is constantly in search of monosyllabic names beginning with the letter 'G'[5]. And there is Wunderlich who cannot do anything but 'lecheln', an amalgamation of 'lächeln' and 'hecheln'. Of course, these men cannot be taken seriously. Like everybody else in the novel, they are non-realistic, exaggerated characters.

In this context, it is very important to note that it was Brussig's intention to illustrate the themes of another book with his novel: those of the psycho-analytical analysis of GDR society by Hans-Joachim Maaz, with the title *Der Gefühlsstau* (1990). According to Escherig (1995) and Lahann (1995), Brussig was very affected by Maaz's analysis of GDR society as mainly repressed and wanted to write a literary text that complemented Maaz's empirical analysis. Brussig illustrates Maaz's hypotheses about the repressive education system, the omnipresent power of the Stasi, the authoritarian approach in school, in sports, and at home. Maaz's does not want to illustrate the behaviour of individual people in the GDR but the general mechanisms of repression and human reaction to it. Brussig's characters are likewise symptoms. Maaz stresses that the first sign of a 'sichtbare[n] Gesundung eines Volkes' (Maaz 1990:146) was the demonstration of the 4 November 1989 – and, in this context, Brussig's last chapter also speaks about a 'healing'[6]. Indeed, one can read the two works alongside each other as different descriptions of the types of social behaviour that transcend individuals and, therefore, individual memories.

A-Wop-Bop A-Loo-Bop

Another way in which these types of people are parodied in *Helden wie wir* is the way they use language. Klaus's father, as the authoritarian Stasi-man, hardly ever speaks, but when he does address words to the boy, Klaus immediately thinks: 'Ganz der Stasi-Vater! Verhör! Er ist wahrscheinlich Vernehmer' (88).

Klaus's mother, on the other hand, speaks so accurately that Klaus cannot even understand his fellow-classmates. She is characterised as

5 See also *The World According to Garp* in the subsection 'Megalomania', below.
6 See the last chapter, 'Der geheilte Pimmel', 277–323.

a 'Sprachwalterin' (53) and 'Wortmümmlerin' (91): 'Sie schlug sich wie eine Dschungelkriegerin durchs Sprachdickicht, und sie war sich durchaus nicht zu schade, auch durchs Unterholz der Etymologie zu robben' (53). Here, the term 'Muttersprache' itself seems to be parodied. To give one of Klaus's numerous examples, his mother calls his beloved part 'Puller', with the following mind-boggling explanation: 'Der Tischler heißt Tischler, weil er tischlert, der Schneider heißt Schneider, weil er schneidert, und der Puller heißt Puller, weil er pullert' (53). What is true of semantics is also true of pronunciation: '*Sex*, dieses Wort mit dem herrlich stimmlosen S, schneidend wie ein Peitschenknall – sie brachte es nie, nie, niemals über ihre Lippen' (58). After the opening of the Wall, she also coins the term 'Helden wie wir' (299) for people like herself who have nothing to regret.

In contrast to his parents Klaus dreams of an emancipated language. He is already familiar with the attempt to create a new language by the Stasi: 'Ihr sollt lernen, einen Observationsbericht zu schreiben, und zwar, ich will es mal so nennen, in einer *neuen* Sprache' (180). But this is not the language Klaus dreams about. Likewise, he is shocked by the Alexanderplatz speech of Jutta Müller alias Christa Wolf: 'Jede revolutionäre Bewegung befreit auch die Sprache'. Klaus's reaction: 'Das war nicht etwa meine Mutter, die mit Linguisten diskutierte – dieser Satz kam aus den Lautsprechern' (282). With the term 'befreite Sprache', Klaus understands something like the language which Marina uses (Marina is the woman Klaus first had sexual intercourse with). When he met her for the first time, Marina sang more than she spoke: 'tüdelüdüdü tüdelüdüdü' (125), and when Klaus remembers her later, he sings: 'A-wop-Bop-A-loo-Bop' (132) and – for the first time in his life – he feels free. This is the new language of his dreams, and these 'non-sense' sounds are in fact more meaningful than all the talk of his 'mothers' Lucie Uhltzscht, Jutta Müller, Christa Wolf:

> Und wenn schon befreite Sprache, dann richtig: *Hoppla!* ist doch eine starke Verfassungspräambel, oder *A-Wop-Bop A-Loo-Bop*, oder *And now for something completely different*, oder *Mittwoch ist Kinotag* oder *Tüdelüdüdü, tüdelüdüdü* (308/309).

Megalomania

In various articles about *Helden wie wir*, critics claimed that, apart from Maaz's *Der Gefühlsstau*, Brussig was also highly influenced by Philip Roth's *Portnoy's Complaint* and John Irving's *The World According to Garp* (Escherig 1995, Franke 1995, Böttiger 1995). Indeed, Brussig makes numerous allusions to Roth's novel. Most of all, it is Roth's technique of telling a story in which politics and private life are closely intermingled, which might have delighted Brussig. As Helmut Böttiger, one of the very few critics who did not use the category 'Schelmenroman' to characterise Brussig's novel, remarks: 'Die DDR braucht ihr '68!' (Böttiger 1995). If Philip Roth depicts repression in a Jewish childhood and education by having a disturbed person talking about his life, why should that not be possible for somebody socialised in the GDR?

There is also the similarity in a literary form: In both books we find somebody 'confessing'. Alexander Portnoy talks to his psychiatrist Dr. Spielvogel, Klaus Uhltzscht to Mr. Kitzelstein. Both books proceed from childhood and adolescence all the way through to politics and employment, then to women and perversions and, finally, into exile: Portnoy journeys to Israel, Uhltzscht is confined to hospital. But Brussig also inverts the pattern. Portnoy always has a lot of success, particularly with women, but his stay in Israel is a complete catastrophe. Uhlzscht's hospitalisation, on the other hand, brings an end to his inhibitions and anxieties as the accidentally achieved growth of his penis removes his fears and complexes.

And there are numerous other allusions to Roth: the constipated fathers; the loving and caring mothers who desire to enter the locked bathroom just at the moment when the boys Alexander and Klaus are busy with their favourite occupations; the abuse of food for masturbation; the boys obsession with themselves and with headlines in the yellow press. Both heroes possess a strange mixture of inhibition complexes and megalomania. Portnoy calls himself 'Alexander the Great' (Roth 1995:64) and Uhltzscht thinks he is 'das *Missing link* der jüngsten deutschen Geschichte' (323). Maaz described this kind of social behaviour as 'gehemmt-zwanghaft' (Maaz 1990:101) – and again Brussig illustrates this with Uhltzscht's terrible childhood and youth.

The parallel with Irving's *The World According to Garp* is also clear in the text – indeed, the text itself is mentioned. It is the Stasi-character Grabs who is obsessed by names starting with 'G' for his children. When searching the house of an intellectual, Klaus finds 'ein Buch mit dem Titel *Garp – und wie er die Welt sah*' (155). He takes it as proof for Grabs and the registry office, 'daß *Garp* ein gebräuchlicher Vorname ist' (155). Of course, neither Klaus nor Grabs seem to know this book. The registry office turns the name *Garp* down, and Grabs names his new son 'Gleb' (155) instead.

Conclusion

> 'And you're always telling me,' Helen said, 'that autobiographical fiction is the *worst* kind.'
> (Irving 1990: 225)

This paper has sought to illustrate that both the quantity of autobiographical writing after 1989 as well as the revival of literary elements known as 'picaresque' point in the same direction. Both are elements of an autobiographical discourse that seems to dominate the East German literary scene at the moment. Obviously, cultural changes bring about an identity crisis for at least part of every population. In the former East, of course, there are many social and economic problems that must not be neglected. But more than these concerns, it might have been the fear of oblivion that triggered a lot of autobiographical writing after 1989. Assmann's model of a final transition from communicative to cultural memory highlights these inevitable processes of remembering and forgetting.

The analysis of Thomas Brussig's novel *Helden wie wir* shows that much of everyday life in the GDR is actually preserved in the satirical elements of the text. But *Helden wie wir* is also a story about education, socialisation and repression: presumably, it reminds not only ex-GDR citizens of their childhood but also many more people outside GDR of their own early years. This is important, because it enables readers from completely different backgrounds to enjoy the novel. As the wide praise of *Helden wie wir* shows, 'Wessis', for example, reacted very positively to the book:

> Wer im Westen wußte, wie sozialistische Puritaner leben, was blaue oder rote Landkarten, was U-Bahn-Schächte und die 'Messe der Meister von morgen' bedeuten können? West lernt, Ost erinnert, West lacht, Ost, nunja, lächelt. (Franke 1995)

Thus, in a novel like *Helden wie wir* one can find as many moments of recollection as in any example of autobiographical writing. What is more, *Helden wie wir* does recall not only facts or typical behaviour patterns; it also evokes a comic perspective on the GDR today – and therefore a way of dealing with the problems after 1989:

> Das Buch liefert überreich, was die meisten ideologischen Pamphlete, Enquete-Kommissions-Papiere und post-oppositionellen Traktate zum Heimgang der Republik so schmerzlich entbehren: den Fleiß des Erzählers, Selbstironie, die Pars-pro-toto-Weisheit erlebter und bewahrter Geschichte(n). (Dieckmann 1995)

And if a would-be hero like Klaus Uhltzscht could succeed in opening the Berlin Wall, what one might expect from the German unification that followed was suggested by Brussig: 'daß ich darin sage, die deutsche Einheit ist derart mißraten, daß sie ohne weiteres einen solchen Urheber (haben kann)' (Brussig in Krekeler 1996).

The type of humour which Brussig uses in his novel can perhaps best be described by Dieter Wellershof's term 'Blödeln' (Wellershof 1976:335). Wellershof characterizes this 'anarchic subculture' of humour as a form of 'freiwilliger Form- und Niveauverlust, dessen Modell [...] der leicht Schwachsinnige ist, also ein mangelhaft sozialisierter, infantil gebliebener Mensch' (338). The silly jokes of *Helden wie wir* mark a step away from serious discourse. Wellershof describes four main elements of 'Blödeln': silly puns, the disparagement of people or historic facts, the frequent eruption into the absurd, and the transition from free association to compulsive thinking. As we have seen, *Helden wie wir* clearly possesses every one of these elements. The novel is a frenetic liberation from the 'adult'-world, pointing out the ridiculous and laughable facts about GDR society. This laughter is able to break through the narrow individual perspective one usually finds in traditional autobiographical writing and to open a much broader perspective on the GDR. *Helden wie wir* is an open invitation to remember and learn about the GDR, and to do so with pleasure – a sure recipe for future recollection. Brussig's laughter is ultimately to be taken seriously.

Bibliography

Assmann, Jan (1997) *Das kulturelle Gedächtnis. Schrift, Erinnerung und politische Identität in frühen Hochkulturen*, München: Beck, 2nd edition

Biermann, Wolf (1996) '"Wenig Wahrheiten und viel Witz". Wolf Biermann über Thomas Brussigs Roman "Helden wie wir"', *Der Spiegel*, 29. 1

Böttiger, Helmut (1995) 'Die DDR braucht ihr 68! Thomas Brussigs Abrechnung mit der sozialistischen Kleinbürgermoral', *Frankfurter Rundschau*, 28. 10

Brumme, Christoph D. (1997) *Tausend Tage*, Köln: Kiepenheuer & Witsch

Brussig, Thomas (1994) *Wasserfarben*, München: dtv

Brussig, Thomas (1995) *Helden wie wir*, Berlin: Volk & Welt

Brussig, Thomas (1999) *Am kürzeren Ende der Sonnenallee*, Berlin: Volk und Welt

Bruyn, Günter de (1994) *Zwischenbilanz*, Frankfurt am Main: Fischer

Bruyn, Günter de (1996) *Vierzig Jahre. Ein Lebensbericht*, Frankfurt am Main: Fischer

de Man, Paul (1984) 'Autobiography as De-Facement', *The Rhethoric of Romanticism*, New York

Escherig, Ursula (1995) 'Kommt jetzt der wilde Osten? Eine neue Stimme vom Prenzlauer Berg', *Der Tagesspiegel*, 31. 8

Franke, Konrad (1995) 'Der Sieger der Geschichte. Thomas Brussig stellt vor: "Helden wie wir"', *Süddeutsche Zeitung*, 11. 10

Fries, Fritz Rudolf (1999) *Der Roncalli-Effekt*, Leipzig: Gustav Kiepenheuer

Fröhling, Jörg et al. (1996) *Wende-Literatur. Bibliographie und Materialien zur Literatur der deutschen Einheit*, Frankfurt am Main: Peter Lang

Groth, Michael (no date) *Götterdämmerung im Zentralkomitee. Tonprotokolle aus den letzten Sitzungen des ZK der SED, Oktober bis Dezember 1989. Eine Dokumentation*, CD Audio, Deutschlandfunk

Hauser, Kornelia (1992) 'DDR-Wirklichkeit als Arbeit am Gedächtnis', *Das Argument* 192, S. 243–253

Hensel, Kerstin (1997) *Tanz am Kanal*, Frankfurt am Main: suhrkamp taschenbuch

Hermand, Jost (1993) 'Diskursive Widersprüche. Fragen an Heiner Müllers "Autobiographie"', *Das Argument* 198, 255–268

Irving, John (1990) *The World According to Garp*, New York: Ballantine Books

Jacobs, Jürgen (1983) *Der deutsche Schelmenroman*, München, Zürich: Artemis

Jurgensen, Manfred (1979) *Das fiktionale Ich*, Bern: Francke

Kant, Hermann (1991) *Abspann. Erinnerungen an meine Gegenwart*, Berlin: Aufbau

Kraft, Thomas (1995) 'An der Charmegrenze der Provokation. Thomas Brussigs Realsatire über 20 Jahre DDR-Geschichte: "Helden wie wir"', *Freitag*, 13. 10

Krause, Tilman (1996) 'Kleine Trompete, zur großen Tuba aufgeblasen. Götz Schubert als darstellerischer Tausendsassa [...]', *Der Tagesspiegel*, 29. 4

Krause, Tilman (1998) 'Alles wird gut oder So tragisch sind wir gar nicht. Was ist neu an der deutschen Literatur seit der Wende von 1989? Ihre Verwestlichung', *Die Welt*, 8. 8

Krekeler, Elmar (1996) '"Da war eine Sehnsucht" Der Schriftsteller Thomas Brussig schreibt, was er lesen will', *Die Welt*, 27/28.4

Krug, Manfred (1996) *Abgehauen*, Berlin: econ Verlag

Lahann, Birgit (1995) 'Der Gigant aus dem Gartenzwerg', *Stern*, 24. 8

Lejeune, Philippe (1975) 'Le pacte autobiographique', transl. by Heydenreich, Niggl (1989), *Die Autobiographie*, Darmstadt: Wiss. Buchgesellschaft, 214–257

Löhndorf, Marion (1995) 'Wer hat die Mauer umgeschmissen? Thomas Brussigs Wenderoman "Helden wie wir"', *Neue Zürcher Zeitung*, 10. 10

Maaz, Hans-Joachim (1990) *Der Gefühlsstau*, Berlin: Argon

Marckwort, Ulf-Heiner (1984) *Der deutsche Schelmenroman der Gegenwart*, Köln: Pahl-Rugenstein

Mayer, Hans (1993) *Der Turm von Babel*, Frankfurt am Main: Suhrkamp

Müller, Heiner (1992) *Krieg ohne Schlacht*, Köln: Kiepenheuer & Witsch

Müller, Klaus Detlef (1976) *Autobiographie und Roman*, Tübingen: Max Niemeyer

Muschg, Adolf (1984) 'Wie echt ist das Ich in der Literatur?', in: Heckmann, Herbert *Literatur aus dem Leben*, München: Hanser, 29–38

Neumann, Bernd (1970) *Identität und Rollenzwang*, Frankfurt am Main: Athenäum

Preece, Julian (1995) 'Damaged lives? (East) German memoirs and autobiographies 1989–1994', in: Durrani, Osman et al. (eds.) *The New Germany. Literature and Society after Unification*, Sheffield: Sheffield Academic Press, 349–364

Roth, Philip (1995) *Portnoy's Complaint*, London: Vintage

Sill, Oliver (1991) *Zerbrochene Spiegel. Studien zu Theorie und Praxis modernen autobiographischen Erzählens*, Berlin, New York: Gruyter

Sparschuh, Jens (1995) *Der Zimmerspringbrunnen*, Köln: Kiepenheuer & Witsch

Walther, Peter (1995) 'Triebkraft der Geschichte', *die tageszeitung*, 9./10. 9

Wellershof, Dieter (1976) 'Infantilismus als Revolte oder das ausgeschlagene Erbe – Zur Theorie des Blödelns, in Preisendanz, Wolfgang/Warning, Rainer (eds.) *Das Komische*, München: Fink, 335–357

Wellershof, Dieter (1991) 'Double, Alter ego und Schatten-Ich. Schreiben und Lesen als mimetische Kur', *Manuskripte* 113/31, 3–11

Wille, Franz (1996) 'Entfesselt verklemmt! Thomas Brussigs Wenderoman "Helden wie wir" als Monodram im Berliner Deutschen Theater', *Theater heute* 6, 36–39

Zachau, Reinhard K. (1997) '"Das Volk jedenfalls war's nicht!" Thomas Brussigs Abrechnungen mit der DDR', *Colloquia Germanica* 4, 387–395

GERTRUD REERSHEMIUS

Language Change – Low German in North-West Germany

In Ostfriesland, the north-westernmost part of Germany bordering on the Netherlands, a variety of Low German is spoken which is in many aspects structurally different from the Low German of neighbouring areas because of a most remarkable history of language contact and language change in the region. Over the centuries Low German in Ostfriesland has been shaped by Frisian, Hanseatic Low German, Dutch and Standard German. This paper will give a short overview of the history of the language and will then proceed with the presentation and analysis of data from modern spoken Low German recorded in a village in the north-west of the area. The paper will examine the quality of language alternation which can be found in the data.

Low German in Ostfriesland – a history of language contact

Unlike other Low German varieties in Lower Saxony, Low German in Ostfriesland is based on a Frisian substratum (Scheuermann 1995). Frisian was the spoken and sometimes even the written language alongside Latin in Ostfriesland until the 14th century. Hanseatic Low German, the so-called 'Hansesprache', was the written and spoken lingua franca of trade and politics in Northern Europe in those days. But it only became dominant in Ostfriesland when the country was occupied in 1400 and in 1433 by armed forces from Hamburg and Bremen as a reaction to East-Frisian collaboration with the pirates around Klaus Störtebeker and Gödeke Michel (Lengen 1995).

Frisian-speaking Ostfriesland took over Hanseatic Low German, which was different in many features from the Low German varieties spoken in the Oldenburger Land in the south and the Groninger Land in the west. Furthermore, Low German in Ostfriesland kept a Frisian substratum, especially in the lexicon but also in phonology, morphology and syntax (Remmers 1994; 1995; 1996). Nowadays, Frisian is still spoken in three rather isolated villages in the area by 1500 to 2000 speakers (Ford 1997).

In the 16th century, however, Low German as a written language with a high degree of standardisation was already in decline (see e.g. Maas 1982, Maas 1986, McAlister-Hermann 1982). By the time of the Reformation, two other languages had taken over the functions of written language and high variety in the area: Lutherans wrote, preached and prayed in High German, Calvinists in Dutch (Kempen 1981). By the end of the 16th century, Ostfriesland turned out to be mainly Calvinist in the south-west and mainly Lutheran in the north-east. The area was divided linguistically as well as with regard to religion. Both parts, however, were connected by Low German as the spoken variety, which underwent a process of differentiation into regional dialects.

Dutch influence remained strong. For some years, between 1806 and 1810, Ostfriesland even belonged to the Netherlands. After Napoleon's surrender, Ostfriesland became part of the Kingdom of Hanover. The new government tried to weaken the Dutch influence in Ostfriesland, but until the end of the 19th century in Calvinist communities hymn and prayer books remained Dutch. Older people in the Calvinist parts of Ostfriesland can still remember that their grandparents used to read and write in Dutch. As a result of this contact, East-Frisian Low German contains up to 500 words of Dutch origin (de Smet 1983). Although Ostfriesland had always had lively trade relations with its southern neighbours, the influence of Westphalian Low German remained weak (Borchling 1928).

Since the beginning of the 20th century, Standard German has served as written language and high variety in Ostfriesland. For the first half of the 20th century, a stable diglossic situation emerged: Low German was the first language of most children born in the area. Only in school did they learn to speak and to write Standard German, which is called 'Dütsch' as opposed to 'Platt' for Low German and which was used for formal and institutional purposes only.

This changed dramatically after World War II. Most of the slave-labourers from the occupied countries who were forced to work on the local farms during the war had had to learn Low German. Then came the so-called 'Flüchtlinge', who were expelled from former German areas in the East. With these people, the only language in common was Standard German, although their children adapted to Low German very quickly.

Growing influence of the media, especially TV, and a restrictive language policy by schools since the early sixties are the main reasons why Low German nowadays is a language in decline. There are almost no monolingual speakers left. Parents stopped speaking Low German to their children because they feared disadvantage at school. Among children and teenagers, only very few native speakers of Low German are left, although a majority understand it (Kruse 1993). The general attitude towards the language, however, has changed. Low German is regarded nowadays as part of the regional culture and heritage and a lot of effort is put into preserving it. In 1998, Low German became the second official language in all public institutions thanks to the European Charter of Regional and Minority Languages. Thirty kindergartens in the area started to educate small children in both Low German and Standard German. The future of Low German, however, very much depends on parents of young children: Can they be convinced of the value of speaking Low German to their children or is the fear of educational disadvantage still too dominant?

Contemporary Low German – a case-study

It is not only a declining number of speakers that endangers the future of Low German. A comparison between native speakers of Low German from two different generations, born in the same village and with the same educational background, shows a significantly higher degree of codeswitching to Standard German with the younger speakers (Reershemius 1997). This paper will focus on the example of a comparatively young speaker who is 33 years old and analyse the contact phenomena between Low German and Standard German. The data were recorded in 1998 in the village of Campen in the north-west of Ostfriesland.

The matrix language of the conversation in the following transcript is Low German with frequent codeswitches into Standard German. All three speakers were raised with Low German as their first language. They learned Standard German at the age of six when they started school. Speaker B is 62 years old, C 36 and A 33.

A, B and C are talking about a play the three of them have been watching. The play was a co-production between a Bavarian and an East-Frisian village and its subject was cultural differences. A and her family plan to spend their next holidays in Bavaria to meet their new friends again.

(1) A: Jaa, **also** då^{r} hem wi ouk dåecht, dan • kun man dat
Ja, also da haben wir auch gedacht, dann könnte man das
ouk ja / dan ha^{r} man dat ouk ja mål zäjn, **also**
auch ja / dann hätte man das auch ja mal gesehen, also
irgendwie.
irgendwie.

(2) B: Ja. Ja. Hm.

(3) A: Un / un **vor allen Dingen** is dat ouk ja zou, zou föl
Und / und vor allen Dingen ist das auch ja so, so viel
Urlaub hem wi dan ja ouk näj, dat wi zou • nåch
Urlaub haben wir dann ja auch nicht, daß wir so noch
mål dan **extra** wechfå^{r}n, wen däj då nå twäj
mal dann extra wegfahren, wenn die da nach zwei
wejk wee^{r}koum.
Wochen wiederkommen.

(4) Dat was ja • dit jå^{r} al zou rå^{r}.
Das war ja dieses Jahr schon so merkwürdig.

(5) B: Zün dan dej feerien nejchst jå^{r} um dej tiid?
Sind denn die Ferien nächstes Jahr um dieselbe Zeit?

(6) A: Ja, dej kine hem, ik löw, äjn dach låte feerien as dit jå^{r}.
Ja, die Kinder haben, ich glaube, einen Tag später
Ferien als dieses Jahr.

(7) B: **Stimmt**. Ja. Ja.

(8) C: O.

(9) A: **Also**, dat • haut fa ...
Also, das haut fa ...
Un dej Bayern hem wal ime **fast parallel**.
Und die Bayern haben wohl immer fast parallel.

(10) B: Ime. Hm. **Stimmt**.
Immer. Hm. Stimmt.

(11) C: Dat wäjst du fan diin **Gäste**.
Das weißt du von deinen Gästen.

(12) A: Ja, dej ...
Ja, die ...

(13) B: Ja. Dej hem ime t zülwichst tiid.
Ja. Die haben immer dieselbe Zeit.

(14) A: Ja, dej / **anscheinend** is dat wal / dej fang dan,
Ja, die / anscheinend ist das wohl / die fangen dann,
löw ik um ...
glaube ich um ...

(15) B: Dej rutään näj mit.
Die rotieren nicht mit.

(16) A: Nej?
Nein?
Wau, dej hem ime in däj ...
Wie, die haben immer in der ...

(17) B: Ime in dise tiid.
Immer in dieser Zeit.

(18) A: O, dej he / **weil** ik löw un dan dej jå^{r} drup • hem
O, die ha / weil ich glaube und dann da Jahr darauf haben
wi t häjl frau.
wir e ganz früh.

(19) B: Hm. Dan wå^{r}t wee^{r} frau.
Hm. Dann wird es wieder früh.

(20) A: Un dat hem däj näj?
Und das haben die nicht?
Dat däj zou **mitrotiern** ?
Daß die so mitrotieren?
(21) B: Nej. Nej. Nej.
Nein. Nein. Nein.
(22) A: Wau kumt dat?
Wie kommt das?
(23) B: Bayern is ja ime fö^{r} zük.
Bayern ist ja immer für sich.
((4 Sekunden))
(24) A: Ja, is ja ...
Ja, ist ja ...
Ik heb nåch dåecht: Ouk dat **Stück**: Et wist ja dåch
Ich habe noch gedacht: Auch das Stück: Es zeigt ja doch
up, et givt zou föl **Paralleln** • un et is dåch wee^{r} häjl anes.
auf, es gibt so viel Parallelen und es ist doch wieder ganz anders.
(25) C: Hm.
(26) A: **Also**, ee / ee/ of bin ji nåch näj då^{r} west?
Also / oder seid ihr noch nicht da gewesen?
(27) B/C: Ja. Ja.
(28) A: **Also**, ik fun dat ja zou / as däj då^{r} inkuam, mit ziin
Also, ich fand das ja so / als die da reinkamen, mit seiner
bääkiest un dej kejkn ja aal as wen dej zäegn
Bierkiste und die guckten ja alle als wenn die sagen
wuln: Wå^{r} bin wi hi^{r} nu wal lant, wa?
wollten: Wo sind wir hier nun wohl gelandet, was?
(29) B/C: ((Lachen))
(30) A: **Also**, ik fun dat ja zou **toll**. ((Lacht))
Also, ich fand das ja so toll.
(31) Mit däj ...
Mit den ...
(32) B: Mit dej hi^{r} **Flossen** tüschn toun un / un däj äjn bäjn.
Mit den hier Flossen zwischen den Zehen und / und dem einen Bein.

(33) A: Ja.
(34) Un dej maude, dej / dej hi^{r} / dej brügns maud
Und die Mutter, die / die hier / die Mutter des Bräutigams
ha^{r} in jäjde hant zoun laang schtejwel, dat hö^{r}
hatte in jeder hand so einen langen Stiefel, damit ihr
aam jung hi^{r} blout näj zou fezuupn dej.
armer Jung hier bloß nicht ertrinken würde.
(35) Då^{r} heb ik ja zou owe laacht.
Da habe ich ja so drüber gelacht.

The transcript shows various contact phenomena which are typical for speaker A., and which fall into three different categories:

Lexical items	**Syntax**	**Discourse markers**
Urlaub	et	also
extra		also irgendwie
fast parallel		vor allen Dingen
Gäste		stimmt
Stück		also
Parallelen		stimmt
Toll		anscheinend
Flossen		also
rotieren		also
		also
		weil

The distribution of these three classes of contact phenomena is quite representative for the whole recording, which lasts 60 minutes altogether. The transcript shows contact phenomena but the fundamental question that needs to be asked in this context is: what does their existence mean for the Low German language in general? Spoken Standard German, for example, is full of English elements which are certainly not regarded as a threat to the German language. How can contact phenomena and their consequences for a language be classified?

I would like to introduce a model of language contact phenomena which was developed by Matras (1998). The model is based on the assumption that contact phenomena originate out of the pragmatic needs of communication. The model distinguishes between four types of language contact:

1. **Differentiation** Bilingual speakers use Language B for emphasising or contrasting procedures in Language A. An utterance in B can e.g. be used as a footnote to the main narrative line. The systems remain separate and the speakers choose to use B for certain communicative purposes.
2. **Integration** Elements of the B-system are integrated into A to enhance A. B-elements are treated as quasi-A-elements. Integration is usually restricted to the lexicon of B.
3. **Convergence** An attempt to apply the same processing and organisation strategies to both systems while pretending on the surface to keep to the A-system.
4. **Fusion** The wholesale adaptation of a syntactical category from B into A. The B-element is not perceived as an imported component any more. Fusion can obviously lead to language change.

Using this model we can analyse the speaker's communicative motivation for using an item or a structure from the B-system.

If we apply our list of contact phenomena, we can state that there is no example of differentiation to be found in the transcript.

The elements in the category termed 'lexical items' are cases of integration: lexical elements of the B-system are integrated into A to enhance A and to fill in lexical gaps in A. These gaps can exist for the individual speaker because there are either no concepts for the words in A, or because the speaker does not know them.

Interesting to note in this context is the fact that the 62-year-old speaker B integrates the word *rotieren* phonologically into Low German whereas the younger speaker A does not.

Et ... in segment (24) is an example of *convergence*. It is clearly an attempt to apply the Standard German construction 'es zeigt sich, daß....' into Low German, although in the East-Frisian variety of speaker A, *et* does not exist, either as a personal pronoun or as a filler for an empty subject position. Interestingly, A integrates the Standard German 'es' phonologically into Low German.

The last category to be examined on the list of discourse phenomena is discourse markers. Since Deborah Schiffrin's book

Discourse Markers (1987) there has been an extended discussion on the definition of this phenomenon. This study does not aim to take part in that particular debate but will use the so called maximal classification which includes conjunctions, sentence particles, fillers, hesitation markers and tags (Matras 1998). Discourse markers are elements through which a speaker tries to monitor and direct the way a propositional unit is processed and accepted by the hearer. Discourse markers therefore build the directing and monitoring frame of conversations, i.e signalling, continuation (addition), intervention (contrast), etc.

Discourse markers are preferred targets for codeswitching, as has been observed in a number of studies on different languages, e.g. Maschler (1994) on Hebrew-English contact phenomena, De Rooij (1996) on Shaba Swahili and French, or Salmons (1990) on American English-German, to mention but a few. But why are discourse markers so especially prone to language alternation? They are comparatively easy to integrate into a different language system because most discourse markers are free morphemes (Thomason and Kaufmann 1988), and they are usually situated at the sentence frame (Stolz and Stolz 1996). By using discourse markers in a second – probably prestigious – language, bilinguals reshape their A-system into a special bilingual register (Poplack 1980). Matras (forthcomimg) explains the ease with which discourse markers are affected by language alternation by emphasising their pragmatic function: bilingual speakers attempt to reduce the cognitive load by eliminating the choice between the two systems available to them. This is because the monitoring and directing tasks are cognitively more complex in that they cover a range of mental activities such as back-processing, planning ahead, anticipation and controlling reactions, interpreting gestures and intervening to dissuade the hearer from any undesired communicative activity.

If we return to the Low German data we can observe that there are hardly any Low German discourse markers left. It would appear that the whole class has been replaced by the younger speakers with Standard German elements, a process which is called fusion in the above-mentioned model.

Coming back to the question of what the listed contact phenomena actually mean for the Low German language, we can conclude that there was no example of differentiation in the transcript. Differentiation is the conscious use of language B elements within the system of language A, which means that the two systems are on an equal level.

The data do, however, show evidence of integration and convergence, both modes of language contact where language A is enhanced and enriched by language B-elements. Furthermore, the use of exclusively Standard German discourse markers can be taken as an example of fusion, a subconscious non-separation of two language systems.

These findings allow the conclusion that Low German is in the process of language change towards the dominant contact language, namely Standard German.

Bibliography

Borchling, Conrad (1928) 'Die westfälischen Einflüsse der niederdeutschen Sprache Ostfrieslands', *Niederdeutsches Jahrbuch* 54, 122–135

Ford, Marron C. (1997) 'Sprachkontakte in Mitteleuropa: Deutsch – Ostfriesisch', in: Steger, Hugo/Wiegand, Herbert Ernst (eds.) *Handbücher zur Sprach- und Kommunikationswissenschaft*, Volume 12.2, Berlin/New York: de Gruyter, 1786–1790

Kempen, Josef (1981) 'Ostfriesland – einst Teil des niederländischen Sprachraums', *Muttersprache* 91, 360–365

Kruse, Antje (1993) 'Zur Lage des Plattdeutschen im nordwestlichen Ostfriesland', *Quickborn* 83, 64–83

Lengen, Hajo van (1995) 'Bauernfreiheit und Häuptlingsherrlichkeit', in: Behre, Karl-Ernst/Lengen, Hajo van (eds.) *Ostfriesland. Geschichte und Gestalt einer Kulturlandschaft*, Aurich: Ostfriesische Landschaft, 113–134

Maas, Utz (1982) 'Der Wechsel vom Niederdeutschen zum Hochdeutschen in den norddeutschen Städten in der frühen Neuzeit', in: Cramer, Thomas (ed.) *Literatur und Sprache im historischen Prozeß*, Volume 2: *Sprache*, Tübingen: Niemeyer, 114–129

Maas, Utz (1986) 'Die "Modernisierung" der sprachlichen Verhältnisse in Norddeutschland seit dem späten Mittelalter', *Der Deutschunterricht* 4, 37–51

Maschler, Yael (1994) 'Metalanguaging and discourse markers in bilingual conversation', *Language in Society* 23, 325–366

Matras, Yaron (1998) 'Utterance modifiers and universals of grammatical borrowing', *Linguistics*, 36, 281–331

Matras, Yaron (forthcoming) 'Fusion and the cognitive basis for bilingual discourse markers', to appear in *International Journal of Bilingualism*

McAlister-Hermann, Judith (1982) 'Mestmaker contra Mestmaker: Ehescheidungsakten aus dem 17. Jh. als Beleg für die Umstellung auf Hochdeutsch in Osnabrück', in: Cramer, Thomas (ed.) *Literatur und Sprache im historischen Prozeß*, Volume 2: Sprache, Tübingen: Niemeyer, 130–149

Poplack, Shana (1980) 'Sometimes I'll start a sentence in Spanish y termino en español: toward a typology of code-switching', *Linguistics* 18, 581–618

Reershemius, Gertrud (1997) 'Niederdeutsch in Ostfriesland', *Osnabrücker Beiträge zur Sprachtheorie*, 54, 104–127

Remmers, Arend (1994) 'Zum ostfriesischen Niederdeutsch I', *Jahrbuch des Vereins für niederdeutsche Sprachforschung* 117, 130–168

Remmers, Arend (1995) 'Zum ostfriesichen Niederdeutsch II', *Jahrbuch des Vereins für niederdeutsche Sprachforschung* 118, 211–244

Remmers, Arend (1996) 'Zum ostfriesischen Niederdeutsch III', *Jahrbuch des Vereins für niederdeutsche Sprachforschung* 119, 140–177

Rooij, Vincent A. de (1996) *Cohesion Through Contrast: Discourse Structure in Shaba Swahili/French Conversation*, Amsterdam: IFOTT

Salmons, Joe (1990) 'Bilingual discourse marking: code switching, borrowing, and convergence in some German-American dialects', *Linguistics* 28, 453–492

Sankoff, Gillian/Thibauld, Pierette/Nagy, Naomi/Blondeau, Helene/Fonollosa, Marie-Odile/Gagnon, Lucie (1997) 'Variation in the use of discourse markers in a language contact situation', *Language Variation and Change* 9, 191–217

Scheuermann, Ulrich (1995) 'Sprache in Ostfriesland', in: Behre, Karl-Ernst & Lengen, Hajo van (eds.) *Ostfriesland. Geschichte und Gestalt einer Kulturlandschaft*, Aurich: Ostfriesische Landschaft, 341–352

Schiffrin, Deborah (1987) *Discourse markers*, Cambridge: Cambridge University Press

Smet, Gilbert de (1983) 'Niederländische Einflüsse im Niederdeutschen', in: Cordes, Gerhard/Möhn, Dieter (eds.) *Handbuch zur niederdeutschen Sprach- und Literaturwissenschaft*, Berlin: Schmidt, 730–761

Stolz, Christel/Stolz, Thomas (1996) 'Funktionswortentlehnung in Mesoamerika. Spanisch-amerindischer Sprachkontakt (Hispanoindiana II)' *Sprachtypologie und Universalienforschung* 49 (1), 86–123

Thomason, Sarah Grey/Terence Kaufman (1988) *Language contact, creolization and genetic linguistics*, Berkeley: University of California Press

GERALDINE HORAN AND CHRISTIAN FANDRYCH

First Steps Towards the Year Abroad: A Multi-Media Language and Culture Course

Some basic assumptions

Designing a course for the preparation of students for their third year abroad will in most cases prove to be a very challenging task. Where should we start? Can we identify common problem areas and general strategies to tackle them – or is each case different and requires different – and individual – solutions? Can students absorb what we teach them about the target context and its specific communicative requirements before they actually live in that target environment? How general or specific should the preparation be – should we prioritise general (intercultural) discourse competence, linguistic survival strategies for the respective institutional target contexts – or types and norms of discourse and text specific to seminars and lectures?

This paper presents and critically assesses a pilot language and culture course based at the Department of German, King's College London[1]. In this course, we have tried to address some of the above questions, based on three general assumptions:

1. Any preparatory course should put a strong emphasis on the linguistic (including the textual and discursive) aspects specific to the target context. Many technical, sociological and cultural differences and difficulties are in some way crystallised in text

1 The course was piloted in 1998–1999. Christian Fandrych co-ordinated the project and was responsible for the overall design and organisation of the course, while Geraldine Horan developed the syllabus, the specific course contents and materials and was the course teacher. In the light of our experiences, we have now designed a permanent course integrating various parts of the pilot project. The course was funded by the College Teaching Fund in 1998–1999.

forms, text norms, forms of oral discourse, etc., and they play a crucial role in helping the students to adapt to their respective environments.

2. A preparatory course should, wherever possible, give students the chance to experience a direct exchange with the target culture, more specifically, with peer groups working and living in the target context. This offers a host of advantages (but is not without its own difficulties, see below), including the opportunity to practise their language, to compare the different study systems and the experiences made with them, thus developing a comparative and intercultural dimension from the students' perspective.
3. The new media (in particular: email, the Internet, video-conferencing) allow for more forms of 'direct' exchange (whether we want to call it 'virtual' or not), and can play an important role in such a preparatory course – both as an interactive tool and as an information resource. To enable students to make use of such tools and forms of communication also entails teaching them important transferable skills they will find useful not only during their year abroad, but also for their professional careers.

While the idea of a direct exchange with a partner group as a preparatory exercise for an actual period abroad seems to be quite compelling, the practical, technical, methodological and organisational details often seem rather daunting. How exactly can we build such an element into a language course for the benefit of both groups? Which activities lend themselves best to what type of objective? Is such an exchange too much of a burden for students and teachers? What impact does the use of the new media have on course planning, teaching methodology, students' and teachers' activities, and educational discourse? We will address some of these issues in more detail below.

Before moving on to such questions of teaching methodology, it is necessary to provide a brief outline of the institutional background of the course, as well as of the general course objectives.

Institutional background

For a number of reasons, the Year Abroad is now a fully assessed, integral part of the degree course for most students of German at King's College (with the exception of a few joint honours programmes).

Students can select between four options for the Year Abroad:
- Studying as part of an exchange scheme (the department has 5 SOCRATES-links)
- Studying at an institution not as part of an existing exchange scheme
- Working as an assistant teacher abroad
- Finding a work placement in a private company (to be approved by the Department)[2].

While abroad, students have to write two essays on academic topics, one of which has to be written in German. Alternatively, those participating in an exchange scheme whilst abroad can produce *Seminararbeiten* to replace one or both of the essays. Additionally, all students have to take a practical language examination on their return, consisting of a text presentation and follow-up discussion, as well as a viewing comprehension. These pieces of assessment, therefore, all test elements that we could describe as '*allgemeine Wissenschafts-sprache*' ('ordinary academic language', see e.g. Ehlich 1995, 2000; Graefen 1999)[3]. 'Macro-level' differences such as different text and

2 In 1998–1999, 12 students opted for the first option, 3 for the second, 7 for the third and 1 for the last option. The number of students who take the first option has increased since the European Studies degree has been fully integrated into King's in 1999. European Studies students taking the German option will also spend their year abroad under an exchange scheme at a German university. For more information about pathways and regulations, see our departmental homepage at www.kcl.ac.uk/kis/schools/hums/german/top.html.

3 The concept of *Allgemeine Wissenschaftssprache* reflects the fact that, apart from the very specialised language of each discipline, there is a pool of linguistic expressions and devices common to all disciplines – irrespective of the science/humanities distinction. Mostly by way of metaphorisation, these expressions have experienced semantic shift and modifications to their typical

discourse norms and forms also play an important role in the year abroad, not just because they impact upon students' ability to function in a different academic context, but also because they constitute expressions of potentially different academic discourse and text traditions, reflecting to a certain degree systemic differences between the two countries.

It is these linguistic, pragmatic and cultural aspects for which the pilot language and culture course should prepare students, whereas the more technical aspects (application procedures, accommodation, health insurance etc.) are dealt with outside the course. While the pilot course was intended to be of benefit to all students, no matter what their plans for the year abroad were, it clearly focused on the target context of those studying abroad. There is a number of reasons why this should be so: apart from the fact that the majority of students actually opt for going abroad as students, it is this environment which seems to be the most complex and often problematic, for many well-known reasons (the mass character of the university system in the German-speaking countires, the lack of a tutor system, the different formats of seminars and lectures etc.). The course was nevertheless open to – and was attended by – students who were preparing to become assistant teachers.

The course was therefore intended to address the following core areas:

- similar and different text genres, cultural and linguistic norms and conventions in academic style (academic language culture) in the target culture;
- specific forms of study and related study skills;
- the institutional and cultural background of these forms of learning and teaching, i.e. the university system *from a student's*

---

collocations in order to adapt to the different purposes of academic discourse. Examples are typical 'speech act verbs', such as *to show, to point out, zeigen, aufzeigen*, with their specific collocations and specialised meanings; certain 'stylistic' conventions, e.g. the use of 'pseudo-agentive constructions' in English (*this article discusses* ...) and passive constructions containing modal verbs in German (*in diesem Artikel soll... diskutiert werden*), the language-specific use of deictic and phoric procedures, etc. For a contrastive analysis of some of these devices see Fandrych and Graefen (forthcoming).

perspective, the practical and personal implications of such a study system.

The following types of texts and patterns of discourse are relevant here[4]:

a) Academic texts (handbooks, dictionaries, monographs, academic articles, etc.): developing reading/comprehension strategies, awareness of language-specific forms of text-organisation on a macro- and micro-level (text norms, text structure, style)
b) 'study texts' and 'study discourse': *Seminararbeiten, Referate, Protokolle, Thesenpapiere, Seminardiskussion* (German context) vs. *essays, exam papers, class presentations* (British context): differing text types and types of academic discourse; text norms and text evaluation; step-by-step guide to the production of study texts; practising relevant language skills, etc.
c) related study skills: bibliography search; reading skills, note taking, summarising, drafting, presenting, discussion skills
d) 'academic style', language-specific ways of organising texts, text commenting, typical collocations, forms of non-agentive style, etc.

Recent research has shown that academic texts and academic discourse vary along disciplinary, but also cultural and linguistic lines, and that text conventions, preferences of text organisation, text commentary and reader-orientation are far from being universal, although the general social purpose of academic communication is comparable across cultures[5]. There is a great need for more linguistic investigation into these differences, not least to enable us to develop better preparatory language courses and to equip our students with the knowledge and proficiency necessary for studying and working in an academic environment abroad[6].

---

4 See Göttert (1999), Jakobs (1997), Mangasser-Wahl (1997), Püschel (1997), Sandig (1997), amongst others.

5 See Clyne (1987), Fandrych and Graefen (forthcoming), and Hufeisen (1998), amongst others.

6 For empirical investigations of German instructional discourse at university level, see Schlabach (1999), Wiesmann (1999).

Of course, it is impossible to achieve a thorough preparation of students for all these aspects in a weekly two-hour language course. What we hoped to achieve, though, was to sensitise students to these kinds of differences, to equip them with some strategies of how to cope with the multiple challenges that lay ahead of them, and to offer them the opportunity to start practising some key skills, both on a 'macro-' (text and discourse genre) and 'micro-level' (text organisation, academic style, use of specific linguistic devices, etc.).

Exchange element

We organised the exchange with a group of students of English at Martin Luther University, Halle-Wittenberg[7]. By a fortunate coincidence they also succeeded in securing funding for this project, which even provided us with the opportunity to organise mutual visits, which proved to be a very motivating element of the course. The Halle students attended a *Hauptseminar* in English linguistics ('Linguistics, Email and the Internet'), starting slightly after the beginning of our term, and ending six weeks before the end of our second term. We synchronised our timetable in order to allow for video-conferencing exchanges to be held during the normal sessions of the course. The course required intensive planning and co-ordination between the two institutions, including a detailed definition of the phases and stages of the different exchange elements, as well as a negotiation of the topics to be treated. A significant difference between the two groups of students arose from the fact that, while our course was a language and culture course (offered on a voluntary basis), the Halle seminar was a credit bearing linguistics seminar, where students had to write coursework on linguistic topics. These slightly diverging interests had to be taken into account, which also meant that both groups had to make some compromises when it came to course contents and activities.

7 The organiser of the exchange at Halle was Professor Eija Ventola, *Institut für Anglistik und Amerikanistik*, Martin Luther Universität Halle Wittenberg. For an analysis and evaluation of the Halle project, see Ventola et al. (1999).

The multi-media language and culture course

In the following we would like to provide an outline of key aspects of the course and multi-media components, before moving on to discuss briefly some advantages and problems in using the new media in language teaching. We will conclude by evaluating the results and experiences of the pilot course and by putting forward suggestions for the further development of such a course.

The pilot course consisted of one two-hour class per week over two semesters, which was supplemented by two hours of self-study in the computer centre each week to enable students to communicate via email and complete tasks set during the class. The language of spoken and written communication throughout was German, apart from video-conferencing sessions, when both German and English were employed by participants. An outline of the course structure is given in the appendix.

Multi-media components

Email tandem

The email tandem component was designed to enable students to create a range of texts on specific topics in German, and to benefit from feedback, including corrections and comments on language, style and content, from their native speaker partners. The participants created the texts either during or immediately after each class and emailed them to their partner(s), and the responses received were discussed in the following session. The written activities included:

1. Composing a draft of a homepage in which the participants introduced themselves, their studies, hobbies and interests.
2. Constructing a guide to student life in London, providing information and advice on student accommodation, enrolling at a university, culture and entertainment possibilities. The homepages were to be published in final format on a students' website.

3. A critical analysis of the coverage of the 1998 German Elections in the German and British media respectively.
4. A summary of comments, responses and experiences arising from the video-conferencing sessions.

Before embarking on the email tandem exchanges, students were given some guidance on how to correct and amend partner texts. It was suggested that corrections on grammatical or stylistic points should be imbedded within the text itself, in upper case, for example, and students were encouraged to add comments after the partner text, consisting of general explanations of style, or of idiomatic expressions or particular collocational patterns.

Video-conferences

The video-conferencing element took place over six sessions. In the introductory classroom session, we familiarised students with the form and functions of the video-conference, and provided some practical guidelines on video-conferencing etiquette, based on information taken from previous studies on the subject, such as Goodfellow et al. (1996)[8]. As students were supposed to hold *Referate*, we also focused on the practical and linguistic characteristics of the German *Referat* as an academic and communicative form, using extracts from Bünting et al. (1996), Kruse (1998), and contributions in Jakobs and Knorr (1997).

The first video-conference familiarised participants with the technical and practical aspects of the medium, and gave them the opportunity to introduce themselves and ask questions about student life in King's College and Halle. During the remaining conferences, each student gave a brief presentation on a scholarly topic of their

8 A sizeable amount of information can also be found on the WWW, see for example, the Language Centre's website on video-conferencing at University College London (www.ucl.ac.uk/language-centre/dvc/dvc.htm); the SIMA Project (Support Initiative for Multimedia Applications) (www.man.ac.uk/mvc/SIMA/video4/toc.html), and the video-conferencing project involving Northern Illinois University, the University of Illinois Urbana-Champaign, and Illinois State University (http://coe.cedu.niu.edu/lc/vcp).

choice. Each *Referat* was followed by questions on content, and comments on delivery, grammar and style from all participants (students were informed in advance that they would be expected to give their reactions to other presentations). The individual *Referate* were then discussed and analysed in more detail during a feedback session in the classroom, when we viewed the contributions once again on video.

Classroom/Internet sessions

The classroom and Internet sessions concentrated on developing the necessary knowledge and skills required to function fully within the German-speaking academic environment. We worked in particular towards developing an understanding of the structure of German-speaking school and higher education systems; towards developing practical and technical study skills (outlined in the introduction to this article); and towards familiarisation with the characteristics of academic writing and communication skills, with a view to producing them successfully. In each of these components, we moved from theoretical descriptions and discussions to practical exercises, and throughout, the comparative and intercultural dimension played an important role. A socio-political component was also incorporated into the classroom and Internet sessions, which explored the German political system, the role of the media, focusing in particular on the German elections. The following outline, however, focuses specifically on the academic tasks and activities.

Structure of university systems in the German-speaking countries

Here the Internet provided an easily accessible, authentic source of information. Students accessed a German university webpage, which enabled them to become familiar with relevant vocabulary and expressions for organisational terms, academic faculties, subjects, and types of courses. As a practical exercise, students were asked to find out details about certain seminars using university webpages, and to summarise and report the information gathered to their peers.

Academic study skills

We began by identifying study skills required in the home institution and contrasted them with the possible requirements of the host university, using information from Bünting et al. (1996) and Kruse (1998). Students were also given practical information on useful bibliographies, databases and aspects of research methodology. This was followed again by guided exercises, in which students located certain titles in university libraries through the Internet, compiled a practice bibliography, and read and summarised a scholarly article.

Academic writing and communication skills

The first stage of this process was to identify the main characteristics of academic writing in German in terms of structure, layout and presentation. Examples of actual *Hausarbeiten* and *Seminararbeiten,* taken from a range of disciplines, were downloaded from the Internet for students to analyse. We discussed formal, stylistic and rhetorical characteristics of the texts, and students made comparisons with their own academic written work. Students were then given language exercises practising the use of the passive, nominal style, extended epithets, the subjunctive, modal verbs, and practising structuring arguments and creating cohesive texts.

Advantages and potential problems of the new media in language teaching

We would now like to focus briefly on the advantages and problems concerning the new media which reflect the specific experiences of the pilot course, but which also are relevant to other language teaching environments.

Advantages

Authenticity: there may be some doubts about whether multi-media creates a 'pseudo-authenticity' in language use, and whether email and video-conferencing create a virtual communicative environment which could lull students into a false sense of security or promote over-confidence in their assessment of certain target language situations. However, it has been our experience that students are able enough to distinguish between 'virtual' and face-to-face communication; and we would argue that as virtual communication becomes an ever more integral part of our personal and professional lives, the ability to communicate in, and move between, 'virtual' and face-to-face environments will prove to be an essential skill (Warschauer and Healey 1998).

Accessibility/immediacy: the Internet allows teachers and students rapid access to texts and information which would previously have proved difficult or even impossible to obtain, seen, for example, in our use of *Hausarbeiten* downloaded from the Internet. Also, the immediacy in spoken communication afforded by the 'virtual visit' in video-conferencing, as previously mentioned, cannot be paralleled other than through face-to-face communication.

Variety of sources/information: students can experience the target language in spoken and written form through email partnerships and informational texts on the Internet, and as participants in video-conferencing. Thus the teacher's role is not that of sole provider, source, or even 'filter' for target language output and information, and this expansion in sources can prove challenging, but ultimately also enriching to the teacher and student alike (Breindl 1997; Warschauer and Healey 1998).

Learner autonomy: through the email partnership, the burden of responsibility is on the student to communicate, receive and process information successfully. In order for students to benefit fully from the autonomy granted by email tandems, they first have to be trained in the skills involved in planning and communicating on an individual level, and this initial step should not be overlooked (Little and Ushioda 1998; Wolff 1998).

Learner motivation: the so-called 'novelty effect' for students, and the opportunity to develop learner autonomy are often seen as motivating factors (Breindl 1997). Some students who have considerable experience in using the Internet, email, and computing facilities in general (in some cases surpassing that of the teacher!) may be excited and challenged by the different learning environment created by computers and video-conferencing (Warschauer and Healey 1998). In particular, the linguistically more confident and more extrovert students may welcome the opportunity to 'perform' by giving a presentation via video-conference, for example.

Potential Problems

Time management: adapting oneself to the use of the Internet, email and/or video-conferencing, and devising how to integrate the new media successfully in language teaching can be time-consuming, and as has been stated in previous research, the teacher must consider to what extent the use of multi-media tools will actually enhance the learning environment, and will not merely involve substituting the keyboard for the pen (Breindl 1997). In classes where the teacher intends to employ the new media, s/he has to be flexible and well-prepared enough to have alternative strategies prepared in case of a breakdown in accessing Internet sites, or problems establishing contact, pictures and sound during a video-conference.

Teacher control: using the Internet, the teacher is also faced with the question of how to control and modify the texts accessed by students. Editing, shortening, or manipulating authentic texts which are accessed and viewed during classes is not possible (Richter 1998). One could argue, however, that this is, in fact, of advantage and constitutes a useful practical experience, as unadulterated access to a wealth of texts reflects the kind of situations students are likely to encounter in a learning environment abroad, where printed and electronic academic texts will not necessarily be specifically selected and altered to suit their levels of ability and needs as non-native speakers.

In two-way video-conferencing sessions led by a teacher at the home and remote sites, co-ordinating proceedings and contributions can often prove problematic. An agreed agenda is needed, which maps out when each teacher will lead proceedings, request contributions, solicit questions or encourage feedback, thereby ensuring that the session does not become disjointed.

Lack of reciprocity: the principle of reciprocity in tandem language learning, as outlined in Little and Brammerts (1996), (see also Little and Ushioda 1998), is central to a successful relationship and learning experience. If this does not occur, and there is an obvious imbalance in the input between partners, or indeed, the level of ability in the foreign language differs significantly, then the tandem relationship will be hindered by feelings of confusion or resentment among the participants, and the tandem partnership will rapidly disintegrate.

Learner demotivation: research into language learning has shown that different learner types respond to different learning activities. Some students will feel threatened and inhibited by the experience, before they even come to expressing themselves in spoken or written form in the foreign language. Yet this is not to say that students cannot develop an interest and confidence in using the multi-media precisely through language courses.

Evaluation of the results of the pilot course

Of all the multi-media components, the email tandem exchange proved the most problematic component of the course. The imbalance in the number of participants, and the fact that the King's College students were assigned two or more partners weakened the success rate for secure one-to-one tandem partnerships. Because most of the email texts were created outside the course, monitoring the frequency and content of the messages proved difficult. Also, as mentioned above, the differing requirements of the courses (voluntary versus credit bearing) meant that King's College students were generally less motivated to spend their own time responding to partner texts and preferred to communicate on a more informal level. In the case of respective learning objectives, whereas Halle students required primarily linguistic and stylistic feedback on their texts, King's

College students seemed to place great importance on obtaining practical, cultural information from their partners, and thus were more content with communicating informally. In an evaluation of an email tandem project between students of German at Trinity College Dublin and students of English at the Ruhr-Universität Bochum, David Little and Ema Ushioda (1998) reported that the low level of successful regular partnerships proved a problem in the tandem learning component, and suggested that in future, email partnerships should be more closely monitored and regulated. The experience from the pilot course at King's College echoes these conclusions to a large extent[9].

On a personal level, however, informal contact between the students was successful, and several of the email partnerships still endure. The email contact did provide important examples of cultural and pragmatic differences in communication, for example, with regard to the perceived levels of politeness. To mention one – rather trivial – example: in an exchange where, in her introductory homepage, a British student asked her partner if she had ever been to the 'Love Parade' festival in Berlin, she received the reply that the partner had never been to this parade, as this kind of event did not appeal to her at all. This is an anecdotal, but nevertheless useful example of a cross-cultural misunderstanding, as the British partner interpreted the response as hostile and therefore 'face-threatening'. Such experiences enabled students to consider contrasts in aspects of youth culture and student life in Britain and Germany (Woodin 1997; Richter 1998). Thus, the email partnership can serve as the introductory step in communicating with native speaker peers, and can prepare students for the problems in communication which could possibly arise – all within a certain 'sanctuary of the classroom' (Rösler 2000).

The video-conferencing sessions were a very successful part of the multi-media component. Video-conferencing provided an ideal medium for mini-presentations and feedback from the home and remote sites, and gave participants the opportunity to see and hear native speakers in a real-time, synchronous communicative situation. In the future, video-conferencing could even be extended to include a

9 See also Warschauer and Healey (1998).

sample lecture from a German-speaking university, to familiarise students with different types of courses and spoken academic discourse in a lecture format. However, video-conferencing sessions do require careful preparation and even trial sessions. During video-conferencing sessions, free, unguided discussions and spontaneous exchanges between home and remote groups are difficult to achieve. Predictably, it is often the more confident students who contribute most frequently, whilst other students feel inhibited by the medium as a whole, and are less willing to contribute spontaneously. Just as with any other learning environment, it is therefore important to devise activities which ensure the active input of as many students as possible (Goodfellow et al. 1996).

What was achieved in the pilot course through the classroom and computing sessions was to *sensitise* students to different forms of academic texts, and to provide limited training and practice in related study skills and in employing 'academic style' in their academic work in German. The course incorporated an ambitious range of topics and activities designed to prepare students on linguistic, pragmatic and cultural levels for their year abroad, and consequently, the opportunities for students to produce substantial pieces of academic writing in German were limited. Given the differing academic writing skills demanded by German and British higher education systems, much time was justifiably devoted to introducing students to the core areas of academic discourse traditions and study skills in German. The understanding of differing traditions is essential to being able to produce an authentic academic text in German, and from our experience, this generally constitutes a large gap in students' knowledge. The majority of students are unaware that such (considerable) differences exist, and thus the step to producing an assessed formal piece of writing in the foreign language is a difficult one. Davies (1997), whilst providing useful exercises in aiding students to create competent, cohesive texts in German, nevertheless adheres to the form and style of the British essay, and includes exercises practising the construction of paragraphs using key sentences, for example. As such, students are trained to produce texts which adhere to the requirements demanded by schools and higher education institutions in Britain. The hybrid texts which result from this combination are acceptable with the British system, yet do not bring us much closer to the German text norms, and as such these texts have little validity in the German-speaking system (Hufeisen 1998). The awareness of differing academic textual formats and styles is, of course, not only relevant for students of foreign languages, but has implications for international academic discourse in general, as Clyne (1987) has shown.

In course evaluation forms, the responses from the students were overwhelmingly positive. Interestingly, students were in general very enthusiastic about the email component of the course, despite the irregularity of communication on an organised, academic level. Students also remarked that, through the video-conferencing sessions, they felt that they had 'got to know' their counterparts in Halle before meeting them in person through the reciprocal visits. Students praised the benefits of being able to communicate with native speakers on a regular basis, and in particular, welcomed the opportunity to present an aspect of their academic work in German to a native speaker audience. Students stated that their knowledge about life in Germany and the year abroad had greatly increased, and that they had acquired a more in-depth awareness and understanding of the academic tasks required of them in a German-speaking university. These are, of course, highly subjective and personal judgements from the students. Once the academic writing course has become established, actual linguistic progress in German could be monitored through the assessment of written work, language exercises and class presentations.

Conclusions and suggestions for further development

Despite certain practical and organisational difficulties which arose, such a course is undoubtedly useful in facilitating authentic language practice, in allowing contact with native speakers and in providing rapid access to a range of target language texts. There are without doubt limitations in the level of authenticity which can be achieved: the use of email, video-conferencing and the Internet cannot mimic or replace face-to-face contact in the foreign country, but they do offer an important extension of traditional classroom teaching and resources, and constitute an intermediate step in the familiarisation process (Breindl 1997). A future course could focus on developing academic writing/study skills from the outset, through a series of written assignments, which would gradually build up students' written competence. Here, an email tandem could play an integrated and tightly controlled function, with students sending drafts of their written academic texts to their partners for corrections, which would then be overseen and monitored by the course leader.

A preparatory course should work towards reducing the time it takes students to become familiar and at ease with the new language community. The pilot project has also revealed that preparatory training can help students to make positive and informed choices about where and what they study in the year abroad. One must, of course, also be aware of possible dangers inherent in wishing to prevent or diminish 'culture shock' prior to residence abroad. Given the complex interchange between practical, personal and intellectual factors which affect the success of the year abroad for the individual, it is well-nigh impossible and even undesirable to anticipate fully the kind of situations the individual student will encounter in the foreign country. One must at all costs avoid generalising aspects of student life and experiences in Germany or reinforcing cultural stereotypes. Modern Languages departments are becoming increasingly aware of the need to make residence abroad a worthwhile experience for students, as evidenced by projects such as the National Residence Abroad Database (University of Portsmouth), Learning and Residence Abroad (Oxford Brookes), and the Inter-culture Project (Lancaster University). From the King's College pilot project, we conclude that a multi-media preparatory language and culture course should aim to raise students' awareness and understanding of possible differences between home and host university systems, so as to ensure that any new experiences are not automatically interpreted as negative by students. On a linguistic level, the course should aim to encourage students to integrate into the German-speaking academic environment, and therefore to function as active participants within it. We are confident that email, the Internet and video-conferencing can help in achieving these aims, provided that their role is well defined and is made transparent to both students and teachers. Thus, with careful planning and implementation, these forms of the media can prove to be invaluable teaching and learning tools.

Appendix: Outline of course structure

Session	Topic	Media	Activity	Objectives
1	Course introduction	C/room *	Discussion of plans/ expectations of the year abroad.	Familiarising students with aims and objectives of course.
2	Introduction to university websites.	Internet	Discussion of GB/German systems. Information searches, translation. Reading comprehension. Discussion of registers and styles.	Promoting understanding of German-speaking university systems. Building useful organisational, institutional vocabulary.
3	Textual, technical features of personal homepages.	Email Internet	Practice in using email. Writing a draft of a homepage.	Understanding and employing different styles and registers.
4-5	University systems in German-speaking countries.	C/room Internet	Analysing informational texts. Reading comprehension; summarising texts, vocabulary exercises.	Familiarising students with academic vocabulary.
6	Guide to student life (KC).	Internet Email	Describing aspects of student life at King's College London.	Creating informational texts.
7	Guide to communicating via video-conference.	C/room VC	Practical advice on video-conferencing format and etiquette. Introductory video-conference.	Familiarising students with the VC medium. Developing spoken communication skills in German.

8	Exchange visit. Joint session: KC/Halle.	C/room	Comparing and contrasting German/British university systems.	Practising spoken skills, explaining, discussing, expressing opinions.
9-10	German/British political systems. Media coverage of German Elections.	C/room	Analysing, discussing newspaper texts and video-clips.	Sensitising students to cultural, political background, developing awareness of media language.
11-15	Presenting a *Referat.*	VC C/room Email	Individual *Referate*, questions and comments. Feedback on results.	Practising academic communication skills.
16-18	Skills for studying in German-speaking university systems.	C/room Internet	Literature searches. Compiling and presenting a bibliography. Note-taking. Summarising extracts from scholarly literature.	Developing and/or practising practical academic skills.
19-22	Academic writing.	C/room Internet	Discussing linguistic and stylistic features of *Hausarbeiten.* Grammar exercises on aspects of formal written German.	Familiarising students with academic discourse, text-types, improving written linguistic competence.

* 'C/room' stands for 'Classroom'

Table 1: Course outline

Bibliography

Breindl, Eva (1997) 'DaF goes Internet: Neue Entwicklungen in Deutsch als Fremdsprache', *Deutsche Sprache* 25/4, 289–342

Bünting, Karl-Dietrich/Bitterlich, Axel/Pospiech, Ulrike (eds.) (1996) *Schreiben im Studium. Ein Trainingsprogramm*, Berlin: Cornelsen Scriptor

Clyne, Michael (1987) 'Cultural differences in the organization of academic texts', *Journal of Pragmatics* 11, 211–247

Davies, Winifred V. (1997) *Essay-writing in German. A Students' Guide*, Manchester and New York: MUP

Ehlich, Konrad (1995) 'Die Lehre der deutschen Wissenschaftssprache: sprachliche Strukturen, didaktische Desiderate', in: Kretzenbacher, H.L./Weinrich, H. (eds.), *Linguistik der Wissenschaftssprache*, Berlin, New York: de Gruyter, 325–351

Ehlich, Konrad (2000) 'Deutsch als Wissenschaftssprache für das 21. Jahrhundert', *German as a Foreign Language* 1/1, www.gfl-journal.com

Fandrych, Christian/Graefen, Gabriele (forthcoming) 'Text-commenting devices in English and German Academic Texts'

Göttert, Karl-Heinz (1999) *Kleine Schreibschule für Studierende*, Munich: Fink.

Goodfellow, Robin/Jeffreys, Ingrid/Miles, Terry/Shirra, Tim (1996) 'Face-to-face language learning at a distance? A study of a videoconference try-out', *ReCALL* 8/2, 5–16

Graefen, Gabriele (1999) 'Wie formuliert man wissenschaftlich?', in: Barkowski, H./Wolff, A., (eds.), *Materialien Deutsch als Fremdsprache 52*, Regensburg

Hufeisen, Britta (1998) 'Schreibenlernen an der Universität? Schreiblernangebote im Bereich Deutsch als Fremdsprache an Sprachenzentren deutscher Universitäten und an einigen kanadischen Germanistikabteilungen', *Zeitschrift für Interkulturellen Fremdsprachenunterricht* 1/3, 25 pp., www.ualberta.ca/~german/ejournal/house.htm

Jakobs, E. M./Knorr, D. (eds.) (1997) *Schreiben in den Wissenschaften,* Frankfurt am Main: Lang

Jakobs, Eva Maria (1997) 'Lesen und Textproduzieren. Source reading als typisches Merkmal wissenschaftlicher Textproduktion', in: Jakobs, E.M./Knorr, D. (eds.), 75–90

Kruse, Otto (1998) *Keine Angst vor dem leeren Blatt. Ohne Schreibblockaden durchs Studium*, Frankfurt am Main: Campus

Little, David/Brammerts, Helmut (eds.) (1996) *A guide to language learning in tandem via the Internet*, CLCS Occasional Paper No. 46, Dublin: Trinity College, Centre for Language and Communication Studies

Little, David/Ushioda, Ema (1998) 'Designing, implementing and evaluating a project in tandem language learning via e-mail', *ReCALL* 10/1, 95–101.

Mangasser-Wahl, Martina (1997) 'Saarbrücker Schreibtutorien', in: Jakobs, E. M./Knorr, D. (eds.), 183–192

Püschel, Ulrich (1997) 'Überlegungen zu einer Anleitung zum Schreiben von Hausarbeiten', in: Jakobs, E. M./Knorr, D. (eds.), 193–200

Richter, Regina (1998) 'Interkulturelles Lernen via Internet?', *Zeitschrift für Interkulturellen Fremdsprachenunterricht* [Online], 3/2, 20 pp. Available at: www.ualberta.ca/~german/ejournal/richter1.htm

Rösler, Dietmar (2000) 'Foreign-language learning with the new media: between the sanctuary of the classroom and the open terrain of natural language acquisition', *German as a Foreign Language* 1/1, www.gfl-journal.com.

Sandig, Barbara (1997) 'Formulieren und Textmuster. Am Beispiel von Wissenschaftstexten', in: Jakobs, E. M./Knorr, D. (eds.), 25–44

Schlabach, Joachim (1999) 'Deutschsprachige Wirtschaftsvorlesungen aus fremdsprachendidaktischer Sicht', in: Barkowski, H./Wolff, A. (eds.), *Materialien DaF 52*, Regensburg, 255–268

Ventola, Eija/Spillner, Sandra/Hezcko, Martin (1999) *Students Go On-Line and Practise Videoconferencing*, Projektbericht, Martin Luther Universität Halle/ Wittenberg: Institut für Anglistik und Amerikanistik

Warschauer, Mark/Healey, Deborah (1998) 'Computers and language learning: an overview', *Language Teaching* 31, 57–71

Wiesmann, Bettina (1999) 'Universitäre Unterrichtsdiskurse – Strukturen und Anforderungen an Studierende', in: Bührig, K./Grießhaber, W. (eds.), *Sprache in der Hochschullehre, Osnabrücker Beiträge zur Sprachtheorie* 59, 13–42

Wolff, Dieter (1998) 'Neue Technologien und fremdsprachliches Lernen. Versuch einer Bestandsaufnahme (II)', *Deutsch als Fremdsprache. Zeitschrift zur Theorie und Praxis des Deutschunterrichts für Ausländer*, 35/4, 205–211

Woodin, Jane (1997) 'Email tandem learning and the communicative curriculum', *ReCALL* 9/1, 22–33

WINIFRED V. DAVIES

A Critique of Some Common Assumptions in German Work on Language and Education

Introduction

This paper was inspired by earlier research amongst teachers in parts of central Germany, which established that the informants had a relatively low level of sociolinguistic awareness (Davies in press, a, b). It has also been influenced by the work of British linguists like Romy Clark, Norman Fairclough, Roz Ivanič and Marilyn Martin-Jones, who have contributed a great deal to the debate about language awareness in language education, and have developed the concept of 'critical language awareness' (CLA) (see, for example, Fairclough 1992). Having investigated the sociolinguistic awareness of the practitioners, I decided to turn my attention to the theorists and policy-makers and examine to what extent their pronouncements and prescriptions are based upon what advocates of CLA would regard as contentious theoretical assumptions about language, or have been influenced by 'critical' theories of language and language education. The material which will be examined comes from writings by academics and from school curricula in Baden-Württemberg and Rheinland-Pfalz. I shall discuss a selection of what I consider to be contentious assumptions about language and linguistic variation, explaining why I think they are so.

Assumption 1: Dialect is a problem

Regional non-standard dialects[1] are often referred to as a 'problem'. Two examples serve to illustrate this: (i) Besch et al. (1983) contains

1 The German term *Dialekt* is usually, but not always, reserved by linguists for the basal variety in a locality (*Ortsdialekt*), although lay people often use it to refer to

two articles: 'Probleme des Dialektsprechers beim Erwerb der deutschen Standardsprache' and 'Probleme des Dialektsprechers beim Fremdsprachenerwerb'. Ironically, in the latter article Viereck concludes that sometimes dialect-speakers are at an advantage when learning a foreign language, although the title gives a very different impression; (ii) In the *Lehrplan Deutsch. Gymnasium. Rheinland-Pfalz. 1984,* we find that one of the topics from which the tenth class has to choose is 'Der deutsche Sprachraum und *die sich daraus ergebenden Probleme*' (my emphasis). Recently, there have been some attempts to replace this concept with the notion of 'Dialekt als Chance', e.g. Klotz and Sieber write:

> In den siebziger Jahren standen die Diskussionen um Dialektdidaktik weitgehend unter der Forderung, die Nachteile, welche Dialektsprecher gegenüber den anderen Schülern hätten, mit unterrichtlichen Arrangements zu kompensieren bis hin zur radikalen Forderung der 'Ersetzung des Dialekts durch die Einheitssprache' [...]. Demgegenüber sind in die neuere Diskussion Aspekte hinzugekommen, die Dialektvoraussetzungen nicht einfach negativ als Handicap bestimmen, sondern auch nach Chancen und Bildungsmöglichkeiten suchen, die mit der Verfügungskompetenz über dialektale Register verbunden sind. (1993: 8)

Non-standard dialect is to be seen as a resource rather than as a problem. However, both views are more problematic than may at first appear.

The first view, dialect as a problem, does not always differentiate clearly between dialect as a social problem and dialect as a linguistic problem. Neither does it make clear that research has shown that dialect is not problematic for all speakers in the same way: as Rosenberg points out: 'Nicht, *ob* jemand Dialekt spricht ist also das Problem, sondern ob jemand *nur* (oder fast nur) Dialekt spricht!' (1993:24).

---

non-standard varieties that are closer to standard than traditional rural dialect (what some linguists call *großräumige Regionalsprachen*). Linguists normally label the variety space between standard German and *Dialekt* as *Umgangssprache*, which is usually translated rather vaguely as 'colloquial speech', but most works on *Dialektdidaktik* make some reference to these colloquial varieties as well as the traditional dialect. In this article the term '(regional) non-standard dialect' will refer to *Dialekt* and varieties of *Umgangssprache*.

It has often been assumed that speakers of regional non-standard varieties have problems mastering standard German, especially its written realisation, because of interference from the dialect: there is some truth in that and practitioners ought to be aware of the potential difficulties faced by dialect-speakers, but some of the problems are not peculiar to them. According to Ammon, 'Die Einheitssprache läßt sich unmittelbarer und leichter in die geschriebene Sprache umsetzen' (1982:36), but Barbour (1987:234) shows that not even the speech of highly educated and socially successful middle-class speakers is synonymous with standard written German. Rosenberg's work on Berlin is also relevant in this context. He found that standard-speaking pupils from Hanover as well as dialect-speaking Berlin pupils made mistakes in a test dictation and he concluded that 'Der Bereich, der unter den Verschlußlauten am häufigsten zu Fehlern führt, ist die Stimmhaftigkeitskorrelation [...]. Diese Schwierigkeiten sind allgemeiner umgangssprachlicher Natur' (1986:222). We must therefore differentiate between errors in written German that are due to interference from regional non-standard dialects and those that are due to interference from spoken forms of German.

The negative evaluation of non-standard linguistic varieties by some sections of German society can have repercussions for speakers of those varieties. Often attempts are made to present these evaluations as linguistic ones, which seems to lend them an air of neutrality, i.e. it has been argued that dialect should be eradicated in order to facilitate the learning of standard German. The view that dialect should be eradicated is not voiced very often today, but the use of non-standard varieties is still acceptable only in certain situations, not those which are prestigious: formal, public, official[2]. The use of non-standard dialect in such situations (including school) can still bring sanctions with it, so pupils quickly learn (and are taught) that language varies and that certain varieties are more desirable than others. This is usually explained in terms of the demands of

2 While acknowledging that prestige is not unidimensional and that the survival of non-standard varieties means that they too enjoy a certain prestige amongst their speakers, one has to allow that the domains associated with power are, on the whole, domains of standard German.

appropriacy, but the power relations between different varieties and their speakers are rarely discussed, and the reason quoted most often to account for the convention of using standard German in public/formal/official situations is its greater communicative radius, i.e. its greater intelligibility. In my opinion, however, this is a contestable notion to which I shall return later.

It must be stressed that I am not arguing that children whose vernacular is a regional non-standard dialect never face problems, but we have to be far more specific when describing those problems. As Wagner (1987:131) says, referring to a study in Bavaria, there is no evidence that speakers of non-standard dialect *per se* have problems at school: a correlation between use of a non-standard dialect and a low mark in German was only established for pupils who used broad non-standard dialect forms even in formal situations. Moreover, Viereck (1983:1494–5) shows that speakers of some Austrian non-standard dialects could be at an advantage when learning English because of certain phonological/phonetic similarities, and we know that *all* pupils have problems learning to write standard German (see Barbour 1987). Speakers of regional non-standard dialects may face problems, but it must be made clearer that many of these problems are social not linguistic problems; they are problems of attitudes, which are products of specific historical and social contexts. It is not therefore legitimate, in my opinion, to present dialect-speakers as people with problems *per se*.

The concept of 'Dialekt als Chance' occurs relatively often in the recent academic literature. It usually means two things: (i) regional non-standard dialect as a means of expressing one's identity: it gives information about a person's geographical and social background and can be used to show solidarity with others from the same background; (ii) multilingualism as a valuable resource: speakers of a regional non-standard dialect have an additional register, which is more appropriate in some situations than the standard (cf. Bücherl 1993:72–6). It is usually assumed that the speaker's repertoire also includes standard. This is a rather one-sided view of 'Dialekt als Chance' since there is never any suggestion that monoglot speakers of standard German should acquire a non-standard dialect in order to expand their repertoires.

Assumption 2: Mutual intelligibility is only secured by means of standard German

This is frequently cited as a reason why people need to learn standard German, e.g. by Bayer:

> Die Fähigkeit zum *verständlichen*, präzisen und situationsangemessenen expliziten Ausdruck von Gedanken und zu entsprechendem *Verstehen* ist eine der Voraussetzungen für die Teilnahme an politischen und kulturellen Prozessen, die in einem demokratischen Staat unabdingbar notwendig ist, und nicht zuletzt auch für die sprachliche Bewältigung einer Vielzahl alltäglicher Situationen und für berufliches Fortkommen.
>
> Eine überregionale, syntaktisch und semantisch ausgebaute Standardsprache ist Voraussetzung für die in einem pluralistischen demokratischen Staat notwendige Kritik und *Verständigung* zwischen den einzelnen Gruppierungen (Altersgruppen, Parteien, Verbänden, usw.).
>
> Wenn es auch außer Zweifel steht, daß Dialekte, Schicht- und Gruppensprachen v.a. wichtige emotionale und beziehungsstiftende Funktionen haben und der Standardsprache in speziellen Teilbereichen sogar überlegen sein können, so kann unter demokratischer Zielsetzung dennoch auf die kulturschließende und integrative Funktion der Standardsprache nicht verzichtet werden. Dialekte, Schicht- und Gruppensprachen sind als Ergänzungen zur Standardsprache (auch im Unterricht) nützlich und wünschenswert; sie können diese aber nicht ersetzen, ohne daß die Gesellschaft in eine große Zahl partikulärer Gruppen ohne die Möglichkeit differenzierter gegenseitiger *Verständigung* zerfällt. (1984:318–19, my emphasis)

Ammon, too, is a fierce advocate of the greater communicative radius of standard German:

> [es] besteht allerdings deutlich funktionale Inäquivalenz zwischen Dialekten und Hochsprache. Sie erweist sich z.B. unverkennbar, wenn man Dialekte außerhalb ihres Gebrauchsgebietes zu sprechen versucht; man ruft dann *Verständnisschwierigkeiten* hervor. Dagegen wird die Hochsprache in sämtlichen Dialektgebieten *verstanden.* (1982:42, my emphasis)

The *Bildunsgsplan für das Gymnasium Baden-Württemberg* (1994) for the tenth class refers to the importance of the standard language for mutual intelligibility within Germany: 'Die Schüler und Schülerinnen erkennen die Bedeutung der Standardsprache für die *überregionale Verständigung* und den Eigenwert der Mundart als regional begrenzter Sprachform' (1994:428, my emphasis).

Two issues need to be addressed here: (i) it is assumed that the standard language is a variety which is understood by all, and (ii) the subjective dimension of comprehension is neglected. König (1978:135), however, refers to studies which found that news broadcasts in standard German were not understood by all listeners, or were only partly understood[3]. Ammon's assumption that, with standard German, one can achieve 'mühelose Verständigung im ganzen deutschen Sprachgebiet' (1979:36) implies, too, that standard German is some sort of monolithic and neutral variety and that there is no discussion at all about the meaning of concepts such as 'Freiheit', 'Demokratie', 'Sozialismus'. Wachs was one of the first to contest this appeal to the supraregional radius of standard German:

> Selbst der zunächst plausible Verweis auf die überregionale Reichweite der Standardvarietät wirkt wenig überzeugend, da Ammon den Fehlschluß macht, den regional begrenzten Geltungsbereich der Dialekte mit deren kommunikativer Reichweite gleichzusetzen. Diese Sichtweise basiert zum einen auf der Annahme, daß Dialekt und Standard geschlossene Systeme darstellen, darüber hinaus werden die Variationsbreite der Sprecher und ihre Verstehensbereitschaft vernachlässigt [...]. (1982:332)

Two important points are made here. Firstly, standard German and regional dialects are not closed systems, between which speakers switch as if they were bilinguals switching between two autonomous varieties. This is certainly true of central and southern Germany[4], where speakers move along a continuum between the basal dialect and standard German, varying the frequency with which they use standard or non-standard features depending on social and situational factors (Durrell 1992:20).

---

3 The fact that news broadcasts are not well understood is perhaps unsurprising, since they use a register based very much on formal written German, containing features such as present subjunctives which are otherwise extremely rare in speech (Holly 1995:354). As Barbour (1987:233) says, there are probably few problems of comprehension when colloquial standard is used, but more studies are needed to corroborate this.

4 In those areas of northern Germany where Low German is spoken, the linguistic distance between the dialect and standard German means that speakers do switch between two autonomous varieties like bilinguals, but this is rarely true of speakers in central and southern Germany.

Secondly, the word 'Verstehensbereitschaft' indicates the role of subjective factors, i.e. attitudes, in comprehension. Comprehension is not secured solely on the basis of objectively measurable linguistic distance between varieties, as is illustrated by Wolff's work in Nigeria and Haugen's in Scandinavia. Wolff found that speakers of varieties which were, on the basis of a comparative linguistic analysis, extremely close, often claimed that they could not understand each other, with speakers of the more prestigious varieties usually more likely to claim not to understand other varieties than vice versa (1959: 35–9). Haugen found that the will to understand played a major role in overcoming communication difficulties between speakers of different varieties (1966:280). Lewandowski, too, stresses the social dimension of comprehension when he writes that 'kommunikativer Erfolg in der Regel am besten mit Äußerungen erreicht wird, die der allgemein geltenden Norm entsprechen (oder sie gar überbieten), und daß Fehler jedweder Art in der Lage sind, den Hörer oder Leser zu irritieren' (1982:20). This emphasises that communicative success involves more than just transmission of a message: it involves creating a certain impression on one's addressee, as underlined by Bourdieu when he makes the important point that not everyone gets listened to, however intelligibly they talk or write:

> The competence adequate to produce sentences that are likely to be understood may be quite inadequate to produce sentences that are likely to be *listened to*, likely to be recognized as *acceptable* in all the situations in which there is occasion to speak. [...] social acceptability is not reducible to mere grammaticality. (Bourdieu 1991:54–5)

This underlines the extra-linguistic aspects of comprehension, which must not be neglected in any discussion of mutual intelligibilty between varieties.

Some linguists, however, believe that the role of extra-linguistic factors in ensuring mutual intelligibilty can be over-emphasised. Milroy (1984), for example, thinks that sociolinguists do not know enough about cross-dialectal communication to be able to claim that miscommunication is not a problem. She shows that linguistic and non-linguistic context does not always help speakers to avoid communication breakdowns even when the will to understand is there.

Also, one must be aware that lack of a common standard can cause more problems with written texts because of the relatively context-free nature of writing.

This means that we should not be too dismissive of claims that miscommunication can occur between speakers of different varieties of German, but I would argue that the standard has to be included here. We cannot simply assume that the standard is understood perfectly by speakers of non-standard varieties. We need more information in order to know how much work needs to be done in schools to ensure that effective communication takes place, and pupils need to discuss the concept of 'effective communication' and uncover the linguistic and extra-linguistic factors that affect it. The media could perhaps play a role in making non-standard varieties familiar to larger audiences, and schools could help by making pupils familiar with different accents and dialects, as is suggested by Andersson and Trudgill (1990:170). They suggest that schools should encourage pupils to acquire the ability to understand a wide range of accents and that pupils should be made aware of the importance of being comprehensible to speakers of other accents and to non-native speakers[5].

Some sociolinguists (e.g. Sieber and Sitta 1986:82,172) see a greater stress on 'Sprachverständlichkeitsnormen' rather than 'Sprachrichtigkeitsnormen' as a step towards greater norm tolerance in schools. Laudable as that sentiment might be, there are, however, problems associated with this approach, for example, who is to decide what is comprehensible? Is it what is comprehensible to teachers without too much effort? This approach could mean transmitting norms that are as arbitrary as the 'Sprachrichtigkeitsnormen', but which show as much variability from one teacher to the next[6].

---

5 They suggest that this can be achieved by reducing the tempo of speech and cutting down on fast-speech features such as elisions and assimilations. In the German context, where non-standard varieties can differ from each other and standard German on every level (grammatical, phonological and semantic), more effort may be required by speakers and listeners.

6 See Davies (in press, b) for research into teachers' norm awareness.

Assumption 3: The appropriateness model is less prescriptive and more objective than a model based on correctness

The appropriateness model is based on 'the view that varieties of a language differ in being appropriate for different purposes and different situations' (Fairclough 1992:33), i.e. it is based ultimately on the difference theory of linguistic variation. The difference theory (unlike the deficit theory) assumes the functional equivalence of all varieties of a language, whilst accepting that they are differently evaluated by society (Dittmar 1980:128–31). Dittmar demands a critical approach to this social evaluation (i.e. that non-standard varieties are appropriate only in informal, private and/or non-official domains, which are normally less positively evaluated than formal, public and/or official domains) and a recognition of the socio-historical conditions which have established a particular set of linguistic practices – the standard variety – as dominant and legitimate (1980:128–31). Cameron, too, criticises the uncritical use of the discourse of 'appropriacy' by some proponents of difference theory:

> the way [they] use the language of 'appropriateness' has the effect of treating norms as facts, of obscuring their contingency and thus of blunting critical responses to them. The alternative is to make clear that while norms materially affect people's behaviour [...], these norms are open to challenge and to change. (1995:235)

The curricula examined here are based on an appropriateness model of variation and refer to the fact that pupils should be taught to use different varieties of German in an 'appropriate' fashion, e.g. the *Bildungsplan für die Grundschule Baden-Württemberg. Deutsch* (1994:20), *Bildungsplan für das Gymnasium Baden-Württemberg. Deutsch* (1994:428) and the *Lehrplan Deutsch. Realschule. Rheinland-Pfalz* (1984:7). The following quotation exemplifies this: 'Die Schüler und Schülerinnen erkennen die Bedeutung der Standardsprache für die überregionale Verständigung und den Eigenwert der Mundart als regional begrenzter Sprachform'

(*Bildungsplan für das Gymnasium Baden-Württemberg. Deutsch* 1994:428). Standard German and non-standard dialect are presented as having different functions: one is appropriate for supraregional communication and one for regionally restricted communication. The problems associated with assumptions about intelligibility between varieties have already been mentioned. Although there is no time to go into this in greater detail, another thing to be borne in mind is that features of non-standard dialect which are avoided by speakers in formal situations are often widespread geographically: it is their social radius that is limited not their geographical radius (Davies 1999, Jakob 1985). This pronouncement takes no note of such facts.

The curriculum for the *Gymnasium* in Baden-Württemberg goes on to say:

> Inhalt: Mundart und Standardsprache; Großgliederung des deutschen Sprachgebiets; Funktionen der Mundart (Zusammengehörigkeitsgefühl, Gefühlswerte, Anschaulichkeit); Funktionen der Standardsprache (in Staat und Verwaltung, Handel und Verkehr, Wissenschaft, Literatur, Medien). (1994:428)

Here the two varieties are presented in complementary distribution across public/private and formal/informal domains. The curriculum for the *Orientierungsstufe* in Rheinland-Pfalz says that non-standard dialect is acceptable for 'mündliches Erzählen' (Schlosser 1985:137), but on the whole dialect is hardly mentioned in the curricula, which implies that the school domain is not considered 'appropriate' for non-standard varieties, at least not in theory[7].

Having looked at the curricula, let us now turn to look at what the academics say about 'appropriateness'. Rosenberg (1993:16) writes: 'Didaktisches Ziel [muß] eine funktionale "innere Mehrsprachigkeit" sein, die Kinder zur *situationsadäquaten Varietätenverwendung* [erzieht], ohne ihnen ihre dialektale Primärvarietät austreiben zu wollen' (my emphasis). His is a typical attitude. He also points out (1993:27) that attempts to extend the domains of non-standard dialects have so far failed, as have attempts to introduce a

---

7 Davies (in press, b) shows that many teachers at *Realschulen* in this area claim not to insist on pupils speaking standard German in class, although the standard, as an idea, enjoys considerable support.

'zweisprachige Deutschdidaktik', which would involve teaching dialect (1993:45). He claims that the concept of 'funktionale Mehrsprachigkeit', i.e. distribution of varieties according to function (the appropriateness model again), is more popular, but he thinks that this has had few practical consequences for teachers' practice, as the assumption that non-standard varieties have no official role to play at school is too strong (1993:47). He is right in the sense that teachers seem to spend very little time talking about dialect at all and their own practice seems to consolidate the existing domain distribution (Davies in press, a).

Rosenberg displays a certain ambivalence in his attitude towards non-standard dialects and standard. On the one hand he says: 'Selbstverständlich sollte die normale Unterrichtssprache des Deutschlehrers die Standardsprache sein'(1993:76), but he then goes on to say: 'Unter dem Gesichtspunkt des situativen Sprachgebrauchs muß Dialekt im Unterricht als ein positives "Mehr" begriffen werden'(1993:76). It is, however, difficult to see how it can be presented as a 'Mehr' if it is relegated in practice to non-prestigious and marginal contexts. 'Funktionale Mehrsprachigkeit' is presented (Rosenberg 1993:46) as an educational aim which could be used to increase the linguistic self-confidence of dialect-speakers; however, whilst this might be feasible in central and southern Germany (roughly south of the Main), it is not so in the north where switching between dialect and standard is governed more by social factors than situative ones (cf. Durrell 1992:19). Even in the south, it is difficult to see how this can do much to help pupils' self-confidence as long as it means that non-standard dialects are confirmed as the language of less prestigious domains and as long as it is clear to pupils that speakers of standard or standard-like varieties do not need to code-switch or -shift to the same degree. The latter may suffer in certain situations because they do not speak a local dialect, but they are less likely to suffer in economic terms because of this gap in their repertoire than will those who have not mastered standard or a standard-like variety.

The discourse of appropriateness appears to accept the demands of liberalism and pluralism, whilst in reality not rocking the boat at all. The hegemony of the standard variety is not affected (Fairclough 1992:43) and divisions in society are camouflaged because the implication is that there are shared sociolinguistic norms amongst all members of society. However, if these norms really were shared to such an extent, there would be no need for the whole tradition of 'Sprachpflege' or 'Sprachkritik' in German. I agree with Sealey (who is referring to policy documents on the teaching of standard English): 'It is difficult to have full confidence in a language curriculum which neglects to mention the non-consensual dimensions of language' (1999:88) and which fails to point out, as Bourdieu (1991:21) and Tollefson (1991:77) do, that some speakers benefit more than others from the rules for 'appropriate' linguistic practices.

One important way of creating a critical sociolinguistic awareness is to adopt a historical perspective and to show how the relationship between the standard variety and the non-standard varieties has developed and how the linguistic value systems of speakers have changed over the years. The curricula (*Bildungspläne*) make some reference to this, e.g.

> Baden-Württemberg, Realschule, Klasse 9: (Entwicklung einer einheitlichen deutschen Hochsprache = Wahlinhalt).
> Baden-Württemberg, Gymnasium, Klasse 11: Die Schülerinnen und Schüler sollen die Geschichtlichkeit der Sprache erkennen, um so einen Zugang zu den älteren Werken der Literatur zu finden, die geschichtliche Bedingtheit des eigenen Sprachgebrauchs zu erfahren und kulturgeschichtliche Zusammenhänge zu erkennen.
> Rheinland-Pfalz, Realschule und Gymnasium, ab Klasse 9: Lerninhalte: Eines der folgenden Themen: Probleme der Sprachnormierung; der historische Wandel der Sprache.

In Rheinland-Pfalz, this topic is discussed earlier than in Baden-Württemberg: in the latter, only grammar-school pupils preparing for the *Abitur* have to learn something about the historical development of German. It could be argued that pupils in that situation are not those who most need to have their (linguistic) self-confidence boosted by learning that the non-standard varieties they speak have a history just as the standard variety does, and are not simply, to quote Grimm, "verderbte Hochsprache" (Reitmajer 1980:74). The topics mentioned for both *Länder* could all be used to raise critical language awareness of the links between linguistic developments and social and political factors; they could, however, also be used simply to present students with descriptions of linguistic changes: how these topics are taught is very much up to individual teachers, and my investigation into language awareness amongst teachers at *Realschulen* in this area (Davies in press, a) found that few have the ability to transmit a critical approach to linguistic variation.

Conclusion

This paper argues for a more critical approach to some common presuppositions about the nature of linguistic variation in present-day Germany, an approach that exposes the social dimension of many judgements which are passed off as 'linguistic' (and therefore more acceptable, since it seems to be less offensive to make value judgements about linguistic varieties than their speakers). A critical approach would acknowledge that power is distributed unevenly in society and that this is reflected in the distribution of language practices (Fairclough 1992:48, Bourdieu 1991)[8]. The present distribution of standard and non-standard varieties of German is the result of years of struggle – it is not the result of inherent structural linguistic differences between the varieties. The fact that the 'appropriateness' rules for standard and non-standard varieties are not the same in northern and southern Germany and that certain shifts in domain distribution have taken place over the last ten or fifteen years[9] should be a living reminder to pupils that social and political factors have played a role in producing the current sociolinguistic situation

8 Whilst it is clear that use of a particular linguistic variety does not correlate with social class nearly as closely as in England (Durrell 1992:20), it is nevertheless true that children from the middle-class tend to be more likely to attend a *Gymnasium* and university, which means that they are exposed for longer to standard German and to what Bourdieu (1991:62) calls 'educational monitoring, correction and sanction' (Hradil 1981:42–9; *Basic and structural data 1998/99*: 92).

9 For more information on the so-called dialect renaissance see Clyne (1995:110–12).

10 The teacher would also lack credibility as pupils learn about linguistic value systems at home and on the street as well as at school.

and could provide a starting point for a discussion of how patterns of language use are not static but dynamic (cf. Bhatt/Martin-Jones 1992:292).

This critique of the appropriateness model does not mean that I am suggesting that pupils who do not speak standard German should not have the opportunity to learn it. To do that would be to fall into the same error which has been criticised in others: an ahistorical and asocial approach to variation. It would be unfair if teachers were to conceal from their pupils the advantages that mastery of standard German entails, and pupils must be aware that going against dominant conventions, i.e. using language 'inappropriately', can be costly (Janks and Ivanič 1992:330)[10]. What I am arguing, however, is that critical language awareness can help people to realise that it is possible to question and even change linguistic conventions that they may have taken for granted as a natural order, and this can be empowering (Janks and Ivanič 1992). Pateman (1975:9) says that people in our society are encouraged to engage in idle discourse, i.e. they are encouraged to treat definitions as closed and not as possible subjects for rational dispute. I would suggest that this applies to the language practices discussed above: we should be encouraging teachers to help their pupils to engage in rational dispute with them in order to pave the way to a more conscious use and understanding of language.

Bibliography

Ammon, Ulrich (1979) 'Regionaldialekte und Einheitssprache in der Bundesrepublik Deutschland', *International Journal of the Sociology of Language* 21, 25–40

Ammon, Ulrich (1982) 'Zum Versuch der soziolinguistischen Legitimation sozialer Sprachungleichheit – am Beispiel von Schullehrzielen in der Bundesrepublik Deutschland – kritische Anmerkungen', in Van De Craen Piet/Willemyns Roland (eds.) *Sociolinguistiek en Ideologie,* Brussels: Universiteit Brussel

Andersson, Lars-Gunnar/Trudgill, Peter (1990) *Bad language,* Harmondsworth: Penguin

Barbour, Stephen (1987) 'Dialects and the teaching of a standard language: some West German work', *Language in Society* 16, 227–44

Basic and structural data 1998/99 (1998), published by the Federal Ministry of Education and Research, Bonn

Bayer, K. (1984) 'Mündliche Kommunikation', in Hopster, Norbert (ed.) *Handbuch 'Deutsch'. Sekundarstufe 1,* Paderborn, München, Wien, Zürich: Ferdinand Schöningh, 307–33

Besch, Werner/Knoop, Ulrich/Putschke, Wolfgang/Wiegand, Herbert, Ernst, (eds.) (1983) *Dialektologie. Ein Handbuch zur deutschen und allgemeinen Dialektforschung,* 2. Halbband, Berlin: de Gruyter

Bhatt, Arvindh/Martin-Jones, Marilyn (1992) 'Whose resource? Minority languages, bilingual learners and language awareness', in Fairclough, Norman (ed.), 285–301

Bildungsplan für die Realschule Baden-Württemberg. Deutsch (1994), Villingen-Schwenningen: Neckar-Verlag

Bildungsplan für die Grundschule Baden-Württemberg. Deutsch (1994), Villingen-Schwenningen: Neckar-Verlag

Bildungsplan für das Gymnasium Baden-Württemberg. Deutsch (1994), Villingen-Schwenningen: Neckar-Verlag

Bourdieu, Pierre (1991) *Language and symbolic power,* edited and introduced by John B. Thompson, Cambridge: Polity Press

Bücherl, Rainald (1993) 'Dialekt als Chance', in Klotz, Peter/Sieber, Peter (eds.) *Vielerlei Deutsch,* Stuttgart: Klett, 68–77

Cameron, Deborah (1985) *Feminism and linguistic theory,* London: Macmillan

Cameron, Deborah (1995) *Verbal hygiene,* London, New York: Routledge

Clyne, Michael (1995) *The German language in a changing Europe,* Cambridge: CUP

Davies, Winifred (1999) 'Geregeltes Miteinander oder ungeregeltes Durcheinander? Versuch einer Beschreibung der sogenannten "Umgangssprache" in Mannheim-Neckarau', *Linguistische Berichte* 178, 205–29

Davies, Winifred (in press, a) 'Language awareness amongst teachers in a central German dialect area,' *Language Awareness*

Davies, Winifred (in press, b) 'Linguistic norms at school: a survey of secondary-school teachers in a central German dialect area', *Zeitschrift für Dialektologie und Linguistik*

Dittmar, Norbert (1980) *Soziolinguistik,* 4th, corrected edition, Königstein/Taunus: Athenäum

Durrell, Martin (1992) 'Pygmalion-Deutsch: attitudes to language in England and Germany', *London German Studies* IV, 1–26

Fairclough, Norman (1992) 'The appropriacy of appropriateness', in Fairclough, Norman (ed.), 33–56

Fairclough, Norman (ed.) (1992) *Critical language awareness,* London, New York: Longman

Haugen, Einar (1966) 'Semicommunication: the language gap in Scandinavia', *Sociological Enquiry* 36, 280–97

Holly, Werner (1995) 'Language and television', in Stevenson, Patrick (ed.) *The German language and the real world*, Oxford: Clarendon Press, 339–73

Hradil, Stefan (1981) *Soziale Schichtung in der Bundesrepublik,* 3. Aufl., München: Ehrenwirth

Jakob, Karlheinz (1985) *Dialekt und Regionalsprache im Raum Heilbronn. Teil 1: Textband*, Marburg: N. G. Elwert

Janks, Hilary/Ivanič Roz (1992) 'Critical language awareness and emancipatory discourse', in Fairclough, Norman (ed.), 305–31

Klotz, Peter/Sieber, Peter (eds.) (1993) *Vielerlei Deutsch,* Stuttgart: Klett

König, Werner (1978) *dtv-Atlas zur deutschen Sprache,* München: dtv

Lehrplan Deutsch. Realschule. Rheinland-Pfalz (1984), Grünstadt: Emil Sommer Verlag für das Schulwesen

Lehrplan Deutsch. Gymnasium. Rheinland-Pfalz (1984), Grünstadt: Emil Sommer Verlag für das Schulwesen

Lewandowski, Theodor (1982) 'Normen im deutschen Schulunterricht. Mündliche Kommunikation und gesprochene Sprache,' in *Schulen für einen guten Sprachgebrauch,* bearbeitet von Birgitta Mogge und Ingulf Radtke (= Der öffentliche Sprachgebrauch Bd 3), Stuttgart: Klett-Cotta, 15–26

Milroy, Lesley (1984) 'Comprehension and context: successful communication and communication breakdown', in Trudgill, Peter (ed.) *Applied sociolinguistics,* London: Academic Press, 7–31

Pateman, Trevor (1975) *Language, truth and politics.* Reading: Jean Stroud and Trevor Pateman

Reitmajer, Valentin (1980) 'Die Bedeutung des Dialekts im schulischen Kommunikationsprozeß', *Linguistische Berichte* 67, 68–81

Rosenberg, Peter (1986) *Der Berliner Dialekt und seine Folgen für die Schüler,* Tübingen: Niemeyer

Rosenberg, Peter (1993) 'Dialekt und Schule: Bilanz und Aufgaben eines Forschungsgebiets', in Klotz, Peter/Sieber, Peter (eds.) *Vielerlei Deutsch,* Stuttgart: Klett, 12–58

Schlosser, Horst Dieter (1985) *Dialektgebrauch in der Schule,* Alsbach/Bergstraße: Leuchtturm

Sealey, Alison (1999) 'Teaching primary school children about the English language: a critique of current policy documents', *Language Awareness* 8, 84–97

Sieber, Peter/Sitta, Horst (1986) *Mundart und Standardsprache als Problem der Schule*, Aarau/Frankfurt am Main: Sauerländer

Tollefson, James W. (1991) *Planning language, planning inequality: language policy in the community,* London, New York: Longman

Viereck, Wolfgang (1983) 'Probleme des Dialektsprechers beim Fremdsprachenerwerb', in Besch, Werner et al. (eds.), 1493–98

Wachs, Inge (1982) 'Dialekt als Sprachbarriere? Soziolinguistische Überlegungen zur Berücksichtigung regionaler Variation in der Schule', in *Linguistische Arbeiten Berichte* 18, 235–65

Wagner, Eberhard (1987) *Das fränkische Dialektbuch*, München: C.H. Beck

Wolff, Hans (1959) 'Intelligibility and interethnic attitudes', *Anthropological Linguistics* 1, 34–41

CHRISTOPHER HALL

The Effectiveness of CALL in Grammar Teaching. An Evaluation Using Error Analysis

Introduction

The need for research into the effectiveness of CALL has been stated repeatedly in recent years:

1) There was a lively exchange of views on the EUROCALL discussion list following the EUROCALL 96 conference in Szombathely (Hungary), bemoaning the lack of papers on the evaluation of CALL materials and stressing the need for more research. In fact, as the proceedings show, EUROCALL 96 did contain three papers on evaluation (Davies and Yu Hong Wei 1997, Ensinger 1997, Neunzig 1997), the latter two in German, which is perhaps the reason why they were overlooked by some of the contributors to the EUROCALL discussion list.

EUROCALL president Graham Davies pointed out in a contribution to the discussion list that the data for evaluation is not easy to come by:

> The main problem I found when carrying out the survey for the Lingua Bureau in 1994 was that a lot of effort was being put into the *development* of CALL materials, but our team found it extremely difficult to find institutions that were actually *using* the materials that had been developed or that were undergoing development. (14.9.96)

2) In his editorial in *Computer Assisted Language Learning* (10/1, 1997), Keith Cameron wrote:

> As a believer in the importance of CALL in education I am surprised by the lack of actual proof I can offer the sceptics. Recently I was asked to name publications which would point to the efficacy of CALL and show how evaluation had

> substantiated the claims certain practitioners make. I must admit that in response to the enquiry I cited above all this journal (p. 2).

This contention was certainly borne out by recent searches I have done for literature on CALL evaluation in the *FirstSearch* bibliographic databases. Two major databases, *ArticleFirst* and *MLA* did not respond with a single item, even though I entered all the terms I could think of to describe the subject area. A third database *WorldCat* did come up with a number of very interesting titles on CALL evaluation, but they were mainly MA theses at American universities and therefore difficult, if not impossible, to obtain. Certainly there seems to be some good work going on here which students should be encouraged to publish, if it is of publishable quality.

Of course, these databases, though very large, do not contain everything which is published. Conference proceedings like the EUROCALL 96 volume (Kohn et al. 1997) are not included.

3) Sometimes doubts about the effectiveness of CALL surface even in the work of CALL specialists. In their article describing an innovative project involving what they call 'role reversal CALL' (i.e. getting students to learn about the language by writing CALL exercises), Smith et al. (1997:213) describe the doubts about traditional CALL exercises which led them to embark upon their project. They write:

> From a teacher's point of view the greatest concern was that students were failing to exploit the potential of the new technologies to their best effect. At its worst CALL activities seemed to promote a passive attitude to learning amongst some students. Gap-filling exercises, text reconstructions and grammar primer exercises, it seemed, were a short-term activity restricted to the classroom, from which the student did not appear to draw any long-term benefit. Successful completion of the prescribed tasks on the computer did not necessarily entail that the student had internalised the corresponding grammar rules being tested.

This view is apparently based not on research, but rather on the authors' feelings and observations. The verb 'seem' is used twice, 'did not appear' once. Nevertheless, it does point to the need for research into the effectiveness of the more traditional CALL exercises, and it must be taken seriously, coming as it does from

CALL practitioners at Coventry University, one of the pioneers of CALL among British universities.

A glance at recent numbers of CALL journals and conference proceedings shows that it is still the case that far more effort is put into producing than into evaluating CALL materials. However, progress in evaluation has been made, notably in conjunction with the TELL Consortium project[1], which included detailed evaluation reports both during development (formative evaluation) and in use after completion (summative evaluation), see Laurillard (1996) and Hewer (1998). These reports are interesting not only for the information they give about the TELL Consortium's products, but also because they provide, for the first time, a detailed, well-thought out strategy for the evaluation of CALL materials.

The evaluation methods used in the formative evaluation were observation, interviews, questionnaires, and pre- and post-tests (Laurillard 1996:4) and in the summative evaluation student logs, post-programme student questionnaires, post-programme stuctured staff interviews and, in one case only, an open discussion with students (Hewer 1998:6). This is clearly a varied array of data gathering methods, which is likely to produce a great deal of relevant information about the effectiveness of the products in language learning. However, because the post-tests and the post-programme questionnaires and interviews took place immediately or very soon after the students had worked with the programmes, they can only provide information about short-term effects[2]. It is my intention in the present study to seek information about longer term effects of a CALL programme. The method used in this study therefore complements the methods used in the TELL evaluation projects and elsewhere.

---

1 The TELL Consortium (Technology Enhanced Language Learning) is a British government funded project which has produced a range of new language learning courseware. For more information see the website: www.hull.ac.uk/cti/tell.htm.

2 This is also the case with some other studies on the effects of CALL, e.g. Laufer and Hill (2000).

The wider debate on the effectiveness of grammar teaching

The evaluation of the effectiveness of CALL in grammar teaching presupposes that grammar teaching itself is effective, i.e. that it contributes to language learning. This is by no means universally accepted. On the contrary, there has been a lively debate on this issue over the last three decades, which is by no means over yet, although I think it is safe to say that the issues are becoming clearer[3].

In his monumental survey of Second Language Acquisition research, Ellis (1994:659) comes to the conclusion 'The case for formal instruction is strengthening and the case for the zero option is weakening.' This is a relatively cautious position. One of the leading German authorities on SLA, Lutz Götze, is more forthright. He writes:

> Daß Grammatik im Fremdsprachenunterricht notwendig sei, gilt – nach einigen Jahren gegenteiliger Auffassung – heute wieder als unbestritten, wenn nicht gar als trivial (1996:136).

Götze distinguishes between two kinds of grammatical rules: rules of the system and rules of usage (1996:136). The rules of the system need to be described and learned as completely as possible (p. 137). The rules of language use (the great majority) are influenced by the context, the intention of the speaker/writer, the communicative situation and the text type and cannot be learned in this way. Götze implies that formal grammar exercises for passives are of no use ('formale Spielerei oder genauer "Sprachstroh"', 'verschaffen allenfalls die Befriedigung bei Lehrenden und Lernenden, in die schwierige Grammatik des Deutschen eingetaucht zu sein', 1996:138).

The teaching and practising of explicit grammar is a way of dividing up the massive field of language into manageable chunks and can be compared to practice in other areas e.g. drawing in art school, scales and arpeggios in music, the training of specific elements in sport (e.g. the start in a sprint race), practising individual steps in

---

3 For an informative survey and discussion of the debate on the effect of formal instruction, see Ellis (1994:611–663).

dancing, etc., etc. All of these are (like language) activities which come naturally to human beings: drawing, music, running, dancing, but in order to become especially proficient at them we need repeated practice of individual elements.

Traditional grammar (based on Latin grammar) was used for centuries to teach countless generations Latin and later other foreign languages. It obviously worked, otherwise it would not have survived so long. This is not to claim that it is the most pleasant, interesting or effective form of language teaching, but it does mean that it cannot be dismissed out of hand (see also Götze 1996:138). Language use could not be taught in this way (I learned Latin and Greek at school for six and five years respectively without learning how to say 'yes' or 'no' in either language!). The rules of language use are best learned in authentic communication, and the average learner seems better equipped to pick up these rules than the rules of the language system.

Harald Weydt (1993:119f.) questions the effectiveness of grammar teaching. He lists four arguments against explicit grammar teaching, and among other things reports that in his grammar classes some foreign students achieve excellent results in the tests, but still make mistakes when they use the language. However, he continues:

> Andererseits is völlig evident, daß Grammatik unbedingt gelehrt werden muß. Alle Erfahrungen mit ungesteuertem Zweitsprachenerwerb zeigen, daß jugendliche und erwachsene Lerner ohne grammatischen Unterricht, der z.B. im selbständigen Konsultieren von Grammatiken bestehen kann, über ein sehr primitives Niveau der neuen Sprache nicht hinauskommen und nicht zu einer fehlerfreien Beherrschung vorstoßen (1993:120).

It seems clear that this is the majority view today, which is also reflected in the Language Awareness movement (see for example James et al. 1991)[4]. I would now like to look at how the teaching of

---

4 This view is not universally held, of course, and there have been recent studies which challenge the usefulness of grammar teaching. For example, in a much-quoted paper Alderson et al. (1997) examined the relationship between students' metalinguistic knowledge and their actual proficiency in a foreign language. They found that learners with a good knowledge of metalanguage were no more proficient than those with a poor knowledge. However, a knowledge of metalanguage is only one aspect of formal grammar teaching, so their results, although interesting, are not conclusive.

grammar by means of CALL fits into this picture and describe my research.

The background to the present study

By chance, ideal conditions for a study into the effectiveness of CALL arose at Leicester University as a result of the modularisation of courses. A CALL element was introduced for first-year students of German in 1993 and was originally compulsory for all students. The CALL material was designed to accompany the textbook used with our first-year students, *Eindrücke-Einblicke* by Karl-Heinz Drochner and Dieter Föhr (published by Langenscheidt). The workbook belonging to this course contains a large number of grammar and vocabulary exercises, and these formed the basis for a set of CALL exercises which I developed to accompany the course (later published as Hall 1996). This is a rather traditional, DOS-based CALL package consisting of exercises on grammar (largely gap-filling exercises), vocabulary, word-formation and text reconstruction exercises. The CALL exercises are accompanied by a series of 12 lectures on the relevant aspects of German grammar. The students attend the lectures first and then do the CALL exercises.

Two years after the introduction of this course, our degree programmes were modularised and we found that there was simply no room on the timetable for the CALL element in some of the programmes. For these students CALL had to be dropped or made optional. This left us with two groups of students who have identical entry requirements as far as their prior knowledge of German is concerned, who follow the same German language programme and sit the same end-of-year examination. As far as the German language teaching they receive is concerned, the only difference between the two groups is that one attends the CALL module and the other does not. For the purposes of testing the effects of the CALL material, our students thus fall naturally into a test group and a control group.

With CALL	Without CALL
Single Subject German (major) Joint French-German Joint German-Italian European Studies (CALL optional)	Modern Language Studies Combined Studies Supplementary German (minor) European Studies (CALL optional)

Fig. 1: Degree programmes involving German

In the four years 1995–96 to 1998–99 we had a total of 182 students in the first year of these degree programmes, but some were excluded from this study for a number of reasons:

- Single Subject German students, who spend more time on German than other students, and also probably have a greater commitment to the subject, which presumably means that they will be prepared to devote more energy to it. On the other hand, Supplementary German students spend one third of their time on German, which is the same as for Modern Language Studies and Combined Studies, but they take German for only one or two years, so their commitment to the subject may be less than that of other students. For similar reasons, Combined Studies students, many of whom drop German after two years, were also excluded.
- Those with foreign qualifications (Austrian and German, but also Dutch, Finnish, French and Italian). These students had a considerably better knowledge of German grammar than the average British student, and would have distorted the results of the study had they been counted in either group.
- Those who failed or did not complete the CALL element.

This left a total of 103 students in the years 1995–1999 who were included in the study. They divide reasonably evenly into 47 students on degree programmes with CALL and 56 on degree programmes without.

CALL group (n=47)	**Non-CALL group** (n=56)
Joint French-German Joint German-Italian European Studies (CALL optional)	Modern Language Studies European Studies (CALL optional)

Fig. 2: Students involved in the study

Although they are following different degree programmes, these students form a relatively homogeneous group with respect to their command of German. The entrance requirements are the same for all degree programmes with a German component. All students must have a minimum grade C at A level[5] in German for our courses, but a small number of students come in with a grade D if they have good grades in other subjects. Over the four years in question, the average A level grades for students on degree programmes with CALL and those without were very similar:

CALL group (n=47)	**Non-CALL group** (n=56)
6.88	7.10

Fig. 3: Average A level scores in German 1995–98

The slightly higher average grade of the students on degree programmes without CALL reflects the greater popularity of theses programmes in recent years, which means that there is tougher competition to get in and that students with lower grades are more likely to be rejected.

The first-year German language teaching is the same for all these students, with the exception of the CALL module. They all take the same modules in written and spoken German, and they all sit the same first-year language examination. The various degree programmes differ in the amount of other German elements the students take, e.g. modules in German literature, linguistics or history.

---

5 Five pass grades are awarded in the British A level exam, from A to E. A point score is also used, with A being equivalent to 10 points, B to 8 points, and so on down to E, which is worth 2 points.

The average marks in first-year written German examination show that the CALL group, which was slightly weaker on the basis of their A level results, has overtaken the non-CALL group by the end of the first year:

CALL group (n=47)	**Non-CALL group** (n=56)
53.8%	49.1%

Fig. 4: Average marks in first-year written German examination 1996–99

Over the four years in question data was collected on the students belonging to both these groups, and the written German produced in the end-of-year examination has been subjected to an error analysis, in order to establish to what extent the CALL exercises have helped in the learning of German grammar.

The error analysis

If the CALL exercises have any lasting impact on the students' command of German grammar, it should make a difference to the German they write in the the end-of-year examinations. So I undertook an error analysis of these examination papers. Clearly this error analysis had to be focussed in order to make it manageable with such a large number of students, and it also had to be limited to aspects of German grammar which are (a) given good coverage in the *Eindrücke-Einblicke* CALL exercises and (b) occur in sufficient numbers in the examination papers. I chose four grammar points, representing different areas of German grammar:

- passive constructions
- relative clauses
- adjective endings
- weak nouns

The errors made in each of these areas were collected, classified and analysed, and figures will be presented for each. In each of the four years the exam paper had the same format, consisting of three questions:

1. a translation from English into German
2. a letter in German
3. an essay in German

Because of the open-ended nature of the questions, there is no absolute number against which performances can be measured. Instead, I have counted all of the occurrences of each structure, whether correct or incorrect, and expressed the correct occurrences as a percentage of the total number.

Passive constructions

In German the passive is formed by means of an auxiliary verb and the past participle of the main verb. Both passive constructions, the *werden* passive (indicating a process) and the *sein* passive (indicating a state) were included, as the CALL exercises cover both these types. The passive is a complex structure involving several elements. This allows wide scope for errors, which typically occurred in:

- choice of auxiliary: **Mehr als gebraucht* ***ist*** *für eine gute Allgemeinbildung*
- case of the subject: **Vor kurzem wurde* ***einen*** *Mann mit einem Messer angegriffen.*
- subject-verb agreement: **Die Reformen* ***wäre*** *kritisiert [...]*
- past participle of main verb: **Milch, die mit [nur 1,5% Fett]* ***kaufen*** *werden kann.*
- past participle of *werden*: **Die Oberstufen des Gynmasiums sind reformiert* ***geworden***
- position of the past participle in the sentence (esp. in compound tenses): **Ich bin* ***worden*** *geboren.*
- omission of essential elements: **ihre andere Ersatzstoffe müssen [...] ersetzen*______.

Frequently we find combinations of these errors, but each incorrect passive construction was counted only once, and concomitant errors – errors which follow on from incorrect choices made by the learner (James 1998:116) – were ignored.

Errors in passive clauses which are not connected with the passive construction were not counted under this heading: word order errors such as the wrong position of the verb in subordinate clauses (error of syntax) or the form of the past participle of the main verb, e.g. **gehelft worden* (for *geholfen worden*). This is clearly an error of verb morphology, not in the formation of the passive. It is not always possible to distinguish between errors of verb morphology and passive errors, e.g. in the case of **ersetzen worden.* Is the infinitive intended here, in which case it is a passive error, or does the learner think that *ersetzen* is the past participle, in which case it is an error of verb morphology? Only an 'authoritative reconstruction', in which we can ask the learner what is meant, could help here.

Cases like *Ich war erstaunt/überrascht/begeistert* were not counted as passives, as these are presumably used as adjectives[6].

Fig. 5 contains the statistics of the passive errors:

CALL group (n=47)	**Non-CALL group** (n=56)
Correct use: 60.1% Average use per student: 3.8 max. 7 min. 1	Correct use: 46.3% Average use per student: 3.5 max. 7 min. 2

Fig. 5: Passive constructions

Relative clauses

German relative clauses involve a relative pronoun and subordinate clause word order (SOV). The most common German relative pronoun is *der, die, das*, which in the majority of cases is identical to the definite article and is thus very familiar to students. The case where it is not identical to the definite article (the genitive singular

---

6 Interestingly, forms like these are generally listed as adjectives in bilingual dictionaries (e.g. Langenscheidt *Handwörterbuch English*, *Oxford Duden Großwörterbuch Englisch*), but only as verbs in monolingual dictionaries (e.g. Wahrig *Deutsches Wörterbuch*, *Duden Deutsches Universalwörterbuch A–Z*, *Duden Rechtschreibung*).

and plural, and the dative plural) are clearly those with which the students experience the greatest difficulties. German relative pronouns have to agree with their antecedents in number and gender, which proved to be a frequent source of error. Typical relative clause errors were:

- form of relative pronoun: **Eine gute Schule..., in* ***deren*** *Schüler unter nicht zuviel Druck sind.*
- agreement with antecedent: **Schulen,* ***daß*** *nicht interessant genug sind.*[7]
- agreement between subject and verb: **Freunde..., die ich besser* ***verstehen****.*
- omission of relative pronoun: *...*trotz des Zeit sie zusammen haben*
- subordinate clause word order: **Dinge..., die ich* ***mag*** *nicht.*
- Other errors were not counted under this heading, e.g. word order errors involving adverbs, comma errors, which belong to punctuation rather than grammar.

Fig. 6 contains the statistics of the relative clause errors:

CALL group (n=47)	**Non-CALL group** (n=56)
Correct use: 67.6%	Correct use: 59.5%
Average use per student: 8.9	Average use per student: 10.4
max. 21	max. 22
min. 3	min. 4

Fig. 6: Relative clauses

Adjective endings

The declension of the attributive adjective in modern standard German is quite complicated. The basic system consists of two sets of endings: the strong endings, which give relatively full information on the case, number and gender of the noun they accompany, and the

7 This is a very common error, which is clearly caused by transfer from English, in which *that* functions both as a conjunction and a relative pronoun.

weak endings which have only minimal distinctions and are used when there is a word such as an article present with an ending which already gives this information (Durrell 1996:119). It should not be beyond students of German to learn this basic system. There are real complications in the German system, but they come with adjectives after certain other determiners such as *mancher* and *solcher*, where there is a degree of variablility and indeed uncertainty even among native speakers of German. However, the purpose of the CALL exercises was to practise the basic system, and the difficult cases were not included.

Whereas some errors are clearly due to a lack of knowledge of the declension system of German adjectives (confusion of the strong and weak declensions, impossible forms), others may be due to a wrong choice of gender or case on the part of the learner, e.g. **ein sehr großes fettes Person* (*Person* treated as neuter?), *mit die andere* (singular: *mit* treated as taking the accusative? If this is a plural form, the ending is incorrect anyway, as it should be weak after *die*). Unless it could be shown that the student was aware of the correct gender or case, which was rare, such cases were disregarded in accordance with the policy of not counting concomitant errors. Thus although errors in adjective endings are simple to identify, they are not always easy to interpret.

Only attributive adjectives were included in the analysis, as predicative adjectives do not take endings in German. There were actually some errors caused by students adding endings to predicative adjectives, e.g. **wenn man* ***ältere*** *geworden ist*, but these were few in number. Nominalised adjectives and participles were included in the study, as they have the same endings as adjectives.

The errors in adjective endings which were counted are:

- confusion of weak and strong endings: **das* ***großes*** *Problem; *für* ***fremden*** *Studenten*
- endings which are not possible in either the strong or weak declension: **ein großen Zahl von Fächern, *das wichtigster Faktor*
- omission of endings: **für das* ***ganz*** *Europa*

Fig. 7 contains the statistics of the errors in adjective endings:

CALL group (n=47)	**Non-CALL group** (n=56)
Correct use: 74.2% Average use per student: 37 max. 52 min. 22	Correct use: 70% Average use per student: 35.2 max. 52 min. 19

Fig. 7: Adjective endings

Weak nouns

Weak nouns are a relatively small class of German nouns which have an *–n* or *–en* ending in all cases except the nominative singular (the oblique cases).

	Singular	Plural
Nom.	der Mensch	die Menschen
Acc.	den Menschen	die Menschen
Gen.	des Menschen	der Menschen
Dat.	dem Menschen	den Menschen

Because these nouns are so different from the great majority of German nouns, they cause problems for learners and I had expected them to cause problems for the students in the present survey. However, this turned out not to be the case. Firstly there were very few weak nouns used (some students didn't use any at all), and secondly both groups achieved a very high percentage of correct forms.

The errors that were made were almost exclusively in the accusative, genitive and dative singular, e.g. **für ein Student*, **das Nutzen den Name*. There was only one error in the plural of weak nouns: **Deutsche und Französe*.

Fig. 8 contains the statistics of the errors in weak nouns:

CALL group (n=47)	**Non-CALL group** (n=56)
Correct use: 85.7% Average use per student: 3.5 max. 14 min. 0	Correct use: 90.3% Average use per student: 3 max. 7 min. 0

Fig. 8: Weak nouns

Discussion of results

The results of the study, summarised in the following table, reveal that the students in the CALL group outperformed those in the non-CALL group in three out of the four grammar points. On the fourth point, the non-CALL group performed better.

	CALL group (n=47)		**Non-CALL group** (n=56)	
	Correct	**Av. use**	**Correct**	**Av. use**
Passives	60.1%	3.8	46.3%	3.5
Relative clauses	67.6%	8.9	59.5%	10.4
Adjective endings	74.2%	37	70%	35.2
Weak nouns	85.7%	3.5	90.3%	3

Fig.9: Summary table

I would like to pick out a number of features of these results for comment.

1) *Passives*: The passive, clearly the most complex of the four structures studied here, has produced the lowest success rate and the clearest difference between the CALL and non-CALL groups. Interestingly in the light of what Götze said about the usefulness of grammar exercises for the passive and how it is much more difficult to learn the rules of use than the form of grammar points like this (see

above), there were no examples of inappropriate use of the passive, all the errors had to do with the form of the passive.

2) *Adjective endings*: The difference between the two groups is markedly smaller than for passives or relative clauses, but the CALL group still has a clear lead. The study provides evidence that the system is not learned as a whole, but that practically all students have a partial command of it. Very few errors occurred with the strong ending *–e* in the nominative and accusative plural and also nominative and accusative singular feminine. Similarly, there were relatively few errors in the dative plural, in which both the strong and weak ending is *–en*. The role of *–n* as the almost universal dative plural ending seems to be well understood. There were far more errors in the confusion of the strong and weak endings in the masculine and neuter singular. There is enough material here for a further study of precisely how the German adjective ending system is acquired.

3) *Weak nouns*: There were no errors at all in the nominative singular and only one in the plural. Almost all the errors occurred in the oblique cases of the singular, and these occur much less frequently than the nominative. The great majority of weak nouns in my material were in the unproblematic nominative singular or plural forms, which explains the very high success rate. The weak nouns used were also predominantly high-frequency items such as *Student* and *Mensch.* This does not explain why the non-CALL group achieved better results, but it does suggest that the present material is perhaps not sufficient to make generalisations about students' command of weak nouns.

4) *High number of correct forms*: When doing an error analysis, we tend to concentrate on the errors and neglect the positive sides of learners' performances. In this study, both correct and incorrect instances of grammatical structures have been counted, so it is not a one-sidedly negative view. It is worth noting that, with the one exception of the passive construction in the non-CALL group, students in both groups achieved over 50% correct scores on all the grammar points.

5) *Comparison of the CALL and non-CALL groups*: The better performance of the CALL group in the structures examined here provides clear evidence that they had an advantage. The advantage

was not restricted to these four structures, as they also achieved higher average marks in the written examination than the non-CALL group, in spite of starting from a slightly weaker level, as indicated by their A level scores.

The major difference between the two groups is that one of them attended the module involving the CALL exercises while the other did not. Other factors have been largely eliminated by excluding students who spent the most time on German (more courses in German literature, history, etc.) and who might be considered to be the most highly motivated (Single Subject German students) as well as those who could be thought of as having the least commitment to the subject (Supplementary subject and Combined Studies students). Therefore it seems justified to conclude that the CALL exercises were effective in improving the performance of the more successful group, and that this study provides evidence of a longer term beneficial effect of CALL exercises in addition to the short-term effect which has been reported elsewhere.

It is hardly necessary to say that a single study like this cannot be regarded as conclusive and that further studies involving substantial numbers of students would be highly desirable.

Bibliography

Alderson, J. Charles/Clapham, Caroline/Steel, David (1997) 'Metalinguistic knowledge, language aptitude and language proficiency' *Language Teaching Research* 1, 93–121

Davies, Graham/Yu Hong Wei (1997) 'Do grammar checkers work? A report on research into the effectiveness of Grammatik V based on samples of authentic essays by EFL students', in Kohn, Janos/Rüschoff, Bernd/Wolff, Dieter (eds.), 169–88

Durrell, Martin (1996) *Hammer's German Grammar and Usage*, 3rd edition, London: Edward Arnold

Ellis, Rod (1994) *The study of second language acquisition,* Oxford: OUP

Ensinger, Doris (1997): 'Die Effizienz computergestützter Übungsformen. Eine Untersuchung im Rahmen des Landeskundeunterrichts für Fortgeschrittene', in: Kohn, Janos/Rüschoff, Bernd/Wolff, Dieter (eds.), 223–30

Götze, Lutz (1996) 'Grammatikmodelle und ihre Didaktisierung in Deutsch als Fremdsprache', *Deutsch als Fremdsprache* 33, 136–43

Hall, Christopher (1996) *Eindrücke–Einblicke Computerübungen*, Berlin and Munich: Langenscheidt

Hewer, Sue (1998) *Optimising the use of TELL products: an evaluative investigation into TELL products in use*, available on-line at: www.hull.ac.uk/cti/eval.htm

James, Carl (1998) *Errors in language learning and use*, London and New York: Longman

James, Carl/Garett, Peter/Candlin, Christopher N. (eds.) (1991) *Language Awareness in the Classroom*, London etc.: Addison Wesley Longman

Kohn, Janos/Rüschoff, Bernd/Wolff, Dieter (eds.) (1997) *New Horizons in CALL. Proceedings of EUROCALL 96*, Szombathely: Daniel Berszenyi College

Laufer, Batia/Hill, Monica (2000) 'What lexical information do L2 learners select in a CALL dictionary and how does it affect word retention?', in: *Language Learning & Technology* 3/2, 58–76

Laurillard, Diana (1996) *The TELL Consortium – Formative evaluation report*, available on-line at: www.hull.ac.uk/cti/eval.htm

Neunzig, Willi (1997) 'Die Effizienz computergestützter Übungsformen – eine Untersuchung im Rahmen des Übersetzungsunterrichts', in: Kohn, Janos/ Rüschoff, Bernd/Wolff, Dieter (eds.), 303–11

Smith, Gordon/Courtney, Kathy/Rickers, Wibke/Köhler-Ridley, Monika (1997) 'Role reversal CALL at Coventry University', in *Computer Assisted Language Learning* 10/3, 211–27.

Weydt, Harald (1993) 'Was soll der Lerner von der Grammatik wissen?' in: Harden, Theo/Marsh, Clíona (eds.) *Wieviel Grammatik braucht der Mensch?* Munich: iudicium, 119–137

PETER HOHENHAUS

An Overlooked Type of Word-formation: Dummy-compounds in German and English

Introduction

In the area of nominal compounding, the issue of (semantic) sub-classification has long been a field of heated debate. The difficulty of exhaustively classifying all relationships between constituents in N+N-compounds, in particular, has led some scholars to give up completely. Selkirk (1982:25) goes as far as claiming 'that it is a mistake to attempt to characterise the [...] semantics of non-verbal compounds in any way'; others have suggested reducing such a characterisation of semantic relationships in nominal compounds simply to 'there is a connection between' A and B (Bauer 1979:46; cf. also Heringer 1984).

Interestingly, these approaches all refer to the famous article by Downing (1977) and her statement that 'virtually any relationship' may hold between the constituents of compounds (see Downing 1977:840). However, they all miss the important qualification 'in the appropriate context'. Furthermore, they tend to blur the fact that Downing (1977) did, after all, come up with a finite list of compounding relationships. Downing (1984:74) emphasised again that the fact 'that such lists can be arrived at' in a non-arbitrary fashion is too significant to be ignored. The salient point is that such semantic patterns only apply to what she calls 'classificatory compounds' – denoting generic types of entities, i.e. the 'normal' compounds we (are likely to) find in dictionaries. Such generalisations do not apply, however, to 'non-generic', 'non-classificatory' compounds, which Downing (1977) called 'deictic compounds'. Her famous example for the latter kind was *apple-juice seat* – a compound formed in a single specific situation to deictically pick out one of several seats at a table, namely the one in front of which a glass of apple-juice had been placed.

Highly context-dependent compounds such as this one are not only outside the range of semantic patterns for 'classificatory compounds', and are thus 'unsuitable for lexicalisation' (Downing 1977:822)[1], but they also point towards a rather different view of word-formation. There is also a significant functional difference between giving a (generic) category a label in the form of a complex word and the forming of a complex word solely to serve as a transitory means of deictic reference within a fortuitous context.

Word-formation and text

While, in Downing (1977), functional considerations were only touched upon as a sideline, the focus was directed towards the general functions of word-formation especially in German linguistics, e.g. Kastovsky (1978/1982/1989), Lipka (1981/1987), or Erben (1981). Even though investigations into the functional side of word-formation have been sporadic and often remain rather superficial, at least it has become irrefutably clear that the older assumption of the sole function of word-formation being simply to provide a means of extending a language's lexicon[2] is no longer tenable.

Out of the many suggested functions of word-formations, the concept of a 'pronominalising function', or text-function, has attracted the most attention, and has been specifically investigated by e.g. Wladowa (1975), Seppänen (1978), Dederding (1983), and Wildgen (1980/1982). However, these studies suffer partly from an insufficiently clear distinction between text-deictic functions and 'Textverflechtung' (roughly: a sort of lexical cohesion), and partly from the

1 In fact, this has far-reaching theoretical consequences, which are also supported by other empirical findings, leading to the necessary incorporation of a notion of 'non-lexicalisability' (which also entails an extension of the usual distinction between 'actual' and 'possible words' to include '[im]possible listeme' as well). These theoretical considerations are beyond the scope of this article, but see Hohenhaus (1996 and 1998).

2 See, for example, Motsch (1977:183) for an assertion of this view.

unconvincing nature of the data (which, in turn, is largely due to unfortunate choices of the text-types investigated). Neither are the differences between the use of lexicalised word-formations and the creation of new, i.e. nonce, word-formations made sufficiently explicit.

A crucial difference must be observed, however: the use of an established word, with a view to, for example, enhancing lexical cohesion, does not explain the existence of the formation in the first place. Any textual function associable with these is rather an effect of their use in such a way – but these lexicalised words have been there, in the lexicon, before; i.e. they were formed independently of that particular context.

In the case of nonce-formations, the question of functions is more important, being linked to the 'existence' of the form in question. That is to say, in such a case we also have to ask: Why has this particular complex word been newly formed, instead of employing an established word, or forming a syntactic phrase? The functions of new word-formations can be seen as the *raison d'être* of creative word-formation. Straightforward 'naming', arguably most important from the point of view of the lexicon, plays a rather less prominent role in creative word-formation in actual performance, whereas, as will be seen from the following, text-function stands out as one of its particular strengths.

Dummy-compounds: general features

It must be surprising that in those areas of classifications that are among the most closely investigated, a) subclassifications of nominal compounds, and b) their text-function(s), an entire type could indeed have been overlooked completely. This paper aims to close such a remarkable gap by providing an outline of a type which has, in fact, never before been acknowledged as a productive word-formation-type in its own right, and which I have dubbed 'dummy-compounds'[3]. First, a couple of examples of the phenomenon in question:

> 'I'm sorry to interrupt, Professor Baldwin,' said Lavine. [...] It's just – Well, I've been looking into solstitial winds at Ross, and I think – I think I may have stumbled onto something really big. [...] I'd kind of like to talk to you about it, if that's all right.' [...] 'Tell me about this **Ross thing**,' he [Baldwin] said, and lit the pipe. (*The New Yorker*, 8/5/1989, 44/47)

> *(The whole family, Willy, Kate, Lynn, Brian, and Alf are having dinner)* Willy:'[...] I want to talk about what we're going to do on our vacation. [...] We decided that we should all stay right here.' [*...the conversation digresses...*] Willy: 'Let's just go back to this **vacation thing**, right?' Lynn: 'Yeah. I think we should talk about it. How come we're not going anywhere?' (*ALF,* Lorimar Home Video, Alien Productions Inc., 1987)

> *(in the headmaster's office)* Peppermint Patty: 'Yes, sir, I admit that I have deliberately chosen to defy the school's dress code. I knew that I'd probably be sent to your office… in fact, I was prepared for it…'

> *(later, on the phone)* 'Hello Snoopy? Guess what... We have to appear before the student council tomorrow on this **dress code thing** so I'll see you at school at nine, okay? [...] This **dress code thing** is so piggy!' (Charles M. Schulz, *The Snoopy Festival*, 1974, 118)

Compounds such as the ones highlighted in bold are different from other kinds of compounds. While the categorial form of noun+noun is rather inconspicuous, the semantics involved here can hardly be said to follow the normal pattern of endocentric compounding, 'an AB is a kind of B', by which a broader category is more specifically defined (e.g. a *handbag* is a kind of *bag*). Here, it would not make sense to say e.g. 'a vacation thing is a kind of thing'. Such a paraphrase would rather be misleading; *vacation thing* does not denote a thing in the sense of 'physical object' at all (which such a context-free 'paraphrase' would imply), but is clearly an abstract noun. *Thing* in its more abstract meanings, however, can mean *any*thing, so that the 'kind-of'-paraphrase becomes completely void: everything is a 'kind

3 Never before 1996, that is – the discovery of dummy-compounds was included in my general study of English nonce word-formation published in that year (in German).

of thing' in this sense. *Thing* in such a compound is thus very similar to a grammatical morpheme, a synsemantic word, practically devoid of any lexical meaning whatsoever.

Instead of denoting, or endocentrically defining, these compounds simply refer back to, pick up again, some bit of previous context. Thus, they could generally rather be 'paraphrased' as: 'What has been said above/earlier involving X'. The relationship between the constituents, and the 'meaning' of the head remain unspecified – *thing* serves merely as a universal, empty head constituent; it is a dummy head.

Similar uses of *thing* have been noted by Fronek (1982), although not with reference to word-formation:

> *thing* is much closer to the class of function words than is generally appreciated. [...] it is capable of almost complete desemantisation [...]. It can be readily used to apply to living beings, objects of any shape and description, liquids, abstract concepts, events, etc. In this respect *thing* is much more inclusive than any other pro-form. (Fronek 1982:637)

The comparison to pro-forms is interesting as Kastovsky (1978/ 1982/1989), Lipka (1981/1987), and Seppänen (1978), in discussing text-functions, made an analogy to pronominalisation as well. *Thing* in the compounds given above is actually much closer to pronominalisation proper. Still, this is only an analogy, since real pronouns could not be used as heads in compound-structures; *vacation it* parallel to *vacation thing* would be ungrammatical. The reason for this is the same as the one Fronek (1982:633, 640) notes for '*thing* as a function word' in syntax:

> unlike most other pro-forms it behaves like an autosemantic word in that it can [...] serve as an empty head for all manner of modification, e.g. by articles, adjectival attributes, prepositional phrases, infinitival and participial constructions, and relative clauses.
>
> [...] *thing* is a useful intermediate link between *it* as a purely grammatical substitute (unsuitable because it cannot be modified) and general nouns such as *event, incident, occurrence*. It has the same degree of semantic inclusiveness as *it*, and at the same time, it has the syntactic flexibility of nouns with lexical meaning.

What has to be added to Fronek's enlightening observations is the role *thing* as a 'dummy head' can play in the morphological structure of nominal compounding as well – since we are, in my view, indeed faced with a highly productive regular pattern of compounding.

Recurrence, the most salient criterion for being a 'productive pattern', is indeed borne out by empirical data: dummy-compounds make up nearly 10% of my own collection of authentic nonce-formations (including all sorts of formation, not just compounds)[4]. They are thus likely to be the most productive single kind of nonce-formation (at least in English). Here is a list of the features characterising the type:

(a) From a formal point of view, dummy-compounds consist of X + dummy head, where the dummy head is one out of a very limited range, in particular *thing* or *business*, and X is an element from the preceding context, typically a noun (often itself a complex noun), but phrasal constituents are also common.

(b) In addition, the choice of determiner for a dummy-compound is restricted. Minimally, a definite determiner is obligatory; more commonly, however, it will be demonstrative *this* or *that*. Often complex determiner phrases immediately precede a dummy-compound, in particular *all this/that* __ and *this/that/the whole* __.

More important are the semantic and functional characteristics, in particular:

(c) The dummy head constituents are not used in their primary meanings (in the case of *thing*: 'physical object', i.e. [+ concrete]), but in an abstract and extremely open sense close to that of the pronouns *it* or *something*.

(d) It does not make any difference which of the dummy heads are chosen; they are interchangeable without affecting the meaning/reference, which is evidence of the 'emptiness' of these heads. (This is also shown by the doublets of dummy-compounds with different heads but the same reference in the same context – see below.)

4 An abridged (570-item) version of that collection of attested forms, together with all the necessary contexts, can be found as Appendix 1 in Hohenhaus (1996:381–449).

(e) The relationship between the immediate constituents is neither exocentric nor properly endocentric, but rather unspecified (none of the paraphrase patterns of classificatory compounds apply).

(f) The reference of dummy-compounds is purely (text-)deictic. This also means it is 'unique reference', without any hypostatisation ensuing. Accordingly, dummy-compounds are always singular in form.

These characteristics are, of course, interlinked; it can be said, for instance, that the deictic character of dummy-compounds (f) is additionally *marked* by the obligatorily demonstrative (or at least definite) determiners (b). Interestingly, both *this* and *that* occur indiscriminately; that is, they too seem to be interchangeable without any effect on the meaning/reference.

Admittedly, the class 'dummy-compounds' postulated here is, on closer inspection, not entirely homogeneous, nor does it have absolutely clear boundaries. Further distinctions/subclassifications within the overall type can be made. Also, some marginal cases will have to be considered. The first group of dummy-compounds, however, can confidently be called 'primary' in so far as they fully display all the features listed above.

Primary dummy-compounds

This group comprises not only those dummy-compounds with *thing* as the dummy head, but also those with *business*, which in this function is equally capable of desemantisation (i.e. in a dummy compound it is not used in its common more specific meanings revolving around the field 'commerce'). Both are used in exactly the same way to refer back to preceding context. Consider the following:

> 'Celia Welch speaking.' He [Dixon] felt as if he'd crunched a cracknel biscuit; in his preoccupation he'd forgotten about Mrs Welch. Still, why worry? In an almost normal tone he said: 'Can I speak to Professor Welch, please?' 'That's Mr Dixon, isn't it? [...]' He wanted to scream. His dilated eyes fell on a copy of the local paper that lay nearby. Without stopping to think, he said, distorting his voice [...]: 'No, Mrs Welch, there must be some mistake. This is the *Evening Post* speaking. [...] Well, actually it was Mr Bertrand Welch I wanted to speak to really,' Dixon said, smiling at his own cunning [...]. 'I'm not sure whether he's ... Just a minute.' [...] Better hang on, Dixon thought, and the information, which Mrs Welch had

> obviously gone to get, about where Bertrand could be reached was just what he wanted for the Callaghan girl. He'd be able to ring her up and tell her, too. Yes hang on at all costs. [...] 'This is Bertrand Welch' [...] '*Evening Post* here,' he managed to quaver through his snout. 'Er ... we'd like to do a little paragraph about you for our, for our Saturday page,' he said, beginning to plan. [...] 'As a matter of fact, when your Mrs Callaghan was on the blower to Atkinson ...' 'Who's this Atkinson character? I've never heard of him.' 'Our Mr Atkinson in the London office, sir.' [...]
>
> The Callaghan girl must be carefully coached in the following story: Some unknown calling himself Atkinson had rung her up that morning and, posing as a journalist, discussed Bertrand. He'd talked vaguely about the *Evening Post*, obtained the Welches' phone number, and rung off. When Bertrand came through on the phone, she must greet him at once with the Atkinson story, [...] The danger obviously was that she wouldn't come in with the conspiracy.

This episode in Kingsley Amis' novel *Lucky Jim* (1953, 99ff.) is referred back to several times in the subsequent text (or more precisely: by the novel's characters in conversation – only represented in writing in the novel, but clearly in 'spoken language mode') by means of dummy-compounds:

> 'I never got a chance to thank you for playing up so well over that **phone business**.' (115)
>
> 'I thought the whole of the ***Evening Post*** **business** was brilliantly funny.' (115)
>
> 'You're getting good at this sort of thing, aren't you? First the table, then the ***Evening Post*** **thing**, and now this,' (133)

The last two examples also show the interchangeability of the actual dummy head used: Both compounds have exactly the same reference, despite the formally different head constituent. What these excerpts from the original text also demonstrate well is how powerful a device of reference dummy-compounds can be – note the textual distance between them and what is being referred to (note the page numbers). This could hardly be matched by any other means of textual deictic reference with similar ease, economy of linguistic material, and syntactic flexibility.

Reference by means of dummy-compounds is not necessarily precise. However, the reference does not normally need to be any more precise in such conversational situations. Of course, the use of this means of reference only works if the hearer shares enough knowledge of context with the speaker. Without any such context-knowledge the expression 'that phone business', for example, would remain uninterpretable for a listener. The fact that the decoding of the deictic reference of a dummy-compound depends on a considerable amount of context-knowledge may also explain that dummy-compounds seem to be a special means of *anaphoric* reference only, i.e. they are never cataphoric.

To substantiate the claim that dummy-compounding does indeed constitute a productive pattern, a list of further authentic examples is given below, for brevity's sake without quoting their contexts[5], but retaining the determiner phrases:

> (this) tenure business, (this) bomb thing, (this) kennel business, (this) kitchen thing, (this) Christine business, (the whole) Michael Ellis thing, (the) degree business, (that) up-and-down business, (the) greengages business, (this) 'rude' business, (this whole) inspector business, (all this) rock-throwing business, (the) sherry thing, (this) shed business

The range of possible dummy heads may have to be extended. For instance, *bit* seems to be capable of playing the same role, and be interchangeable with the more common dummy heads, as evidenced by the 'doublets' *Women's Liberation bit* and *Women's Liberation business*, both having the same reference (in the same text – David Lodge, *Changing Places*, 1975, 184–185).

The same could be true for *affair*. Again, 'doublets' can be found (cf. *Summer Ball thing* and *Summer Ball affair*, taken from Kingsley Amis, *Lucky Jim*, 1953, 93–94). Fronek (1982:636) also mentions *affair*, in passing, together with *business*, *matter*, and *stuff*, as words 'of extremely broad semantics.' Thus it can be usable as the head in

5 Normally, adducing nonce-formations should be accompanied with sufficient amount of the original context, otherwise their interpretation will generally be impossible. Here, only the attestation of more forms is important, not their interpretation; the contexts necessary for decoding the reference of these forms, however, can be found in Appendix 1 in Hohenhaus (1996).

dummy-compounds as well[6]. Further possible members of this set could be *style*, *kind*, *type*, or *idea* (cf. the 'doublet' *kennel idea* and *kennel business*, with identical reference in the same *Alf*-context the example *vacation thing* was taken from). However, without more empirical evidence, the suggestion of including all these into the class of dummy-heads has to remain tentative.

In general, *-thing*/*-business*-compounds must be taken to be the most prototypical, and also the most productive, kind of dummy-compounds. Note that the judgement of this type's productivity is not necessarily contingent on frequency of attestation. The type is so flexible for deictic text-reference that it must also be one of the most productive patterns of English compounding in the 'potentiality' sense of the term 'productivity' (cf. Lieber 1992:1–9; Welte 1996:77–79). Almost anything, in a context, can be referred to by using the form of a dummy compound. Try it! If this were not an academic text, reference to parts of it could be made like this: that pronominalisation business, that hypostatisation thing, this recurrence thing, all this productivity business, etc. – it would not be appropriate style here, but in an informal chat with somebody who shares the knowledge of the contexts referred to, I *could* refer to them in this form and be understood.

And I could do so not only in English but also in German. In fact the two languages appear to be virtually parallel with regard to 'primary' dummy-compounding. The equivalent formal frame for English [(*all* +) $\mathrm{DET}_{\mathrm{def/dem}}$ + (*whole* +) *thing*/*business*] in German is [$\mathrm{DET}_{\mathrm{def/dem}}$ + (*ganz-* +) *-Geschichte*/*-Sache*]. Two examples (attested in conversation):

---

6 On the other hand, *affair* is slightly different from *thing* or *business* in that its broad (abstract) semantics are already its 'primary' meaning, so the 'de-semantisation'-criterion does not apply in the same way. Interestingly, *affair* can apparently be used in the 'opposite' way of differing from its 'primary' meaning (compared with *thing*), namely for reference to concrete physical objects (!) – as in the following: 'there's a new university there, you know, one of those **plateglass and poured-concrete affairs** on the edge of the town' (taken from: David Lodge, *Small World*, 1984, 182). However, since this compound is not text-deictic but concrete in meaning and also plural in form, it is not a dummy-compound.

1. In a German television programme, a guest in the studio reported the astonishing fact that Scotland exports sand to Saudi Arabia, the point being, though, that knowledge of this simple fact alone is rather meaningless and loses its remarkability once the important detail is also known that it is a special sort of sand (namely one that is particularly suitable for sandblasting, unlike Saudi Arabia's abundant desert-sand). The interviewee later refers back to all this by using the dummy-compound 'diese *Sandgeschichte*'.

2. A member of a group working on a joint publication suggested that all contributions should perhaps have uniform title pages, but this was not resolved. Next day, another member picked up the issue again by saying: 'Ich finde, wir sollten uns noch mal diese ganze *Titelblatt-Sache* überlegen.'

The compounds used in these contexts exhibit exactly the same characteristics as listed for English dummy-compounds above. They are in the same way text-deictic means of unique reference, marked by demonstrative determiners, with no ensuing hypostatisation; the heads show a similar desemantisation; *-geschichte* and *-sache* here do not mean 'history' (or 'a story') or 'physical object', respectively, which would be their 'primary' meanings. Thus, they could also easily be substituted for one another: 'diese *Sand-Sache*' or 'diese *Titelblatt-Geschichte*' would have been equally possible.

Even though numerous such dummy-compounds can be heard in German informal conversation, the type may be somewhat less frequent/productive than it is in English. If this is so, it may partly be due to the existence in German of a competing, similarly economical, syntactic means for achieving the same sort of text-deictic reference: [*das mit* + $[\mathrm{DET}_{\mathrm{def/dem}} + (\mathrm{AP}\ +)\ \mathrm{N}]_{\mathrm{NP}}]_{\mathrm{NP}}$. In fact, in the first of the two contexts retold above, it is also referred back to by precisely this structure: 'Das mit dem schottischen Sand.'

Secondary dummy-compounds

There are also sets of data sharing essential features of primary dummy-compounds but also displaying additional special features. Thus I shall subclassify them into the following separate 'secondary' types.

Derogatory dummy-compounds

The first such sub-type at first looks very similar to dummy-compounds with *bit*, *affair*, or *idea*, showing less desemantisation than *thing* or *business*, while sharing all the other referential and formal characteristics. However, here this difference in semantics and choice of forms is more systematic. First a couple of examples:

> 'What work do you do?' Dixon asked flatly. 'I am a painter. Not, alas, a painter of houses, [...]. No no; I paint pictures. [....]' Dixon hesitated; Bertrand's speech, which [...] had clearly been delivered before, had annoyed him in more ways than he'd have believed possible. [...]
> 'It would hardly be worth coming just to meet the great painter, would it?' Dixon said [...]. Carol half-closed her eyes [...]. 'What makes you say that? she said. [...] He can be quite entertaining at times, actually, though you're quite right about the **great-painter stuff**.' (Kingsley Amis, *Lucky Jim*, 41/46)

> 'Being married to you is like being slowly swallowed by a python. [...] I want out. I want to be free. I want to be a person again.' 'Look,' he said, 'let's cut out all this **encounter group crap**. It's that student you found me with last summer, isn't it?' 'No, but she'll do to get the divorce.' (David Lodge, *Changing Places*, 40)

The dummy heads in this kind of compound belong to a specific semantic class, words which at least in a second meaning are used as general derogatory words – including, apart from *stuff* and *crap,* also *nonsense*, *rubbish*, *shit*, *bollocks*, and certainly a few more. The strength of the derogatory quality of these words is, of course, not homogenic but forms a scale. *Stuff* is probably the 'weakest', and not unlikely to be found in rather neutral registers as well, while e.g. *crap* is much more stylistically marked and thus restricted in register.

What makes compounds like these different from 'primary' dummy-compounds is that they do not only (neutrally) refer to preceding context, but at the same time also make a (negative) value judgement. The substitution of, say, *thing* for *stuff*, *crap*, etc. would turn such compounds into neutral, 'primary' dummy-compounds, and vice versa. Within this subtype, the dummy heads seem to be interchangeable as well, without affecting the semantics in principle (only in degree of pejorative force). Here is a small set of further examples I have recorded (again, only the determiner is given in brackets, but not the actual context): (this) *Thomas nonsense*, (his load of) *Bulldog Drummond crap*, (all that) *Chinese paintings bollocks*, (this) *'pussy cat' nonsense*.

German appears to follow similar patterns to English 'derogatory' dummy-compounding in virtually the same way as is the case for the 'primary' kind. Possible heads include: *-Kram*, *-Quatsch*, *-Mist*, *-Blödsinn*, *-Scheiße*, etc., which, again, are interchangeable, with only the derogatory force increasing accordingly – roughly in the order of the nouns listed, from mild to strong. One example shall suffice here (again, attested in conversation): in a chat about general politics in Germany, in early May 1998, one of the speakers repeatedly focused on Germany's role in Kosovo at that time. Eventually, one of the other speakers said: 'Jetzt geht mir dieser ganze *Kosovo-Mist* aber langsam auf die Nerven.' (Note that this compound was not meant to refer to and qualify the Kosovo conflict and Germany's role in it as such, but only that part of the previous context it was the topic of.)

For this secondary type, however, I do not yet have a sufficient number of attested examples in either English or German to allow for more than tentative generalisations. I presume, however, that a broader empirical survey of informal spoken language (especially if it covers speech situations of conflict) should reveal a wealth of tokens belonging to the class in question.

Personal deixis dummy-compounds

A better empirical basis is already in place for the second class of 'secondary' dummy-compounds to be introduced here. I have recorded numerous examples such as the following:

'I was wondering about that article of yours. [...] Have you sent it off to anyone else?' 'Yes, that **Caton chap** who advertised in the T.L.S. a couple of months ago. Starting up a new historical review with an international bias, or something. [...]' 'Ah yes, a new journal might be worth trying. There was one advertised in the *Times Literary Supplement* a little while ago. Paton or some such name the **editor fellow** was called.' [...] 'Apparently this **Caton fellow** was in for the chair at Abertawe at the same time as Haines.' (Kingsley Amis, *Lucky Jim*, pp. 14/82)
'But then, when the official part was over, I was nobbled by a man in the English Department. Name of Dempsey.' 'Robin Dempsey,' said Persse. 'Oh, you know him? Not a friend of yours, I hope?' 'Definitely not.' 'Good. Well, as you probably know, this **Dempsey character** is gaga about computers. [...]' (David Lodge, *Small World*, 183)

Mrs Entrail: Then there's Stanley ... he's our eldest [...] the one we hear so much about nowadays is Karen. She married a Canadian – he's a dentist – they live in Alberta [...]

Mr Entrail: [...] a really horrible-looking person, she is. I thought that one would stay on the shelf, but along comes this stupid **dentist git**. He's a real creepy bastard, he is. (Monty Python's Flying Circus, *All the Words*, New York: Pantheon, 1989, Vol. 2, 312f.)

These compounds[7] are very similar to the other kinds of dummy-compounds in that they too are deictic compounds, again typically marked by demonstrative determiners, with unique reference. Here, however, the deixis is not just textual (although that is involved as well), but it is primarily personal deixis – explicit reference to particular people in those contexts. As in the derogatory dummy-compounds discussed in the preceding section, an element of 'emotional deixis' (cf. Hohenhaus 1996:272ff.; van Ek and Robart 1984:159f.) is important here, although to more varying degrees – from very negative to practically neutral. The latter crucially depends on the head constituents. Thus they are not always interchangeable without affecting meaning; while the choice between either *fellow* or *character* hardly seems to make much difference, the choice between *chap* or *git*, for instance, certainly does.

7 More examples without contexts: *Catchpole fellow, Michael Ellis character, marketing girl, Haines character, post office man, Monsour guy, Callaghan girl, Atkinson character* (for the latter two see the context reproduced in section 3.1. for *phone business, Evening Post thing/business*).

Where the first constituent is a proper name, normally the use of the name alone would have done for neutral reference, provided the person of that name is known to both speaker and listener. Thus, the fact that a speaker chooses to form a dummy-compound instead must bear significance, and I would hold that this is linked to the 'emotional' deixis mentioned above, which is specifically given emphasis through this type of formation[8].

In this sense, the 'secondary' type of dummy-compounding under discussion here is similar to the other 'secondary' type of derogatory (but abstract) dummy-compounds; and by the same token, both subtypes are different from 'primary', purely text-deictic dummy-compounding. And it is in the area of personal deixis dummy-compounds that we find more contrastive differences.

Compounds for referring to people in English and German have also been discussed by Hietsch (1984), particularly with regard to the range and semantics of the 'second' elements. Based on constructed examples, rather than attested authentic forms, Hietsch (1984:393) suggests the following:

> In English, for instance, there are a wide variety of ways of referring to a male person who works at the London Foreign Office: 'Foreign Office chap' (the implication is almost invariably neutral-positive), 'Foreign Office bloke' (negative-neutral), 'Foreign Office bod' (negative), 'Foreign Office geezer' (insulting), 'Foreign Office chappie' (patronising), 'Foreign Office johnny' (the speaker is upper-class male), 'Foreign Office guy' (the speaker is probably American).

It could be argued that some of Hietsch's characterisations, especially the last two, may no longer apply in contemporary English. The main focus in Hietsch (1984), however, is placed on compounds with *-man* as the head constituent, and German equivalents with *-mann*/*-mensch*, but he generally fails to acknowledge the nonce nature of such

8 There is also a syntactic alternative which appears to be in between neutral reference and the deictic strength of the compound. It involves the same determiner and lexical constituents, but not in compound form; one example: in the context of the compound *Caton chap* (see above), the same person is later also referred to as 'this chap Caton'.

compounds[9]. Indeed, these forms must be considered to be the most straightforward kind of dummy-compounds of this subtype.

German alternative common nouns for reference to males, parallel to English *-guy*, *-bloke*, *-fellow*, *-chap*, etc. could be considered as well; in particular *-kerl*, *-typ*, *-meister* spring to mind (e.g. *Versicherungsmensch*, *Versicherungskerl*, *Versicherungstyp*, *Versicherungsmeister*, could all be used in the same function with hardly any connotational differences). But Hietsch does not pursue (or even mention) these possibilities either.

What Hietsch (1984:394) does note, however, is a different, rather special category of possible head nouns in such compounds:

> Near synonyms, taken from the rather wide field of Christian names made into common nouns – e.g., *-fritze* as in *Möbelfritze* 'furniture chap', or *Pressefritze* 'newspaper bloke', 'newspaper johnny', and *-heini* as in *Computerheini*, slightly negative, hence 'computer bod' [...] extend the possibilities of semantic differentiation further.

As Hietsch indicates, there seems to be one similar possibility of using a proper name as a dummy head in English, namely *-johnny* (although I have not myself ever come across an authentic attested example). In general, however, such use of proper names appears to be far more restricted in English. If it is synchronically possible at all, there certainly is no equivalent frequency and no choice of proper-name-come-common-noun heads as there is in German.

It will not have escaped the reader that, so far, the choice of data looked at could be regarded as 'male chauvinistic' in as much as only reference to males has been discussed. As far as references to women are concerned, Hietsch (1984:406) considers in passing the possibility of dummy heads based on proper names for reference to females – however, without making concrete suggestions as to what female proper name could be used. In German, I have come across *-triene*, *-liese*, and *-grete* (thus *Möbeltriene*, *Möbelliese*, *Möbelgrete* would be female equivalents to Hietsche's male example *Möbelfritze* above).

9 For instance, he complains that in 'the major dictionaries [they] are not even granted a mention' (Hietsch 1984:394). However, since dummy-compounds are nonce-formations, which never enter the lexicon, lexicography is quite right in not listing them.

Non-proper-names as specifically marked female dummy heads include, of course, *-frau* as the most neutral one[10]. Hietsch (1984:406) claims that *-weib* is 'more familiar', which I would contest, at least for present-day German, in which it has taken on distinctly negative connotations. Another female-only dummy head I have frequently come across is *-tante*, which can also be taken to be somewhat derogatory (e.g. *diese Versicherungstante*), although more in a merely distancing rather than sexist way (which is how I would understand something like *Versicherungsweib*). English equivalents would be *-woman* or *-lady*, both mentioned by Hietsch (1984:406), as neutral ones. Rather more negative common nouns that could be used as dummy heads as well appear to be quite restricted in English, tending to have more specifically sexist implications – such as *-tart*, *-bird*, or *-slapper*[11]. And, unlike in German, no proper names seem to be capable of functioning as female dummy heads in English at all.

German is even more markedly different from English as regards the possible uses of proper names as the first constituent. While this seems absolutely natural in English (cf. *Caton chap*, *Dempsey character*, etc.), with the name being referentially identical to the compound as a whole, the same is impossible in German. If proper names as first elements are possible in German dummy-compounds at all, at least the relationship between that name and the head nouns has to be of a different nature. It cannot be identity. For instance, the only example Hietsch (1984:402) mentions, *Kohlmann*, meaning 'one who works for Helmut Kohl', could thus not be formed to refer to Kohl himself, i.e. with the reading 'man who is (called) Kohl'.

10 Cf. Heringer's (1984) discussion of various context-dependent interpretations of *Fischfrau*.

11 Of course, *-girl* has to be added to the list, restricted in reference with respect to age only rather than being notably sexist. In fact, the context given for *phone business* in section 3.1. also contains an example of this kind: *Callaghan girl*. The same person is, in a different part of the same context, also referred to, rather less favourably so, as *Callaghan piece*.

The importance of the findings

An account of a language's system of word-formation should cover all, and in particular all productive, types of formation. Why is it, then, considering how well-researched English and German morphology is, that dummy-compounding has hitherto been overlooked? I suspect this has to do with empirical bases. Dummy-compounds appear to be specific to only certain 'text-types'. They are almost exclusively found in informal conversation. Such kinds of spoken language, however, are rarely surveyed in research on morphology (instead most studies rely on ready-made collections, in particular in the form of dictionaries). Still, since spoken language is not strictly bound to the spoken *medium*, but also has to include 'written down' informal conversation, e.g. in novels, it remains remarkable that dummy-compounds have slipped the attention of morphological studies.

Another explanation for dummy-compounds having been overlooked for so long may well be that they do not 'stand out'; they do not draw attention to themselves. In fact, I would argue that they are *so* normal that they usually go without notice unless one is specifically attuned to detecting them. According to Lieber's (1992:1-9) concept of productivity, this 'inconspicuousness' (of individual hapaxes) can be taken as a symptom of full productivity. Thus, for the synchronic description of the regularities/possibilities of 'living' word-formation, dummy-compounds deserve to be moved into the spotlight.

The inclusion of dummy-compounding thus not only closes a significant gap in the formal, semantic and functional description of the word-formation systems of English and German. It is also important as part of the study of deixis, text-linguistics/discourse analysis, as well as stylistics. Furthermore, since the systems of dummy-compounding in English and German are not identical, although quite similar, the same applies to contrastive linguistics of the two languages.

Future research

The generalisations and predictions made in this article should lend themselves to being tested with the methods of corpus linguistics. What would be required are large enough computerised corpora containing a representative sample of those informal spoken language text-types in which dummy-compounds tend to occur. If this condition regarding the coverage of the relevant registers in such corpora is fulfilled, it should be possible to search for the range of types outlined above and come up with statistical data to verify the claims made above, and, in particular, test the more tentative ones. This is mostly a line of future research, however, and no concrete results can be reported at this stage.

Bibliography

Bauer, Laurie (1979) 'On the Need for Pragmatics in the Study of Nominal Compounding', *Journal of Pragmatics* 3, 45–50

Dederding, Hans-Martin (1983) 'Wortbildung und Text: Zur Textfunktion (TF) von Nominalkomposita (NK)', *Zeitschrift für Germanistische Linguistik* 11, 49–64

Downing, Pamela (1977) 'On the creation and use of English compound nouns', *Language* 53/4, 810–842

Downing, Pamela (1984) 'The relation between word formation and meaning', *Quaderni di Semantica* 5, 69–77

van Ek, Jan A./Robat, Nico J. (1984) *The Student's Grammar of English*, Oxford: Blackwell

Erben, Johannes (1981) 'Neologismen im Spannungsfeld von System und Norm', in: Geckeler, Horst et al. (eds.), *Logos Semanticos. Studia linguistics in honorem Eugenio Coseriu*, vol. 5, Berlin, New York, Madrid, 37–43

Fronek, Josef (1982) '*Thing* as a function word', *Linguistics* 20, 633–654

Heringer, Hans Jürgen (1984) 'Wortbildung: Sinn aus dem Chaos', *Deutsche Sprache* 12, 1–13

Hietsch, Otto (1984) 'Productive Second Elements in Nominal Compounds: The Matching of English and German', *Linguistica* (Ljubljana) 24, 391–414

Hohenhaus, Peter (1996) *Ad-hoc-Wortbildung: Terminologie, Typologie und Theorie kreativer Wortbildung im Englischen*, Frankfurt am Main, Bern, New York, Paris: Peter Lang

Hohenhaus, Peter (1998) 'Non-Lexicalizability – as a Characteristic Feature of Nonce Word-Formation in English and German', *Lexicology* 4/2, 237–280

Kastovsky, Dieter (1978) 'Zum gegenwärtigen Stand der Wortbildungslehre des Englischen', *Linguistik und Didaktik* 36, 351–366

Kastovsky, Dieter (1982) 'Word-Formation: A Functional View', *Folia Linguistica* 16, 181–198.

Kastovsky, Dieter (1989) 'Word-Formation', in: Dirven, René et al. (eds.), *A User's Grammar of English: Word, Sentence, Text, Interaction, Part A, The Structure of Words and Phrases*, Frankfurt am Main, Bern, New York, Paris: Peter Lang

Lieber, Rochelle (1992) *Deconstructing Morphology: Word Formation in Syntactic Theory*, Chicago, London: University of Chicago Press

Lipka, Leonhard (1981) 'Zur Lexikalisierung im Deutschen und Englischen', in: Lipka, Leonhard/Günther, Hartmut (eds.), *Wortbildung*, Darmstadt: Wissenschaftliche Buchgesellschaft

Lipka, Leonhard (1987) 'Word-Formation and Text in English and German', in: Asbach-Schnitker, B./Roggenhofer, J. (eds.) *Neuere Forschungen zur Wortbildung und Historiographie der Linguistik*, Tübingen, 59–67

Motsch, Wolfgang (1977) 'Ein Plädoyer für die Beschreibung von Wortbildungen auf der Grundlage des Lexikons', in: Brekle, Herbert E./Kastovsky, Dieter (eds.) *Perspektiven der Wortbildungsforschung*. Bonn: Bouvier

Selkirk, Elizabeth (1982) *The Syntax of Words*, Cambridge, Mass.: MIT Press

Seppänen, Lauri (1978) 'Zur Ableitbarkeit der Nominalkomposita', *Zeitschrift für Germanistische Linguistik* 6, 133–155

Welte, Werner (1996) *Englische Morphologie und Wortbildung*, Frankfurt am Main, Bern, New York, Paris: Peter Lang

Wildgen, Wolfgang (1980) 'Textuelle Bedingungen der Einführung und Verwendung ad-hoc gebildeter Komposita', *L.A.U.T., Series A, Paper 80*

Wildgen, Wolfgang (1982) 'Makroprozesse bei der Verwendung nominaler Ad-hoc-Komposita im Deutschen', *Deutsche Sprache* 10, 237–257

Wladowa, E.W. (1975) 'Okkasionelle Wortbildungen mit dem gleichen Stamm als Satz- und Textverflechtungsmttel', *Textlinguistik* 4, 71–87

NILS LANGER

On the Polyfunctionality of the Auxiliary *tun*

The auxiliary use of the verb *tun* is a common property of virtually all West Germanic languages. Its English variety *do* has received a tremendous amount of attention in the research literature, which is partially to do with the dominance of English linguistics in general but also, as this paper will suggest, with the relative ease with which the grammatical properties of the auxiliary can be defined in English. The case is different, however, for auxiliary *tun* in German. It has been shown (Fischer 1998, Langer forthcoming a, Langer forthcoming b) that the construction was widespread throughout the Early New High German period (1350–1650) and it is clear from evidence found in dictionaries and grammars of modern dialects that the construction is still commonplace in many if not all dialects of Modern German. In this paper, I will be discussing the validity of the claim that auxiliary *tun* is polyfunctional, made explicitly in e.g. Ebert (1993), Fischer (1998), and Langer (forthcoming a) and implicitly in many dialect dictionaries, including the *Deutsches Wörterbuch* (*DWB*). Polyfunctionality in this context is understood to mean that one element can have various functions in various distributions, as opposed to a possible definition where an element is seen to have several functions in one distribution. Examing the distribution of *tun* in both ENHG and modern dialects, I will argue that contrary to the prevalent opinion in the research literature, auxiliary *tun* is in fact not polyfunctional but without function and that it is this lack of grammatical specificity that enables it to occur in a large and divergent variety of distributions in German.

Having introduced the problem, I will then provide a brief survey of some of the functions that auxiliary *tun* is said to express or realise in other West Germanic (WGmc) languages. Following this I will examine dialect dictionaries and grammars of modern German dialects to establish distributional patterns and overlaps with the aim of determining the number and type of functions *tun* is said to express in non-standard varieties today. Finally, I will investigate what more recent research literature says about the functions of *tun*; these functions will be correlated with the evidence of my Corpus of ENHG language use of auxiliary *tun*. Crucially, I will not be attempting to refute any postulation of a specific function on the grounds that they are incorrect or implausible. Rather, I will be showing that the evidence in favour of these postulations is inconclusive or improbable on the basis of complementing evidence and that a categorisation of *tun* as a 'dummy' auxiliary will provide the most satisfactory solution.

The Problem

In one of the very few studies todate that concern themselves with the functional distribution of auxiliary *tun* in EHNG, Fischer (1998) concludes that the *tun*-periphrasis can be said to have nine functions:

> This analytic verb form [= auxiliary *tun*; NL] was used to replace synthetic tenses – present and past tense – as well as the synthetic subjunctive. Furthermore it was employed to mark subordinate clauses and – occasionally – to form subjunctives. Moreover it was used as a marker of a topic-comment structure and as a simple periphrasis of a cognitively more elaborate form. Finally the *tun* periphrasis was a supporting syntactic means to express durative Aktionsart and could be seen in connection with imperfective aspect.' (Fischer 1998:134)

Importantly, these suggested functions come from a range of areas of German grammar, ranging from verbal morphology such as tense (present and past), mood (subjunctives), and aspect (durativity, imperfectivity) to sentence-level syntax, such as the marking of subordinate clauses and changing the topic-comment structure. Finally, it is postulated that the auxiliary *tun* functions as a semantico-pragmatic mechanism to facilitate the cognitive processing of the sentence. In Fischer's defence it should be pointed out that she is not claiming that all these functions are necessarily expressed by the inclusion of *tun* in the sentence, a point elaborated on in Abraham and Fischer (1998). Nonetheless, it is striking that in an – admittedly long and dialectologically diverse – period of German, i.e. ENHG, a single auxiliary is said to have such a wide range of functions, taken from very diverse areas of grammar. This apparent polyfunctionality will come under scrutiny in this article. It will be argued that whilst *tun* can co-occur with these functions, they are not expressed by the auxiliary.

In this context, it is interesting to note that a prominent example of regional English *do* has recently been re-analysed with a similar line of argument. It has been a long tradition to identify auxiliary *do* in South-Western English as a marker of habituality, firstly in the nineteenth century but also recently by e.g. Ihalainen (1976), Weltens (1983), Harris (1984), and Trudgill (1986). In a recent article, Klemola investigated these claims and found that in the present tense 'no evidence could be detected in the data to show that the form would be restricted to a habitual function' (Klemola 1998:51) whereas for the past tense, '[t]he conclusion must be that not even the periphrastic *did* form is used exclusively as a marker of habitual aspect in the three corpora [of SW English] investigated, although past habitual is the dominant semantic environment where this grammatical construction is used in the dialect' (Klemola 1998:51). The objection to the analysis of *do* as a habitual marker is therefore not that habituality does not occur in sentences with *do*. On the contrary, Klemola found that between 66% and 85% (depending on the corpus) of his instances of *do* did occur in the 'semantic environment' of habituality. But given the remnant examples that did not co-occur with a habitual interpretation there is serious doubt as to whether auxiliary *do* expressed habituality by virtue of its presence or whether the auxiliary is merely able to co-occur with the function because it is neutral with respect to this aspectual meaning. In this particular respect, it should be pointed out that Fischer (1998) suggests that *tun* is a '*supporting* syntactic means' to express aspect and *Aktionsart*, rather than being the unique or sole marker. Nonetheless, this implies that *tun* has some specific meaning to represent a particular aspect or *Aktionsart*.

Functions of *tun* in WGmc (except German)

Afrikaans is the only West Germanic (WGmc.) language that appears not to have auxiliary *tun* (Ponelis 1979), whilst for Yiddish, Simon (1988:169) attests a durative function in the Middle Ages and in Frisian, the construction of *dwaan* + Inf existed until the late Middle Ages (Stapelkamp 1948). In Dutch, the construction is generally ungrammatical in the standard language with the exception of 'hierbij doe ik u toe komen [...]' in formal letter writing (Ingrid Tieken-Boon van Ostade, personal communication) and causative constructions (since eMD, cf. van der Horst 1998) as in

(1) De zon doet de temperatuur oplopen (Cornips 1998:86)

In non-standard Dutch, auxiliary *doen* is found in child language and language used towards children (Tieken-Boon van Ostade 1990), adult colloquial speech to avoid complex morphology and to thus ease cognition (Duinhoven 1994), as well as various dialects (e.g. Groningen, Twente, Drente, Heerlen) (Cornips 1998). The only dialect use that has received some specific attention is Heerlen Dutch, for which Cornips (1994, 1998) found that *doen* + Inf is only used to express habituality. In the context of this article it is important to note that Heerlen *doen* is not a unique marker of habituality in that dialect and also that it can co-occur with other (adverbial) habituality markers.

The history, distribution and function of auxiliary *do* in English, the 'auxiliary *par excellence*' (Denison 1993:255), is probably the most-discussed issue of verbal morphology and syntax in that language. It originated as a causative construction (Brunner 1962:325) but developed a periphrastic use in the late Middle Ages. In Standard English, auxiliary *do* is fully grammaticalised to enable negations, questions and emphasis, albeit only the latter is directly expressed by *do* whilst in negations and questions, the auxiliary is used as a catalyst (with the negation being expressed by *not* and questions by the marked intonation). As regards regional English, we saw above that SW *do* is often claimed to be habitual in interpretation, although this has recently been disputed partially by Klemola (1998) as shown above.

In sum, auxiliary *tun* is a very common property in virtually all WGmc languages. It is striking, however, that the auxiliary occurs in many different functions across the language varieties, with the most prominent ones being of an aspectual nature.

Functions of *tun* in Modern German dialects

The evidence found in dialect dictionaries and grammars is overwhelming. The most striking observation is that the auxiliary *tun* is found in 28 of 32 seminal works on dialects (cf. section two of the bibliography) and that it is present in all dialect areas of Modern German. As regards the attested functions of *tun*, the picture is confusing, mostly due to the fact that the dictionaries and grammars do or might use different terminology (this is not always clear from the phrasing of the dictionary entries) when referring to the same distribution or function. For reasons of space, I will concentrate on four functions:

- subjunctive
- focus
- aspect
- tense

Altogether, 46 varieties of German are entered in the table below; some varieties are listed by more than one author/work, e.g. Bavarian. The inclusion of Low German varieties is justified because of its *sociolinguistic* status as a modern German dialect. The varieties are listed under the name of the region they are spoken in, and for all cases without a superscript index, the full bibliographical details can be found in the bibliography, section two. For those dialects that are reported via the research literature rather than a dialect grammar or dictionary, the key to the superscript indices is: 1=Erben 1969; 2=Erb 1995; 3=Abraham & Fischer 1998; 4=Eroms 1984; 5=Eroms 1998.

Dialect area	Auxiliary *tun*	No auxiliary *tun*
Standard (n=3)	Duden 'mundartliche Literatursprache'[1]	Wahrig
LG (n=10)	Westphalen, Ostphalen, Nordharz, Hinterpommern, Niedersachsen, Holstein[1], Hamburg[1], Mecklenburg[2], Stavenhagen[1]	Stadt Hannover
WCG (n=11)	Köln[1], Rheinland, Frankfurt, Mainz[1], Südhessen[2], (Niederhessen), Pfalz, Luxemburg, Remscheid, Pennsylvania, Oberhessen[2], Hessen-Nassau[2]	Trier, Waldeck, Barmen
ECG (n=8)	Thüringen, Schlesien, Obersachsen, Aken, Stadt Madgeburg, Leipzig[2] Westsudetenland[1], Egerland[1],	
WUG (n=7)	Baden, Elsass, Lothringen, Schweiz, Bern, Schwaben[2], Bern[3], Zürich[3]	
NUG (n=4)	Würzburg, Franken, Nürnberg, Ostfränkisch[3]	
EUG (n=3)	Bayern, Tirol	

Table 1: Distribution of auxiliary *tun* in Modern German dialects

Firstly, the most striking result is clearly the large number of varieties that contain auxiliary *tun* compared to those that do not. Secondly, it is notable that there appear to be no regional patterns: those dialects that do not allow the construction are part of a dialect area where the vast majority of dialects does contain the periphrasis in their grammar.

Overall, the table shows all too clearly that the auxiliary *tun* is a widely distributed element in modern German dialects, with all dialect areas (as defined for ENHG in Reichmann 1989) containing the construction in a majority of dialects. In the following tables, the distribution of periphrastic *tun* in the modern dialects will be shown with regard to individual grammatical functions. The functions are ordered with decreasing frequency and generally link up to the major functions listed in the previous section.

Subjunctive

Duden lists the subjunctive as one of the functions of auxiliary *tun* but marks it as 'regional'. The table below give evidence that subjunctive is realised by *tun* in all dialect areas. For EUG, Eroms (1998:145f.)

claims that this function is on the brink of being grammaticalised in Bavarian, with nearly 100 % of the informants preferring auxiliary *tun* as a subjunctive marker. Apart from that, the construction occurs elsewhere, with some dictionaries (e.g. Mitzka's *Schlesisches Wörterbuch*) distinguishing further between conditional and optative, whilst others argue that the periphrasis is restricted to certain tenses (cf. Fischer 1998 for a similar classification in ENHG).

Subjunctive	In general	Present	Past	Conditional	Optative
Dialect area					
Standard (n=3)	(Duden)				
LG (n=10)	Nieder-sachsen	Ost-phalen	Nordharz		
WCG (n=11)	Frankfurt Mainz[1]		Süd-hessen[2]	Frankfurt Luxemburg Pfalz	Pfalz
ECG (n=8)	Thüringen Obersachsen Aken Madgeburg			Schlesien	Schlesien
WUG (n=7)	Baden Lothringen Schwaben[5]	Schweiz Baden[2]	Schweiz	Schweiz	
NUG (n=4)	Franken			Nürnberg	
EUG (n=3)	Bayern[4] Bayern[5]		Bayern[5]		

Table 2: Auxiliary *tun* as a marker of subjunctive

Tense

The use of *tun* as an 'umschreibung des präsens' and other tenses had already been suggested by the DWB (1935:444ff.). Above, it was mentioned that this classification is problematic because as a finite verb, auxiliary *tun* must carry tense and thus the objection to the analysis arises that the function 'Umschreibung eines Tempus', which is found very frequently in the dictionaries and grammars, may have been used for lack of evidence of other functions. This is particularly prominent as regards the *Umschreibung* of present and past tense, which, incidentally, are the tenses most frequently realised by *tun*. As with the subjunctive, all dialect areas are represented: it is not regionally marked. Notice also that a number of dialects are claimed to be able to realise both past and present, which, again, maybe suggests that in those instances, *tun* does not realise either of these tenses as such but is there simply because of an independent requirement, namely for finite verbs to carry tense. An exception to this problem is *tun* as an imperative since its morphological form is marked for a single function. Nonetheless, it is doubtful whether one can accurately speak of imperative to be a unique function of *tun*. After all, all lexical and auxiliary verbs can (synthetically) form an imperative, too.

Tense	Present	Past	Future	Imperative
Dialect area				
Standard (n=3)				
LG (n=10)	Mecklenburg[2] Holstein[1] Hamburg[1]	Mecklenburg[2] Holstein[1] Hamburg[1]		
WCG (n=11)	Pfalz[2] Südhessen[2]	Kassel[1] Hessen-Nassau[2]	Pfalz Südhessen[4]	Südhessen[2] Köln[1]
ECG (n=8)	Magdeburg	Schlesien Madgeburg		Obersachsen[1] Westsudeten-land[1], Egerland[1]
WUG (n=7)	Elsass		Elsass	Schweiz
NUG (n=4)	Nürnberg			Nürnberg
EUG (n=3)	Tirol Bayern-Österreich[3]	Bayern-Österreich[3]		Tirol, Bayern[4] Bayern-Österreich[3]

Table 3: Auxiliary *tun* as a marker of tense

Aspect

The problem with the identification of aspectual functions as realised by *tun* has also already been discussed above, in that often aspect is realised by the semantics of the lexical verb (*Aktionsart*) and, possibly, the accompanying adverbials. Nonetheless, four types of aspect are frequently mentioned, as listed below. In comparison to the subjunctive and tense marking shown above, the realisation of aspect appears much less frequent, which suggests that aspect marking may actually be part of the semantics of *tun*, given that the distribution is varied with regard to dialect. Notice that in all dialect areas, *tun* is claimed to have an aspectual function and that in all dialect areas except NUG and ECG, the auxiliary can express more than one aspect, although not necessarily in every individual dialect.

Aspect	Durative	Habitual	Iterative	Progressive
Dialect area				
Standard (n=3)				
LG (n=10)	Mecklenburg[2]	Niedersachsen[3]		
WCG (n=11)		Pennsylvania[2]	Pennsylvania[2]	Pennsylvania
ECG (n=8)	Leipzig[3]			
WUG (n=7)	Schweiz Bern[3]			Zürich[3]
NUG (n=4)		Ostfränkisch[3]		
EUG (n=3)		Bayern[4]		Bayern[4] Tirol[3]

Table 4: Auxiliary *tun* as a marker of aspect

Focus

The issue of focus is particularly difficult as grammatical focus seems to interact and be overruled by phonological focus in German. The existence of grammatical focus has long been recognised and it is generally accepted that theme and rheme occupy distinct positions in the German phrase structure (cf. Abraham 1995). It is thus plausible to suggest that since the presence of an auxiliary will cause the lexical verb to appear in a different position (in most cases the sentence-final, i.e. the rheme position), an auxiliary may be used deliberately to achieve this change in the phrase order and thus in the information structure of the sentence. In cases where a semantically marked auxiliary or modal verb might be used, a default auxiliary could be inserted in the Verb-Second position; that this default auxiliary is probably *tun* is suggested by the table below, where it is used in four syntactic distributions. In this context, it is suggestive to learn that the only distribution of auxiliary *tun* in Standard German as prescribed by the Duden is a focus construction, i.e. a V-topicalisation structure, where the auxiliary appears to have no other function than to be an element to fill the finite verb position, a constraint on German that is independent of focus in general, e.g. *Essen tut Susanne jeden Tag*.

The function of focus is widely distributed, with NUG being the notable exception. The 'Betonung der Tatsächlichkeit', which has been suggested as part of the Rhenish *tun*, is an isolated function and could also be subsumed under the heading *focus in general*. Notice that only V-topicalisation structures provide a syntactic means of identifying the functions with the lexical verb appearing in sentence-initial position and thus preceding the auxiliary; in all other focus structures, it is up to the linguist to make the choice of classification.

Focus	In general	Theme/ Rheme	V-topicalisa-tion	*Tatsächlichkeit*
Dialect area				
Standard (n=3)			Duden	
LG (n=10)	Ostphalen Hinter-pommern Nordharz		Stavenhagen[1]	
WCG (n=11)	Rheinland Frankfurt Pennsylvania	Rheinland		Rheinland
ECG (n=8)		Obersachsen Leipzig[3] Egerland[1]	Thüringen Aken Obersachsen[1]	
WUG (n=7)	Baden Schweiz	Baden Schweiz[1] Schwaben[1]		
NUG (n=4)				
EUG (n=3)	Bayern[4]	Tirol[4]	Südtirol[4] Bayern[5]	

Table 5: Auxiliary *tun* as a marker of focus

The Researchers' View on Functions of *tun* in ENHG

As regards the linguistic function of auxiliary *tun* in ENHG, the opinions of the research community are divided, ranging from virtual semantic redundancy:

> Eine semantische Nuancierung [durch die Präsenz der *tun*-Periphrase] gegenüber den einfachen Formen ergibt sich bei ihr – *wenn überhaupt* – aus der Emphase, die auf der durch den Infinitiv ausgedrückten Verbhandlung liegt [...] (Philipp 1980:75; my emphasis, NL)

to extreme polyfunctionality (Fischer 1998, Langer forthcoming a). It is certainly the case that auxiliary *tun* can co-occur with a range of adverbials, e.g. *immer* and *die ganze Zeit*, which has led researchers to suggest that *tun* is a marker of durativity, iterativity and/or other verbal aspects (Fischer 1998:132ff.). It is not clear, however, whether the auxiliary is the actual marker of the aspect expressed in the sentence, especially in cases where there is a supporting adverbial. Fischer (1998:132) identifies the auxiliary only as a support to express *Aktionsart* or aspect and shows that sentences that contain the *tun* + Infinitive construction, can have durative, habitual and iterative meaning, as already suggested in the DWB (1935:444), saying that *tun* + infinitive occurs 'manchmal mit dem nebenbegriffe des pflegens und der wiederholten handlung':

(2a) der bischoff thete die ganze nacht nachsinen (durativity; Fischer 1998: 132)

(2b) vnd wird dem Pfeiffer sein auffblassene Arbeit an keinen Orth mehr bezahlt als in disen [Wirtshäusern] / auch all Spihl=Leuth vnd Possen=Krammer tun hierinnen ihre Wahr versilbere (habituality; Fischer 1998:133)

(2c) Was ist das maßzehlende? Welches eine gleichheit vnd maß andeüten thut (iterativity; Fischer 1998:133)

Eichinger (1998:362) claims that Grimmelshausen used the *tun*-Periphrase 'in einigen Instanzen' as a marker for imperfective action, whilst on p. 365, he argues that 'die *tun*-Konstruktion die *Erfüllung* eines entsprechenden Schemas [betont]' [my emphasis, NL], i.e. perfectivity. In the light of these attempts at describing the function of *tun*, von Polenz (1994:263) seems justified in claiming that the *tun*-construction is 'semantisch schwer erklärbar'. In addition to the marking of aspect, *tun* is claimed to be a marker of subjunctive mood, although again, '[i]t is not always easy to determine whether a particular form [of *tun*] is subjunctive or not' (Fischer 1998:127), since in ENHG /a/ and /e/ were not conclusively assigned to represent a specific function in the different dialectal variants of *tun* (Solms and Wegera 1993:305f.). Therefore, the modern researcher faces a potential phonological identity of the morphological difference between *theten*$_{\text{SUBJ}}$ and *theten*$_{\text{PAST}}$ and which is an important problem when analysing a specific example as either subjunctive or indicative. Interestingly, neither Philipp (1980:123) nor Ebert (1993:420f.) mention the auxiliary *tun* as a possible marker in their sections on the subjunctive in their grammars of ENHG. Nonetheless, Fischer (1998:127) identifies twelve occurrences of subjunctive *tun* in her corpus. Finally, auxiliary *tun* appears to be a catalyst to change the default emphasis pattern in the clause, by enabling the lexical verb to appear in the V1 position (V-topicalisation) or in the rhematic position of the sentence:

> Manchmal intensivieren solche z.T. sprechsprachlichen Konstruktionen lediglich eine Tätigkeit, z.B. das dialektale *ich tu's schon machen* für *ich mache es*. (Wells 1990:257)

> [*Tun*] makes it possible to form the characteristic German sentence-frame, by means of which the non-finite lexical verb can be moved to the rhematic focus position at the end of the sentence. (Fischer 1998:131, with reference to Abraham 1995:602)

In a similar line of argument, Admoni suggests that the increasing frequency of the auxiliary in ENHG is due to the fact that it enables the formation of the sentence frame, an independent development in the syntax of German:

> Solcher Gebrauch [of *tun* as an auxiliary] entspringt aber der sich immer weiter entwickelnden Tendenz des deutschen Satzes zur Zweiteiligkeit des Verbs und erlaubt die Rahmenbildung auch in solchen Direktsätzen, die sonst rahmenmäßig neutral wären. (Admoni 1990:185)

The reason for this apparent polyfunctionality of *tun* in ENHG, and, for that matter, in modern dialects, too, is seen by Fischer in the fact that the inclusion of *tun* in the sentences can help 'reduce cognitive efforts' (Fischer 1998:132), an idea which was postulated by Erben (1969:46, 52), too, under the heading of 'denkökonomische Formel'. Fischer (1998:132) claims that using *tun* makes the sentence easier to process and understand because it will relieve the speaker from using difficult, i.e. rare ablauts (in past participles) or splitting separable prefixes from their base lexical verbs. As regards the origin of the polyfunctionality of *tun*, Fischer (1998:134) suggests that 'the polyfunctionality of [the] *tun* periphrasis does not seem to have emerged in the course of its historical development, but to have probably existed from the beginning.' However, the ground for the emerging *tun* was and is particularly fertile at a stage when the grammatical system of a language undergoes a change.

> Wherever there are gaps in the system, *tun* seems to be the obvious choice to fill them. [...] This has to do with its special status as a functionally variable, latently existing auxiliary which can be employed in the morphological, syntactic, semantic as well as pragmatic field. (Fischer 1998:134)

Tun and Polyfunctionality

To summarise so far, it is claimed in the literature that the auxiliary *tun* in German is polyfunctional in that it can or does express a variety of functions, implicitly suggesting that these functions would be absent from the sentence if *tun* was absent. Fischer (1998) furthermore suggests a watered-down version in that *tun* is merely a *supporting syntactic means* to express a certain (aspectual) function, therefore in the absence of *tun*, this function would not be there as prominently or strongly as it is with *tun*. The very nature of historical linguistics, i.e. working without native speakers' judgements, makes it very difficult to shed any light on the matter. However, as was shown above, even the evidence from modern dialects is inconclusive. In this section, I will be attempting to cast further doubt on the validity of the claims that *tun* is polyfunctional in ENHG.

Tense and Mood

One of the most convincing examples of a specific function represented by *tun* involves tense and/or mood. It is argued that the clear morphological evidence showing that *tun* carries present tense, past tense, and/or subjunctive was sufficient to postulate that *tun* is a tense or mood marker. Clearly, this is based on a misconception of the idea of 'marker' or 'represents/expresses a function'. Simply because an element is licensed (by the grammar) to carry a certain feature is not to say that this element is the marker of this feature by virtue of the grammar. Compare the following:

(3a) Das Buch kaufte$_{[+\text{SUBJ}]}$ ich gerne, wenn ich mehr Geld hätte.
(3b) Das Buch hätte$_{[+\text{SUBJ}]}$ ich gerne gekauft.
(3c) Das Buch würde$_{[+\text{SUBJ}]}$ ich gerne kaufen.
(3d) Das Buch täte$_{[+\text{SUBJ}]}$ ich gerne kaufen.

In (3b), a form of *haben* carries the subjunctive feature, as is clear from both the interpretation of the sentence and the verbal morphology. However, despite the evidence in (3b), nobody would want to suggest that in German, subjunctive is expressed or marked by *haben*. Similarly, in (3d) the subjunctive marking in this paradigm is not on *tun* but on the finite verb (which in (3d) happens to be a form of *tun*, thus the subjunctive marker is the finite verb (slot) and example (3d) is grammatical not because of the presence of *tun* as such but because of a finite verb, which happens to be *tun*. Note that this view has interesting repercussions on the analysis of *würde* as a subjunctive marker. Following the line of argument presented here, it cannot be said that *würde* is a subjunctive marker! Rather, *würde* is a potential candidate of German that can fill the finite verb slot that is marked [+SUBJ]. Therefore, the reason that *würde* has become the prominent finite verb to mark subjunctive in Modern German is not because of an increased frequency or functional preference of *würde* but rather because diachronically more and more lexical verbs lost their ability, for independent morphological reasons not discussed here, to fill a [+SUBJ] slot. The subjunctive form of *werden*, i.e. *würde*(*n*), however, did not undergo the same development and because of its combinability with lexical verbs (again, independent of the subjunctive marking, as attested by the non-subjunctive *werden* + Inf.), it is frequently used to express subjunctiveness with a range of lexical verbs. To conclude, (3d) is grammatical (in ENHG and modern German dialects) by virtue of *tun* being a (n auxiliary) verb that retains its morphological ability to fill a [+SUBJ] slot. The processes involving subjunctive marking in these varieties of German and Standard German do not differ. What causes the ungrammaticality of (3d) in Standard German is the general ungrammaticality of *tun* as an auxiliary.

The same argument holds for the postulation that auxiliary *tun* functions as a tense marker.

(4a) Ich $\text{lese}_{[+\text{ TENSE}]}$ die Zeitung.
(4b) Ich $\text{habe}_{[+\text{ TENSE}]}$ gestern die Zeitung gelesen.
(4c) Ich $\text{werde}_{[+\text{ TENSE}]}$ morgen die Zeitung lesen.
(4d) Ich $\text{tat}_{[+\text{ TENSE}]}$ gestern die Zeitung lesen.

Again, it is not the case that (4d) is grammatical because *tun* has the specific function of [+past tense] but because *tun* is licensed as an auxiliary. The grammaticality of (4d) follows from that, in that any auxiliary in the finite position must be finite, i.e. carry tense. It is interesting to note in this respect that I have not come across any suggestion that postulates *tun* as a marker for number or person, despite the fact that it will always (in finite verb positions) be specified for these features.

To conclude, auxiliary *tun* cannot be said to function as a *marker* of tense or mood because instances of *tun* with a specification for tense or mood (i.e. all instances, as a finite verb is always specified for these features) are due to the status of *tun* as an auxiliary, not because of any *tun*-specific properties.

Focus

In contrast to Modern English, where the auxiliary *do* itself is focussed by way of audible phonological stress in

(5) Whatever you think, Susl *did* say that she liked me!

the auxiliary *tun* cannot receive phonological stress:

(6a) * Den Kuchen *tust* du jetzt nicht essen.
(6b) Den Kuchen tust du jetzt nicht essen.

However, despite these crucial differences, it is often claimed that *tun* is often used for emphatic purposes. This suggestion has been developed in a little more detail in Abraham and Fischer (1998) where it is argued that the inclusion of auxiliary *tun* in a sentence will alter the theme-rheme structure. This is undoubtedly the case since the insertion of an auxiliary in the Verb-Second (V2) position will cause the lexical verb to surface in the V-final position as in

(7a) Annelie gab Dirk den Kuchen.
(7b) Annelie tat Dirk den Kuchen geben.
(7c) Annelie möchte Dirk den Kuchen geben.

The insertion of *tun* in V2 causes a reorganisation of the theme-rheme distribution with the rheme being *den Kuchen* in (7a) and *geben* in (7b). Speakers use this mechanism to emphasise particular phrases and the use of *tun* in the V2 to achieve certain focal effects follows from more general rules of German grammar. Again, it is not a particular feature of *tun* that activates the mechanism as shown by the grammaticality in (7c). (7c) achieves the same rheme-reorganisation effects as (7b); however, in comparison to (7a), (7c) adds the semantics of *mögen* whilst (7b) is a more neutral alternant to (7a) (except, of course, for the changed theme-rheme structure), due to the semantic vacuity of *tun*. To conclude, it is not surprising that in a grammar which contains auxiliary *tun*, the auxiliary is used, just like any other auxiliary, to alter the theme-rheme structure of a sentence by preventing the lexical verb from occupying the V2 position. This is not to say, however, that *tun* is somehow the default or preferred marker for the theme-rheme alternation strategy or that it is one of the specific functions *tun* to change emphasis. Rather, this property is common to all auxiliaries.

Aspect

The identification of aspectual interpretation of auxiliary *tun* is certainly most problematic due to the difficulty of establishing subtle differences in meaning in historical texts. Abraham and Fischer (1998:39) express some doubt on the verifiable attribution of aspectual marking by *tun* with reference to their list of (modern) examples of aspectual *tun*, noting that the types of aspect suggested to be marked by *tun* are already present in the lexical semantics of the main verbs of their example sentences. Similarly, Eichinger (1998:361) says about his *tun*-examples in the Simplicissimus that the aspectual relationship between the periphrastic and the corresponding synthetic verb phrases is not easy to determine. As cited above, Fischer (1998) formulated very carefully that *tun* is used to 'support' a certain aspectual reading (i.e. durativity or imperfectivity) rather than to solely represent it. Generally, aspect is a grammaticalised category of the verb; the way adopted here to determine aspectual modification by *tun* is to survey a corpus of ENHG *tun* in order to establish with which *Aktionsarten* as marked on lexical verbs and adverbials *tun* can co-occur. If, e.g. it is assumed that *tun* expresses durativity, the following would be ungrammatical and therefore should not be attested:

(8a) * Der Zug tut$_{[+durative]}$ explodieren$_{[+punctual]}$.
(8b) * Das Kind tut$_{[+durative]}$ plötzlich$_{[+punctual]}$ einschlafen.

since there is a direct clash between durativity and punctuality. By way of negative elimination, it could be concluded from a grammatical attestation of (8) that *tun* does *not* mark durativity. My corpus, consisting of 127 texts from the Heidelberg Corpus, which was compiled by Oskar Reichmann to form the basis of the *Frühneuhochdeutsche Wörterbuch* (Reichmann 1989), is divided into dialect areas and scanned for specific *Aktionsarten* that co-occur with auxiliary *tun*:

	No. of *tun*	Perfective				Imperfective	
		inchoa-tive	resulta-tive	punc-tual	causa-tive	iterative	durative
NG	16	4	5	0	4	0	10
WCG	145	7	87	4	7	0	66
ECG	35	3	28	5	3	2	16
WUG	82	1	49	8	4	4	29
NUG	116	1	52	10	5	6	58
EUG	128	18	50	8	13	12	44
Total	522	34	271	35	36	24	223

Table 6: Auxiliary *tun* with a perfective or imperfective lexical verb[1]

The actual numbers should be seen as mere indications of certain tendencies as it is notoriously difficult to assign specific *Aktionsarten* to most verbs, especially as these can vary between its meaning in isolation and in a given sentence:

(9a) Marc isst. (durative)
(9b) Marc isst einen Apfel. (resultative)

Nonetheless, the table shows very clearly that, across all dialect areas, the auxiliary *tun* is just as likely to occur with perfective as with imperfective verbs. The occurrence of *tun* with accompanying adverbials in similarly inconclusive in that only some 129 attestations (of 522) include an adverbial that provides some aspectual meaning. The relative scarcity of adverbials gives some support to Fischer (1998), as an auxiliary *tun* that does have aspectual meaning would not require the presence of an adverbial of the same aspectual interpretation. Nonetheless the compatability of *tun* with all types of *Aktionsarten* indicates that its supporting function with regard to aspect is at most restricted to its ability to move the lexical verb, carrying a specific *Aktionsart*, into the rhematic position and thereby emphasising it. This, however, is not a property specific of *tun* but of any auxiliary.

1 Extra numbers are due to some verbs being categorised for more than one *Aktionsart*.

Conclusion

In this paper, I have argued that the much-cited polyfunctionality of auxiliary *tun* in Modern German dialects as well as in ENHG is ill-founded on a misconception of grammatical marking. I hope to have shown that the auxiliary *tun* behaves no differently from any other auxiliary and that its various 'functions' are common to German auxiliaries in general and not specific to *tun*. In contrast, auxiliary *tun* is semantically vacuous and it is for this reason that it is used more frequently than other auxiliaries in certain distributions, since it can be inserted in the auxiliary position without adding a semantic interpretation to the sentence. It is in this sense that the auxiliary is a dummy auxiliary, 'a true little helper and a general factotum' (Fischer 1998:134).

Bibliography

i. Secondary Literature

Admoni, Wladimir (1990) *Historische Syntax des Deutschen*, Tübingen: Niemeyer

Abraham, Werner (1995) *Deutsche Syntax im Sprachenvergleich*, Tübingen: Narr

Abraham, Werner/Fischer, Annette (1998) 'Das grammatische Optimalisierungs-szenario von *tun* als Hilfsverb', in: Donhauser & Eichinger, 35–47

Brunner, Karl (1962) *Englische Sprachgeschichte*, Tübingen: Niemeyer

Cornips, Leonie (1994) De hardnekkige voorordelen over de regionale doen+infinitief-constructie, *Forum der Letteren 35*, 282–294

Cornips, Leonie (1998) 'Habitual *doen* in Heerlen Dutch', in: Tieken-Boon van Ostade et al. (eds.), 83–102

Denison, David (1993) *English Historical Syntax*, London: Longman

Donhauser, Karin/Eichinger, Ludwig M. (eds.) (1998) *Deutsche Grammatik – Thema in Variationen. Festschrift für Hans-Werner Eroms zum 60. Geburtstag*, Heidelberg: Winter

Duinhoven, A.M. (1994) 'Het hulpwerkwoord *doen* heeft afgedaan', *Forum der letteren* 35, 110–131

DWB = Grimm, Jacob/Grimm, Wilhelm (1935) *Deutsches Wörterbuch*, edited by M. Lexer, D. Kralik and the *Arbeitstelle des Deutschen Wörterbuchs*, volume 1, 1. Abteilung, 1.Teil, Leipzig: S.Hirzel

Ebert, Robert Peter (1993) 'Syntax', in: Reichmann, Oskar/Wegera, Klaus-Peter (eds.) *Frühneuhochdeutsche Grammatik*, Tübingen: Niemeyer

Eichinger, Ludwig M. (1998) '"Als ich aber im besten Tun war" – Verwendungsweisen des Verbs *tun* in H.J.Ch. von Grimmelshausen "Simplicius Simplicissimus"', in: Donhauser and Eichinger (eds.), 351–368

Erb, Marie Christine (1995) *Zur Theorie expletiver Verben*, M.A. dissertation, University of Frankfurt am Main

Erben, Johannes (1969) '"Tun" als Hilfsverb im heutigen Deutsch', in: Engel, Ulrich et al. (eds.) *Festschrift für Hugo Moser*, Düsseldorf: Pädagogischer Verlag Schwann

Eroms, Hans-Werner (1984) 'Indikativische periphrastisch Formen von *doa* im Bairischen als Beispiel für latente und virulente syntaktische Regeln', in: Wiesinger, Peter (ed.), *Beiträge zur bairischen und ostfränkischen Dialektologie*, Göppingen: Kümmerle Verlag

Eroms, Hans-Werner (1998) 'Periphrastic *tun* in present-day Bavarian and other German dialects', in: Tieken-Boon van Ostade, I. et al. (eds.) 139–15

Fischer, Annette (1998) '*Tun* periphrasis in Early New High German', in: Tieken-Boon van Ostade, I. et al. (eds.) 121–138

Harris, John (1984) 'Syntactic variation and dialect convergence', *Journal of Linguistics* 20, 303–327

Horst, Joop van der (1998) '*Doen* in Old and Early Middle Dutch: A comparative approach', in: Tieken-Boon van Ostade, I. et al. (eds.) 53–64

Ihalainen, Ossi (1976) 'Periphrastic *Do* in the Dialect of East Somerset', *Neuphilologische Mitteilungen* LXXVII, 608–622

Klemola, Juhani (1998) 'Semantics of DO in southwestern dialects of English English', in: Tieken-Boon van Ostade, I. et al. (eds.), 25–52

Langer, Nils (forthcoming a) 'The Distribution of Lexical and Non-Lexical Do in West Germanic' in: Solms, Hans-Joachim/Watts, Sheila/West, Jonathan (eds.) *The Germanic Verb*, Tübingen: Niemeyer

Langer, Nils (forthcoming b) 'Zur Verteilung der tun-Periphrase im Frühneuhochdeutschen – Wornach die Bürger sonst die Finger lecken tun', *Zeitschrift für Dialektologie und Linguistik*, vol. 68/1

Philipp, Gerhard (1980) *Einführung in das Frühneuhochdeutsche. Sprachgeschichte – Grammatik – Texte*, Heidelberg: Quelle & Meyer

Polenz, Peter von (1994) *Sprachgeschichte vom Spätmittelalter bis zur Gegenwart. Bd. II*, Berlin, New York: de Gruyter

Ponelis, F.A. (1979) *Afrikaanse Syntaksis*, Pretoria: van Schaik

Reichmann, Oskar (1989) *Frühneuhochdeutsches Wörterbuch*, Band I, Berlin, New York: de Gruyter

Simon, B. (1988) *Jiddische Sprachgeschichte. Versuch einer neuen Grundlegung*, Frankfurt: athenäum

Solms, Hans-Joachim/Wegera, Klaus-Peter (1993) 'Flexionsmorphologie' in: Reichmann, Oskar/Wegera, Klaus-Peter (eds.) *Frühneuhochdeutsche Grammatik*, Tübingen: Niemeyer

Stapelkamp, C. (1948) '"Bliken dawen" – "Gijn lichten dwaen" – "Writen dwaen"', *It Beaken* 10, 180–192

Tieken-Boon van Ostade, Ingrid (1990) 'The origin and development of periphrastic auxiliary *do:* a case of destigmatisation', *NOWELE* 16, 3–52

Tieken-Boon van Ostade, Ingrid et al. (eds.) (1998) *Do in English, Dutch and German. History and present-day variation,* Münster: Nodus Publikationen

Trudgill, Peter (1986) *Dialects in contact,* Oxford: Blackwell

Wells, Christopher J. (1990) *Deutsch: eine Sprachgeschichte bis 1945,* Tübingen: Niemeyer

Weltens, B. (1983) 'Non-standard periphrastic *do* in the dialects of South West Britain', *Lore and Language* 3/8, 56–74

ii. Dialect grammars and dictionaries

Bauer, K. (1902) *Waldeckisches Wörterbuch, hrsg. von H. Collitz* (= reprint, Wiesbaden: Sändig Verlag, 1969)

Bergmann, G. (1996) *Wörterbuch der obersächsischen Mundarten, Band 4, S–Z, begr. von Frings, Th. und Große, R.*, Berlin: Akademie Verlag

Bischoff, K. (1977) *Akener Wörterbuch*, Köln: Böhlau

Brückner, Wolfgang (1984) *Frankfurter Wörterbuch, 16. Lieferung S–U, hrsg von Scheimbs, H.O. und Vogt, G.*, Frankfurt: Waldemar Kramer

Christa, P. (1927) *Wörterbuch der Trierer Mundart [...]* (= reprint, Vaduz: Sändig Reprint Verlag, 1969)

Damköhler, E. (1927) *Nordharzer Wörterbuch* (= reprint, Wiesbaden: Sändig Verlag, 1970)

Drosdowski, G. (1989) DUDEN. *Deutsches Universalwörterbuch*, Mannheim: Dudenverlag, 2nd ed.

Follmann, M.F. (1909) *Wörterbuch der deutsch-lothringischen Mundarten*, Leipzig: Quelle & Meyer (= reprint, Hildesheim: Georg Olms, 1971)

Gebhardt, A. (1907) *Grammatik der Nürnberger Mundart*, Leipzig: Breitkopf & Härtel

Greyerz, O. von/Bietenhard, R. (1981) *Berndeutsches Wörterbuch*, Bern: Francke, 2nd ed.

Halbach, G.H. (1951) *Bergischer Sprachschatz. Volkskundliches plattdeutsches Remscheider Wörterbuch*, Remscheid

Hansen, A. (1964) *Holzland-ostfälisches Wörterbuch [...], bearbeitete und herausgegeben von H. Schönfeld*, Ummendorf: Kreisheimatmuseum

Hodler, W. (1969) *Berndeutsche Syntax*, Bern: Francke

Hofmann, F. (1926) *Niederhessisches Wörterbuch [...]*, Marburg: Elwert's Verlagsbuchhandlung

Krämer, J. (1969–1975) *Pfälzisches Wörterbuch, Band III, begr. von E. Christmann,* Wiesbaden: Steiner

Lambert, M.C. (1924) *A Dictionary of the Non-English Words of the Pennsylvania-German Dialect*, Lancaster, PA: The Pennsylvania-German Society

Laude, R. (1995) *Hinterpommersches Wörterbuch des Parsantegebietes*, hrsg. von D. Stellmacher, Köln: Böhlau

Leithaeuser, J. (1929) *Wörterbuch der Barmer Mundart* (= reprint, Vaduz: Sändig Reprint Verlag, 1990)

Ludewig, G. (1987) *Stadthannoversches Wörterbuch, bearbeitet und herausgegeben von D. Stellmacher*, Neumünster: Karl Wachholtz

Luxemburger Wörterbuch (1950) Luxemburg: Linden

Marin, E./Lienhart, H. (1904–1907) *Wörterbuch der elsässischen Mundarten, Bd. II.* (reprint, Berlin: de Gruyter, 1974)

Meisen, K. (1958–1964) *Rheinisches Wörterbuch, bearbeitet von Josef Müller unter Mitarbeit von Heinrich Dittmaier*, Berlin: Erika Klopp Verlag

Mitzka, W. (1965) *Schlesisches Wörterbuch, Band III,* Berlin: de Gruyter

Ochs, E. (1925–1940) *Badisches Wörterbuch, Erster Band, vorbereitet von F. Kluge, A. Götze, L. Sütterlin, F. Wilhelm, E. Ochs*, Lahr: Moritz Schauenburg

Sartorius, J. B. (1862) *Die Mundart der Stadt Würzburg* (= reprint, Vaduz: Sändig Reprint Verlag, 1989)

Schöpf, J.B. (1866) *Tirolisches Idiotikon* (= reprint, Vaduz: Sändig Reprint Verlag, 1985)

Spangenberg, K. et al. (1983–1995) *Thüringisches Wörterbuch*, Sächsische Akademie der Wissenschaften, Berlin: Akademie Verlag

Staub, F./Tobler, L. (1973) *Schweizerisches Idiotikon XIII, Wörterbuch der schweizer-deutschen Sprache, fortgesetzt von A. Bachmann und O. Gröger,* Frauenfeld: Huber & Co

Stellmacher, D. (1993) *Niedersächsisches Wörterbuch, Band III*, Neumünster: Wachholtz

Wagner, E. (1987) *Das fränkische Dialektbuch*, München: C.H. Beck

Weber, A./Bächtold, J.M. (1983) *Zürichdeutsches Wörterbuch*, Zürich: Hans Rohr, 3rd ed.

Woest, F. (1930) *Wörterbuch der westfälischen Mundarten, neu bearbeitet und herausgegeben von E. Nörrenberg* (=reprint, Wiesbaden: Sändig, 1966)

NOTES ON CONTRIBUTORS

INGO CORNILS is Lecturer in the German department at the University of Leeds. His research interests are the Utopian and the Fantastic and he has published on Romanticism, the German Student Movement and German Science Fiction. He is currently working on the political and cultural impact of the German Student Movement on Germany and a comparative study of H.G. Wells and Kurd Lasswitz.

PETER DAVIES is Lecturer in German at the University of Edinburgh. Recent publications include: *Divided Loyalties: East German Writers and the Politics of German Division* and articles on Johannes R. Becher, Alexander Abusch, Hanns Eisler's *Johann Faustus* and Bertolt Brecht in the GDR. He is currently working on a project on autobiographical writing in the German Communist Party. Research for the paper in the present volume was carried out thanks to a Leverhulme Trust Special Research Fellowship at the University of Manchester.

WINIFRED DAVIES is Senior Lecturer in German at the University of Wales Aberystwyth where she teaches German sociolinguistics and German language. She has researched into linguistic variation and attitudes towards it and is currently investigating language awareness amongst teachers and trainee teachers in Central Germany. Among her publications are *Linguistic Variation and Language Attitudes in Mannheim-Neckarau* (1995) and *Essay-Writing in German: A students' guide* (1997).

CHRISTIAN FANDRYCH is Lecturer in German at King's College London. His research interests include various aspects of German linguistics (morphology, text linguistics, academic discourse) and German as a foreign language/Applied Linguistics. Publications include *Klipp und Klar. Übungsgrammatik Grundstufe Deutsch* (2000, with Ulrike Tallowitz), and *Wortart, Wortbildungsart und kommunikative Kommunikation* (1993).

IAN FOSTER lectures in the School of Languages at the University of Salford. He is the author of *The Image of the Habsburg Army in Austrian Prose Fiction, 1888 to 1914* (1991) and has published widely on Austrian Literature.

CHRISTOPHER HALL lectures in German at the University of Leicester and is Visiting Professor of Germanic Philology at the University of Tampere in Finland. His research interests lie in the fields of German linguistics and phonetics, language teaching and testing, computer-assisted language learning, and intercultural communication. In addition to books, articles and reviews, he has published CALL packages for German and Swedish.

PETER HOHENHAUS has been Visiting Lecturer in German and Linguistics in the Department of Modern Languages at the University of Bradford (as *DAAD-Lektor*) since 1996. His main research areas are empirical and theoretical morphology, lexicology, humorology, *DaF*, and corpus linguistics. He is the author of *Ad-Hoc-Wortbildung* (1996).

GERALDINE HORAN is currently Lecturer in German linguistics at the University of Birmingham. Her research interests include German linguistics and socio-linguistics, as well as German language teaching. She has recently completed her PhD-thesis on the topic *'Ebenso echt weiblich wie echt nationalsozialistisch': an analysis of female discourse*.

MARIANNE HOWARTH is Professor and Head of Modern Languages at Nottingham Trent University. She is the author of *Absolute Beginners' Business German* (1994), and she has published several articles on Britain's diplomatic and business relations with Germany.

NILS LANGER has studied and taught German, Linguistics and English at Newcastle upon Tyne, Leiden, Heidelberg, Wolfenbüttel and Dublin. He completed his doctorate on the effectiveness of prescriptive grammarians in Early New High German this year and is currently Lecturer in German at the University of Bristol.

MECHTHILD MATHEJA-THEAKER is Senior Lecturer in German at the University of the West of England in Bristol. Her main research interests are: the situation of women before and after German unification and social transformation after unification. Her publications include *Alternative Emanzipationsvorstellungen in der DDR-Frauenliteratur 1971–1990*, (1996).

TANJA NAUSE is a research student at the University of Bradford, having studied German Literature and Cultural Studies at the Humboldt-University, Berlin, where she graduated in 1998. Her research interests are: post-*Wende* literature, forms of autobiographical writing and cultural memory, and picaresque storytelling.

RACHEL PALFREYMAN gained her PhD on Edgar Reitz's *Heimat* from the University of Manchester in 1999. She has been lecturing at the University of Nottingham since September 1998 and is currently working on Tom Tykwer and constructions of the environment in German film.

STUART PARKES is Professor of German Literature and Society at the University of Sunderland. He has published widely on contemporary German literature in its social context. He is the author of *Writers and Politics in West Germany* (1986) and is co-editor of *Literature on the Threshold* (1990), *German Literature at a Time of Change 1989–1990, The Individual, Identity and Innovation. Signals from Contemporary Literature and the New Germany* (1994), *Contemporary German Writers, Their Aesthetics and Their Language* (1996) and *Literature, Markets and Media in Germany and Austria Today* (2000).

GERTRUD REERSHEMIUS is Lecturer in German at Aston University. Her research interests are: pragmatics, discourse analysis, language contact, bilingualism (especially in Yiddish and Low German). Her recent publications include: *Biographisches Erzählen auf Jiddisch. Grammatische und diskursanalytische Untersuchungen* (1997).

DAVID ROCK lectures in German at the University of Keele. He has published widely on modern German literature and currently specialises in GDR and Romanian-German writers. His most recent publications are *Jurek Becker: A Jew who became a German?* (2000) and *Voices in Times of Change: The Role of Writers, Opposition Movements and the Churches in the Transformation of East Germany* (2000). He is working on a volume on German minorities in Eastern Europe (with Stefan Wolff).

JEAN-MARC TROUILLE is Lecturer in German Studies at the University of Bradford, where he also teaches Dutch. His research interests lie in the field of Franco-German economic, industrial, political and cultural cooperation.

STEFAN WOLFF was educated at the Universities of Leipzig and Cambridge and at the London School of Economics and Political Science. He worked as DAAD-Lektor at the University of Keele (1996–1999) and is currently Lecturer in German Studies at the University of Bath. His main research areas are ethno-territorial cross-border conflicts in Europe and minority rights. His publications include a book (1995) and several articles on Northern Ireland (1998/99), articles on the transformation process in eastern Germany (1998), an article on ethno-territorial cross-border conflicts in western Europe (1999), and two forthcoming edited volumes on German minorities in Europe (2000) and the integration of ethnic German resettlers in the Federal Republic (2001).

CUTG Proceedings

Series editor: Allyson Fiddler

The CUTG series is a new venture presenting a selection of papers given at the annual Conference of University Teachers of German in Great Britain and Ireland (CUTG). The volumes are intentionally broad-based, bringing together articles on literary and cultural studies, language and linguistics, media studies and institutions, to reflect the range of scholarly activity being conducted by Germanists and also to meet the needs of teachers of modern languages whose interests increasingly cover wider areas.

Vol. 1 Steve Giles, Peter Graves (eds): From Classical Shades to Vickers Victorious: Shifting Perspectives in British German Studies.
Papers delivered at the Conference of University Teachers of German, University of Leicester, 6–8 April 1998. 258 pp., 1999.
ISBN 3-906763-03-X / US-ISBN 0-8204-4603-3

Vol. 2 Christopher Hall, David Rock (eds): German Studies towards the Millennium.
Selected papers from the Conference of University Teachers of German, University of Keele, September 1999. 287 pp., 2000.
ISBN 3-906765-65-2 / US-ISBN 0-8204-5304-8